LAW AND ECONOMICS
IN A NUTSHELL

FIFTH EDITION

By

JEFFREY L. HARRISON

Stephen C. O'Connell Chair
College of Law
The University of Florida

WEST®

A Thomson Reuters business

Mat #41060651

Nutshell Series, In a Nutshell and the Nutshell Logo are trademarks registered in the U.S. Patent and Trademark Office.

COPYRIGHT © 1995 WEST PUBLISHING CO.
© West, a Thomson business, 2000, 2003
© 2007 Thomson/West
© 2011 Thomson Reuters

> 610 Opperman Drive
> St. Paul, MN 55123
> 1–800–313–9378

Printed in the United States of America

ISBN: 978–0–314–26753–5

For

McCabe
Casey, and
Conner Blue

PREFACE TO THE FIFTH EDITION

This is the fifth edition of Law and Economics in a Nutshell. It is designed to be understood by those with no prior training in economics and only a moderate understanding of some basic legal principles. The overall goal of the book is not simply to go through each area of law and ask "what would the efficient rule be." It does do that, but it places that question in the context of a larger question of whether the assumptions and values inherent in economic analysis are appropriate for legal analysis. I do not attempt to answer this larger question but to inform the reader about the empirical and philosophical issues raised by the application of economics to law. As a personal matter, in my years of reading and writing about law and economics, I have come to believe that well-informed and open-minded legal decisions are those that consider economic consequences. Indeed, I believe they are often considered at an intuitive level even by those who otherwise express concerns about "law and economics." This does not mean, however, that economic or efficient solutions, even when they can be identified, must be adopted. Economics is simply another source of information.

As with past editions of this book I have done two things. First, many of the examples are updated and corrected where necessary. I appreciate those readers who have been generous enough to communicate with me on matters they felt were less than clear and even, thankfully infrequently, incorrect. Second, there are two new chapters. These chapters are devoted a very basic discussion of economics as applied to marriage and divorce and to taxation. In addition, throughout the book I have included discussions of the implications of the huge amount of research that has been devoted to the study of happiness. This topic, like behavioral economics two decades or so ago, is an important new focus for law and economics. Indeed, it holds out the promise of a reassessment of how efficiency should be viewed. Whether this promise can be kept is a different matter.

I would like to thank my wife, Sarah, and my son, McCabe, for their efforts in making the book more readable. In addition, scores of students, while taking the course on law and economics, have contributed by their questions and observations which have then influenced the content and presentation of that which follows. Finally and with great embarrassment, I would like to thank a reader who sent several pages of notations about typos and substantive matters. From the point of receiving his letter I intended to thank him by name and carefully filed

PREFACE TO THE FIFTH EDITION

his name in a place that was so well preserved that I am now unable to find it. In any case, you know who you are and, I apologize.

JEFFREY L. HARRISON
GAINESVILLE, FLORIDA

May, 2011

OUTLINE

OUTLINE

TABLE OF CASES

References are to Pages

TABLE OF CASES

TABLE OF CASES

LAW AND ECONOMICS
IN A NUTSHELL

FIFTH EDITION

CHAPTER ONE

INTRODUCTION

Although without much fanfare, lawyers have long recognized economics as a complementary discipline. For example, Oliver Wendell Holmes wrote in 1897, "the man of the future is the man of statistics and economics."[1] In addition, the economic underpinnings of the famous Hand Formula, which defines negligence as the absence of cost-justified preventative action, is obvious. Similarly, well before legal scholars began to think and write about law and economics in the late 1960s and early 1970s, economists were hard at work providing litigation assistance to attorneys in the areas of remedies and antitrust.

Economists have always been conscious of the importance of the relationship of law and economics. Evidence of this is found in the earliest studies of economic matters as well as in the writings of Adam Smith and Karl Marx. In the early part of the last century, scholars like John R. Commons, Robert Lee Hale, and Irving Fisher discussed the importance of understanding the impact of legal institutions on economic development and the ways in which economic change may encourage legal

1. Oliver Wendell Holmes, "The Path of the Law," 10 *Harv.L. Rev.* 457 (1987).

1

change.[2] In fact, it is possible that these earlier scholars of law and economics and the "Institutional Economists" made a greater effort to fully address the complex interplay of law and economics than more contemporary writers.[3]

The most recent wave of law and economics, associated with the University of Chicago, roughly began with the appearance of Ronald Coase's famous 1960 article "The Problem of Social Cost"[4]—now the most cited article in legal scholarship. It gained its real impetus among legal academicians with the publication of Richard Posner's *Economic Analysis of Law* which in 2011 was in its seventh edition. The early period of law and economics was marked primarily by efforts to describe what law would look like if courts adopted efficiency as their guiding standard. In this respect it is "positive" as opposed to "normative" in its focus since the idea was to be descriptive and objective. Throughout this book, ideas drawn from this approach to law and economics will be referred to as "conventional." Often the conclusion is that law designed to be efficient would look much like it does. The Chicago period has also saw efforts to study the evolution of law in order to determine whether laws move inevitably toward sets of rules that are efficient. In

2. Steven G. Medema, "From Interwar Pluralism to Posner," 30 *History of Political Economy* (Ann. Supp., 202) 1998.

3. See generally, A. Allan Schmidt, "Institutional Law and Economics," 1 *European Journal of Law and Economics* 33 (1994).

4. Ronald Coase, "The Problem of Social Cost," 3 *J. L. & Econ.* 1 (1960).

addition, there have been attempts to address the moral justifications for adoption of efficiency as a desirable standard.

More recently, there have been increased efforts to assess individual behavior in legal contexts with empirical studies. In particular, a conventional approach to economics typically involves the assumption that people are rational maximizers of self interest. The behavioral question is whether this assumption holds up. This is an especially provocative question in the context of law in which people may feel compelled by a sense of duty or right and wrong. The legitimacy of this work was affirmed in 2002 when the Nobel Prize in economics was awarded to Daniel Kaheman and Vernon Smith, two of the leaders in economic experimentation.

Even more recently, economists and psychologists have focused on happiness and its relationship to law as well as economics.[5] This relatively new and fascinating area of study goes to the core of economics because it raises a fundamental question. Conventional notions of efficiency rely on the choices people make and then assume those choices maximize utility. The problem is there is little or no follow up. In other words how do we know if choices made really do maximize utility or happiness. Researchers who focus on happiness are largely interested in

5. See e,g. *Law and Happiness* (eds. Matthew Adler & Eric A. Posner, 2010); Peter Henry Huang, Happiness Studies and Legal Policy. 6 *Ann. Rev. of Law & Social Science* (December 2010); Jeffrey L. Harrison, Happiness, Efficiency and the Promise of Decisional Equity: From Outcome to Process. 36 *Pepperdine Law Review* 935 (2009);

what actually happens. Ideally, this is what economics should be about but it is not an easy task. The problem is pinning down what it means to be happy and what sorts of things are consistent with happiness. Perhaps most important, is happiness an absolute or relative concept?

This book proceeds from the assumption that a properly taught course in law and economics, whether in an economics department or in a law school, will include more than a single-minded examination of the conventional application of economic analysis to law. This means not simple examining the criticisms of law and economic but exploring the implications of economics for a discipline—law—that is fundamentally normative. Examining the criticisms of law and economics as well as its normative implications can lead to a broader understanding of when and how the use of economic analysis is useful. Similarly, it is valuable to consider the ways in which the theory of law and economics can be improved by considering information about human behavior and ultimate happiness provided by other disciplines.

The next Chapter is an introduction to basic price theory, including the fundamentals of supply and demand, and to concepts of efficiency. Although the concepts are not always obviously connected, it makes sense to become acquainted with them as they are likely to be relied upon at various points throughout the remainder of the book. Much of what is described in Chapter Two will be elaborated upon in Chapter Nine in the context of antitrust law. Chapter Three focuses on some of the controversies that arise in the application of economics to law.

Chapter Four discusses the foundation of law and economics—the Coase Theorem—and many of its applications to property-related issues. Chapter Five examines the various concepts typically found in a course on contracts and contract remedies. Chapter Six does the same with respect to tort law with emphasis on unintentional torts and the Hand formula. The premise of Chapter Six is that the economic function of tort law is to minimize the sum of accident costs and efforts to prevent them. Chapter Seven focuses on the economics of settlement. Why do most cases settle and what explains those that do not?

Chapter Eight applies economic analysis to criminal law. This is a sometimes controversial application of economics to law because it can lead to the conclusion that it is efficient for some levels of criminal conduct to take place.

Chapter Nine covers much of the economic theory behind most antitrust law. Chapter Ten is devoted to the economic rationales for the regulation of business. These range from "natural monopoly" to the search for social justice. These justifications range from regulating natural monopolies and allocating inherently scarce resources to efforts to control pollution and limit the destruction of endangered species. One issue to keep in mind is whether regulation should be guided by happiness as opposed to conventional cost/benefit analysis. Chapter Eleven extends this analysis to intellectual property.

In Chapter Twelve the theory that the common law evolves to efficient rules and the process of this evolution is fundamentally economic in nature is examined. In Chapter Thirteen the tools of economics are applied to some facets inheritance. Chapter Fourteen focuses on the application of economics to marriage and the family. Finally, in Chapter Fifteen, public choice theory is examined. Public choice has been the focus of social scientists for many years. While conventional economics deals with decision-making and the expression of preferences in traditional markets, public choice addresses the same issues in contexts in which the mode of expression is voting. Public choice may be especially relevant to an understanding of the criticisms of applying economic analysis to law. This is because people may tend to vote in a way that expresses their generalized preferences for certain values or notions of fairness or justice. In traditional markets, they are more likely to vote—with their dollars—in a manner that expresses individualized "tastes."[6] The application of economics to the decisions that involve law probably occupies some middle ground in which both general values and individualized tastes play a role.

Before beginning a detailed examination of law and economics, one final notice is warranted. A

6. See Kenneth Arrow, *Social Choice and Individual Values*, (1963).

study of law and economics requires students to adopt a different orientation from that required for conventional college courses. Law and economics is not really a single topic but a series of topics ranging from microeconomics to game theory, sociology, and jurisprudence. Although one can find a wealth of implied and expressed economic analysis in judicial opinions, the basic materials are really scholarly writings found in law reviews and economics journals. These writings are landmarks in the same sense as judicial opinions are landmarks—they set new standards or signal turning points.

CHAPTER TWO

ECONOMIC TOOLS AND CONCEPTS

This Chapter is devoted to the fundamental tools and concepts that economists apply to law, beginning with a discussion of supply and demand. It then considers elasticity and compares perfect with imperfect competition. These concepts are part of "price theory." For those who wish to follow up on this Chapter's discussion, Chapter Nine extends the analysis to another (but still basic) level in the context of antitrust law. This Chapter also examines externalities and the forms of efficiency that are most commonly discussed in law and economics.

A. DEMAND, SUPPLY AND MARKET EQUILIBRIUM

1. DEMAND

"Demand" has a very specific meaning and is often used in a confusing manner in the popular press. When economists speak of demand, they mean a *range* of prices and the amount of a good or service that individuals are willing and able to purchase in a given market at a given time at those prices. It is critical to note that demand does not account for those who either cannot afford the good or service or are unwilling to pay. This may be particularly important later when the discussion turns to consideration of efficiency and what that term means. Also, you cannot speak about demand without expressly or implicitly limiting the market both time-wise and by location. Thus, you might ask what is the demand for coffee from 7:00 A.M. to 9:00 A.M. on Monday in Oscarville. The appropriate answer to that question would be a list or schedule of possible prices and the amounts of coffee people would be willing and able to purchase during the time specified. Table 1 might be the answer.

Table 1: Demand for Coffee

Price cup of coffee	Quantity
$1.00	800
$1.05	750
$1.10	700
$1.15	650
$1.20	600

From the Table, you can determine the *quantity demanded* of coffee at each price. As the Table indicates, the quantity demanded declines as the price increases. For example, at $1.00 per cup, the quantity demanded is 800 cups. At $1.05, the quantity demanded is 750 cups. Typically, the relationship between price and quantity demanded is depicted on a graph. In Figure 1, the Y or vertical axis is price, and the X or horizontal axis is quantity. If the demand for coffee were graphed, the price/quantity combinations could be connected by a straight line. In Figure 1, D_1 is called a demand curve and is a graphical representation of the demand in Table 1. In this particular graph, only a few of the possible prices and quantities are illustrated.

Figure 1

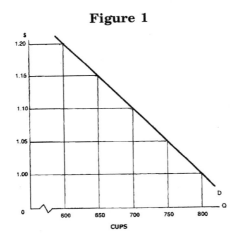

Demand curves almost always slope downward. This is consistent with people being willing and able to purchase less as prices increase. They purchase less both because they look to buy substitutes and because an increase in the price of any product lowers their purchasing power generally. Conversely, when price declines, their income increases in the sense that they can buy more.

A change in demand is represented by a shift of the demand curve so that at all prices the quantity demanded either increases or decreases. In Figure 2, D_2 represents a decrease in demand while D_3 shows an increase in demand. It is important not to confuse a change in demand with a change in the quantity demanded.

Figure 2

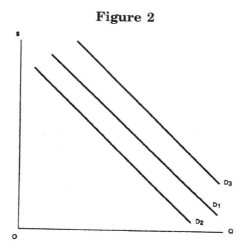

A change in quantity demanded occurs when a change in price results in movement to a new position on the same demand curve. A "shift in demand" or "change in demand" means that the entire curve shifts and that a different quantity is demanded at every price on the schedule.

Shifts in demand can be the result of changes in the tastes and preferences for the good or service. They can also be the result of a change in price of other goods and services. For example, complementary goods are those that are typically used together. Thus, tennis balls and tennis rackets are complementary goods. If the price of tennis rackets increased, the demand for tennis balls would be likely to decrease. If the original demand for tennis balls was D_1 in Figure 2, the new demand curve would be to the left, perhaps D_2, indicating a downward shift in demand.

Another possibility is that goods are substitutes. In other words, to one degree or another, they can be used for the same purposes. Thus, to some extent jogging can be viewed as a substitute for playing tennis. If the price of tennis rackets increases, the demand for jogging shoes may increase. This would be illustrated as a shift to the right of the demand curve for jogging shoes. D_3 in Figure 2 represents an increase in demand over D_1.

2.   SUPPLY

The proper definition of supply is comparable to that of demand. Supply is a schedule of prices and the quantities that would be available for sale at each price in a given market at a given time. Thus, the supply of coffee in Oscarville between 7:00 and 9:00 A.M. might look like Table 2.

Table 2: Supply of Coffee

Price per cup	Quantity
$1.00	600
$1.05	650
$1.10	700
$1.15	750
$1.20	800

As with demand, supply is often plotted on a graph. In Figure 3, the quantity is along the X axis and the price is along the Y axis. S_1 is the supply curve for coffee in Oscarville between 7:00 and 9:00 A.M. As the Table and Figure indicate, quantity supplied generally increases as price increases. To understand why, one must understand the concept of marginal cost. Marginal cost is the increase in cost associated with the production of *one* additional unit of output. Thus, if the total cost of producing 4 units of output is $4.00 and the total cost of producing 5 units of output is $5.00, the marginal cost of the fifth unit is $1.00.

Figure 3

One can plot marginal cost on a graph and illustrate how the costs of producing one more unit of
output change as output increases. This is the marginal cost curve, and the part of that curve that is
relevant for this analysis is upward sloping. In fact,
the relevant part of the marginal cost curve is the
supply curve just as depicted in Figure 3. The
reason why the marginal cost curve and the supply
curve are identical is because a producer will be
willing to sell an additional unit of output as long as
the price offered for that unit is at least equal to the
marginal cost of producing that unit. Thus, in order
to answer the question of how many units will be
made available for sale at each price, the producer

would consider the marginal cost of producing each unit.

Like demand curves, the entire supply curve can shift. Again, it is important to distinguish this from a change in the quantity supplied. A change in quantity supplied occurs when a price change results in movement to a new position on the same supply curve.

Typically, a shift in supply is a response to an increase or decrease in the cost of inputs. Thus, if the item involves the use of labor and the cost of labor on an hourly basis increases, you would expect the supply curve to shift upward and to the left. The same would be true with respect to an increase in the cost of raw materials. In Figure 3, this is illustrated by the curve S_2. In fact, due to the huge increases in the price of coffee beans in recent years, S_2 might be a more accurate representation of the supply of coffee today. At each price along S_2, sellers are willing to sell a lower quantity than they were before the increase in costs. Or, to put it differently, at each quantity, it will now take a higher price to get the producer to make that quantity available for sale. Conversely, a decrease in the price of coffee beans will result in a shift from S_1 to S_3. This is an increase in supply.

3. MARKET EQUILIBRIUM

By combining supply and demand, as depicted in Figure 4, you can determine the equilibrium price and quantity for a given market at a given time.

This does not mean that a price and quantity will be established and not change. Instead, there will be a tendency for the market to gravitate toward the equilibrium price and quantity. In the case of Oscarville, the equilibrium price will be $1.10 and the equilibrium quantity will be 700 cups.

Figure 4

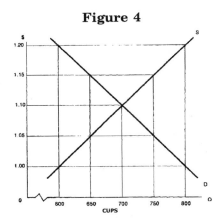

To understand why, consider the reaction if the price were $1.20. The quantity demanded would be 600 cups and the quantity offered for sale would be 800 cups. With more offered for sale than individuals are willing and able to purchase, there is a surplus in the market and price will tend to fall. In effect, suppliers would compete against each other by lowering price to eliminate the excess. At a price of $1.00, the quantity demanded would be 800 cups and the quantity supplied 600 cups. In this case, there is a shortage, and suppliers will find that they can increase price. Only at a price of $1.10 would the quantity supplied equal the quantity demanded. Price will gravitate toward this level and the quantity sold will gravitate toward 700 cups.

B.   ELASTICITY

1.   GENERALLY

Just as important as the fact that demand curves generally slope downward and supply curves upward is the question of just how steep the curves are. Put differently, just how responsive are sellers and buyers to changes in price? The economist's label for this measure of sensitivity is "elasticity." Elasticity is expressed as a number which is:

% change in quantity/% change in price.

In the case of demand, if the percentage change in quantity exceeds the percentage change in price, i.e. the above ratio is greater than one, demand is said to be "elastic." In short, buyers are relatively responsive to price changes. If the ratio of percentage change in quantity to percentage change in price is less than one, demand is said to be "inelastic." The primary factor accounting for the elasticity of demand is the availability of substitutes. If prices increase and many substitutes are available, individuals will move away from the good or the seller who has increased price. A classic example of an inelastic good would be emergency medical care. If you need emergency treatment it is a necessity for which few substitutes exist. An example of an elastic good would be a specific brand of soft drink, because one can easily substitute away from a brand by buying different brands.

The implication of different elasticities is illustrated in Figure 5. The graph includes two demand curves. The slope of D_1 is relatively steep, while the slope of D_2 is relatively slight. At P_1 on both curves, the quantity demanded is Q_1. If price increases to P_2, the quantity demanded on D_1 is Q_2 and the quantity demanded on D_2 is Q_3. In other words, the same price increase results in different responses. The steep curve is relatively inelastic; buyers are relatively unresponsive to the price change. Among other possibilities, this suggests that there are not many good substitutes for the good represented by D_1. Along D_2, the response is greater. D_2 is relatively elastic and buyers alter their spending in response to the price change.

Figure 5

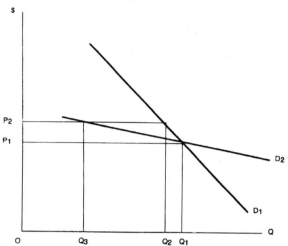

Elasticity of supply can be calculated the same way as the elasticity of demand. Here again, the more responsive sellers are to price increases or decreases, the more elastic the supply curve is said to be. The critical determinant of supply elasticity is the rate at which costs of production increase as output increases. For example, if a seller has excess capacity and if inputs are relatively inexpensive, a small increase in price may result in a large increase in output.

2. INCIDENCE ANALYSIS

Incidence analysis is devoted to determining who actually pays more when costs of production or taxes increase. Elasticity is an important determinant of which groups of possible payers are affected. This can be illustrated using the supply and demand for coffee in Oscarville. In Figure 6, the initial equilibrium price is P_1 and the equilibrium quantity is Q_1. Suppose a new government regulation is enacted that requires all restaurant owners to pay ten cents per cup sold to a fund established for cleaning old Starbucks sites. This would have an impact, initially, on the supply side of the market, making it more expensive to sell coffee. The supply curve would shift upward and to the left. In Figure 6, S_1 is the supply before the regulation and S_2 is the supply after regulation. The curve shifts up by exactly the amount of the charge because at every level of output, the marginal cost of coffee increases by the same amount—in this case, ten cents.

Figure 6

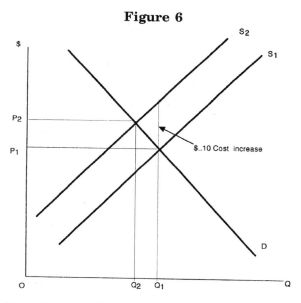

Here the question incidence analysis addresses is how the extra ten cent cost will be allocated between the buyers and sellers. For example, in Figure 6, the cost of coffee increases to P_2 per cup and the quantity sold drops to Q_2. Thus, some consumers pay more and some do not buy as much coffee. The increase in price is not, however, equal to the ten cent increase in the cost of production.

Contrast Figure 6 with Figure 7. Here the two supply curves are the same as in Figure 6, but the demand curve is very steep or relatively inelastic. As the demand curve indicates, price increases do not result in much of a response in terms of quantity demanded. Thus, after the regulation, the price of coffee goes up to P_2 and quantity decreases to Q_2;

most of the extra cost of production is paid by consumers. One could repeat this exercise with a very flat or elastic demand curve and the result would be that the price of coffee would barely rise at all; more of the cost would be absorbed by producers. As it turns out, the elasticity of both supply and demand determine upon whom the extra cost will fall.

Figure 7

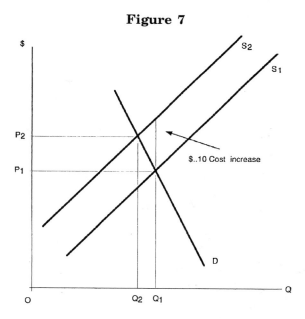

C. PERFECT AND IMPERFECT MARKETS

While supply and demand curves are useful tools for economic analysis of law, they may not be representative of how markets are actually structured. For example, total market demand in Oscarville might be determined by asking each resident how much coffee he or she would be willing to buy at each price along the schedule and then adding those quantities of coffee to get the total market demand. This is called horizontal summation since only the amounts along the X axis are added. The same process might be done on the supply side. All the sellers of coffee might be asked how much they would be willing to sell at each price on the schedule. These quantities would be horizontally summed to get the supply for the market.

The analysis so far assumes that there are in fact a number of suppliers. In this context, the sellers can do no more than passively react to the market-determined price. In fact, the basic demand and supply model involves the assumption that the sellers are selling homogeneous products, that buyers and sellers have complete information about prices and any other relevant factors, that it is easy to enter the industry, and that no seller is large enough to effect price by increasing or decreasing its output. Economists call this perfect competition. Under these conditions, each seller is a "price-taker" and simply sells all it wants to sell at the market-determined price.

If any of the above conditions are absent, the market becomes imperfect. Imperfect markets are ones in which sellers cease to become passive price takers and, for one reason or another, are able to raise prices above what they would be in a competitive market. For example, consumers may not be able to get information easily or one seller may be able to convince prospective buyers that its product is different from the others—that is, it is differentiated. These imperfections can be sources of market power. The more market power a seller has, the more it will be able to raise prices above competitive levels. Moreover, the firm with market power is no longer a price-taker. As market conditions increasingly differ from those under perfect competition, simple demand and supply analysis begins to lose its validity. Instead, individual firms will set prices above competitive prices and decrease output to levels below that under competitive conditions. A more detailed explanation of the economic implications of imperfect competition is reserved for Chapter Nine, but the actual process of determining price is discussed here.

In order to determine how price determination differs, assume all the coffee sellers in Oscarville merge into one big supplier. Assume the new supplier's marginal cost curve would be derived by horizontally summing together the marginal cost curves of all the small firms. In other words, it would be the same as the supply curve for the whole town before the merger. This single firm will also be faced with the entire Oscarville demand.

That does not mean it will price where demand and supply intersect. Instead, it will want to pick the one price that will maximize profit. It will make a profit on each unit sold as long as the addition to total revenue from selling that unit exceeds the increase in total cost associated with producing that unit—marginal cost. The extra revenue from selling an additional unit is the marginal revenue.

It is now useful to turn to Figure 8. The demand from Figure 2 is included in the graph as is the supply from Figure 2. Here it is labeled MC for marginal cost and not S for supply because the firm really is not willing to offer different amounts for sale at different prices but is searching for a single price. The curve that is new is labeled MR for marginal revenue. Marginal revenue—again, the extra revenue from selling one more unit—is consistently lower than the price for which that unit is sold. The reason for this is simple. If the seller wants to sell more, it must lower the price for all units. Thus, the increase in revenue from selling additional units when price is lowered is partially or completely offset by the decreased revenue from all those units that now have lower prices.

Figure 8

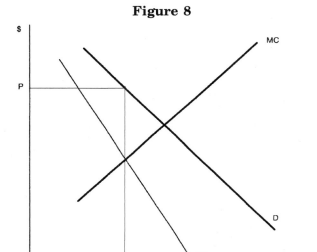

The firm would like to sell all those units that generate more in terms of marginal revenue than their marginal cost. In the graph, this is true for all units for which the marginal revenue curve is higher than the marginal cost curve. Thus, the firm will produce and sell up to level Q. Of course, it will want to set the highest price possible for Q. The price on the demand curve that corresponds to quantity Q is price P. This will be *the* price set by the seller.

Obviously, the degree of competitiveness has many important implications. Although explored more fully in Chapter Nine, it is worthwhile to point out some of them here. First, under perfectly competitive conditions, firms will tend to make the minimum profit necessary to stay in business. This is called a "normal profit" and economists treat it as a cost along with other costs of production. A profit in excess of a normal profit is called an "economic profit." The reason why firms in perfectly competitive industries tend to make only a normal profit is because entry into the industry is so easy that anything above a normal profit will attract competitors and the increase in supply will drive prices and profits down. Under imperfect competition, this is less likely to occur and firms can make long term economic profits. In addition, prices will tend to be higher under imperfect conditions and the level of output lower. This, as one might expect, has important implications for antitrust policy.

The competitiveness of the industry also plays a role in incidence analysis. Under perfectly competitive conditions, any costs that are passed on at all must be passed on to consumers. This is because the firms in the industry are only earning a normal profit—the minimum necessary to survive. This does not mean that prices will necessarily rise by the full amount of the cost increase. As firms raise prices to cover the cost increase, some consumers will drop out of the market and fewer firms will be needed to serve the remaining buyers. With fewer firms, the demand for the inputs used in that industry will fall and the price of inputs may decline. If so, the cost increase may be partially offset by a decrease in the price of other inputs and, overall, price will not increase by the full amount of the cost increase. If anyone "absorbs" the cost increase, it is the consumers who continue to buy, those who have left the market to buy less desirable products, and the firms that have left the market.

On the other hand, if the industry is imperfectly competitive, it may be that firms are enjoying economic profits or "rents." In these instances, the part of the cost increase that is not passed on to consumers may be absorbed by the firms that remain in the market in the form of lower profits.

D. MARGINAL ANALYSIS GENERAL

An important tool of economic analysis generally and in the application of economic analysis to law is marginal analysis. Marginal analysis is essentially a decision-making technique in which one compares the benefits and costs of decisions. As already described, in its most traditional economic application, firms apply marginal analysis to determine the profit maximizing level of output.

For example, in the context of criminal law, one might reason that a motorist will speed as long as the advantage from speeding exceeds the expected fine for speeding. Here the expected fine would be the fine if caught multiplied by the probability of being caught. The marginal benefit would be whatever advantage is gained by arriving earlier than if the speed limit were observed.

The usefulness of marginal analysis is obvious and many would say that it is the "rational approach" to decision-making. For example, suppose an inventor spent several years and several thousand dollars attempting to invent a special wrinkle remover and was getting no closer to the magic formula. He might reason, "I can't stop now, I have already devoted so much time and expense to the effort." This would not be marginal analysis. The time and money spent are "sunk costs." The supposedly rational approach would be to ask what the costs of further efforts are likely to be and what are the likely benefits. This may be, however, a bit of an oversimplification in that there may be adverse psychological effects associated with giving up on a project. Even this does not mean that marginal analysis as a decision-making strategy is flawed. It suggests that there is a tendency in economics to define the marginal costs and benefits of decisions too narrowly.

E. EFFICIENCY

In one form or another, the concept of "efficiency" is an important tool in the study of law and economics. Typically, the term "efficiency" is associated with the notion of accomplishing an outcome at the lowest possible cost. The term for that type of efficiency is "productive efficiency." Productive efficiency is, however, just one of a number of "types" of efficiency you will encounters in law and economics.

1. ALLOCATIVE EFFICIENCY

Allocative efficiency is typically reserved for considerations of whether an industry is producing the "right" amount of a specific good or service. This is different from the question of productive efficiency, which deals with whether any particular level of output is produced at the lowest possible cost. Allocative efficiency can be understood by referring to the basic supply and demand model. The demand curve tells what a particular product is worth to individuals. As one moves down the demand curve, the value of additional units of output decline; that is, the price people are willing to pay decreases.

The supply curve, on the other hand, reflects the cost of producing additional units of output. This is because when the seller is considering how much he or she will offer for sale at each price, a direct comparison is made of the price offered to the cost of producing additional units. The cost of producing additional units is determined by the cost of inputs and the cost of those inputs is determined by the price others are offering to use the inputs in the production of other goods. Thus, in a real sense, when an input is used to produce one good, the "social cost" is the value placed on the use of the input in the production of other goods.

It makes sense, in terms of efficient resource allocation, to produce an item as long as the value attributed to it by buyers exceeds the social cost of its production. Since demand tells us the value attributed to the item being produced and supply tells us the social cost of producing extra units, it makes sense to produce until demand and supply intersect.

This can be seen in Figure 9, the demand and supply for Vespa motor scooters. Demand and supply intersect at 15 Vespas. At the quantity of 14 Vespas, the price people are willing and able to pay exceeds the cost, as indicated by the supply curve, of additional production. Thus, society values the production of additional units more than the social cost of additional units. At 16 Vespas, production would be too high. Since demand lies below the supply curve at this level of output, the social cost of the 16th unit exceeds the value of that unit. The "right" amount of inputs is "drawn" into the production of Vepas at 15 units. This is said to be allocatively efficient.

There is an important caveat to this explanation of allocative efficiency. The entire analysis, since it is dependent on supply and demand, is based on preferences and the strength of those preferences as they are expressed in markets. And, as indicated earlier, supply and demand depend on "willingness and ability to pay." It is possible that it is desirable to produce goods and services that people cannot afford. This does not mean that the economist's definition of allocative efficiency is necessarily wrong. Instead, it just means that one may legitimately believe that allocative efficiency is but one concept to be weighed in making normative decisions.

Figure 9

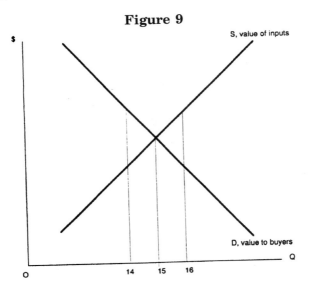

2. THE THEORY OF SECOND BEST

Now that you have learned about supply and demand and how competitive markets result in allocative efficiency, an important additional concept comes into play. The "theory of second best" has received scant attention in the field of law and economics.[1] This is unfortunate, as its implications are important and have the potential to undermine a great deal of economic-based policy. One can

1. The work of Richard Markovits is an important exception. See Richard Markovits, "A Basic Structure for Microeconomic Policy Analysis in our Worse–Than–Second–Best World: A Proposal and Related Critique of the Chicago Approach to the Study of Law and Economics," 1975 *Wisc. L. Rev.* 950.

understand the theory by thinking back to the concept of allocative efficiency. Demand indicates the value attributed to the good by buyers and supply indicates the cost of production in terms of resources used that could be used to produce other goods. Presumably, the efficient amount of inputs are drawn into the production of the good at the level of output determined by demand and supply.

Suppose, however, that there are two goods—buttons and zippers—and that they use the same inputs except that buttons require plastic and zippers do not. In addition, assume all inputs are sold under competitive conditions except plastic. Since the price of plastic will be determined under imperfect market conditions, its price will be higher than it would otherwise be. In addition, due to this inflated price, the supply of buttons will be lower and the price higher than it would be if plastic were sold under competitive conditions. Unlike the model used to describe allocative efficiency, now the supply curve does not tell us the cost of button-making in terms of the cost of resources.

In addition, since the price of buttons is higher, consumers will shift their purchases to zippers, a good substitute for most purposes. Resources will flow into zipper production even though, but for the imperfect conditions in the plastic market, those resources would be more efficiently used in the production of buttons.

The solution to the problem may seem simple: somehow arrange for the plastic market to behave competitively. As one might expect, though, this may very well be impossible. If one decides that all the markets cannot be competitive, the question then becomes whether it makes sense from the standpoint of efficiency to make as many markets competitive as possible. The answer is that efficiency may not be furthered by a policy of making as many markets as possible competitive when you know that ultimately all markets will not be competitive. In fact, there may be a "second best" solution that actually allocates resources more efficiently by allowing for comparable levels of imperfection.

The theory of second best illustrates the interdependence of markets. It also calls into question analyses that speak in terms of efficient levels of damages or sanctions without examining the structure of the "market" involved and related markets.

3. PARETO OPTIMALITY AND SUPERIORITY

The concepts of Pareto optimality and Pareto superiority are discussed in any study of law and economics. A resource allocation is Pareto *optimal* if any movement from that allocation would make at least one person worse off. A change from one resources allocation to another is Pareto *superior* if it means at least one person is better off and no one is made worse off.

For a better understanding, consider Jack, who would like to sell his 1965 Ford Mustang, and Sally, who would like to buy the Mustang. Suppose Jack asks for a price of $10,000, but would be willing to accept an offer of $8,000. This means that Jack would prefer or feel better off with any sum in excess of $8,000 than he would feel if he continued to possess the car. Put differently, Jack would derive more utility from $8,000 than he would from possessing the Ford. Similarly, suppose Sally offered Jack $7,000, but was willing to pay as much as $9,000. Here again it can be said that Sally would feel better owning the car than she would feel if she possessed anything else $9,000 could buy.

Obviously, we have a range of possible prices— $8,000—$9,000—that would leave both Jack and Sally feeling better off. A price within this range would be consistent with increasing the utility of both parties. Sometimes this range of prices is referred to as the "contract curve." It describes a number of prices that would make both Jack and Sally feel better off. The exchange of the car for a price between $8,000 and $9,000 would be Pareto superior.

Suppose an exchange does take place—the car for $8,500—and we then consider adjusting the price. In other words, having chosen a position on the contract curve, we then consider the possibility of adjusting the exchange so that it is at another place on the contract curve. For example, one might decide to let Sally have the car and require Jack to refund $100. Or one might allow Sally to keep the car but pay Jack $200 more. In both of these cases, the movement from one price to another would not make both parties feel better off. In fact, any movement from the $8,500 would leave either Jack or Sally worse off. When resources are distributed in such a way that they cannot be reallocated without at least one party feeling worse off, the original distribution is said to be Pareto optimal.

Although voluntary exchanges are the best way of assuring that a Pareto superior allocation is achieved, it is also possible to achieve Pareto superiority through involuntary means. For example, Sally may simply take the Mustang from Jack and leave him 85 crisp one-hundred dollar bills. If the money makes Jack feel better off than possessing what Sally took and no one else is adversely affected, the outcome is Pareto superior.

The problem is that there are only three sources of information that tell us what amount Jack needs to make him feel at least as well off as he did before Sally took his car. Sally is one source, but there is no guarantee that she can accurately determine how much Jack valued the Mustang. Jack might be another source, but it is not clear that Jack will be dependable when, after the fact, he is asked what amount the court should require Sally to pay in order to restore him to at least his previous level of well-being. Finally, there could be outside sources that would testify as to the fair market value of the car. The problem here is that Jack may attribute a greater value to the car than the fair market value. Thus, if the involuntary exchange achieves Pareto superiority, it may be more a matter of coincidence than anything else.

The public policy implications of Pareto standards of efficiency are extremely confining. Strict adherence to these standards would either rule out all involuntary exchanges or require one to employ inherently unreliable *ex post* measures of compensation. For example, it may seem quite clear that resources would be allocated more efficiently if money were taken from the very wealthy and then used to pay for food and shelter for the neediest. And, for all anyone knows, the amount of benefit for the poor would greatly exceed the loss experienced by those from whom the money is taken. While this may seem obvious to some, the problem is that economics as a science is not equipped to make any assurances about the relative gains and losses from such a redistribution. Such an analysis involves what economists call an "interpersonal comparison of utility." Pareto standards avoid these comparisons, but their application would result in a public policy straitjacket.

There is one more complication with an application of Paretian standards. Suppose Jack and Sally make a voluntary exchange because they each believe the exchange will make the feel better off. Suppose further that Jack then pines to have his car back and Sally finds owning a vintage Mustang not as much fun as she had hoped. Has there been a Pareto Superior exchange? In a sense there has been if one goes only by the choices they have made. On the other hand, the actual outcome in terms of satisfaction, utility or happiness, is not superior. Conventional economics tends to focus on the choice that is made. Increasingly, though, social scientists interested in happiness, are looking at actual outcomes.

4.   KALDOR–HICKS EFFICIENCY

Paretian concepts of efficiency, if applied to all public policy decisions, could lead to very limited government action. After all, everyone would have to agree with the policy. Another version of efficiency, Kaldor–Hicks or wealth maximization, responds to this problem. For something to be Kaldor–Hicks efficient, those individuals made better off by the policy or change would have to be made sufficiently better off that they *could* compensate those who are made worse off. The key here is that the compensation is "potential," not actual.

Two aspects of Kaldor–Hicks efficiency are critical. The first is that the unit of measurement for well-being is not utility but "wealth," "value," or "price." This introduces the notion of "ability to pay." What is maximized is an imperfect substitute for utility and for actual well-being. For example, suppose two individuals—one rich and one poor—both desire a cup of milk. The poor person wants it desperately and is willing to give his or her last dollar for the milk. On the other hand, the rich person does not care for the milk but thinks it would be fun to open the container and pour the milk into a storm drain and, therefore, is willing to pay $1.50 for the milk. Under wealth maximization principles, the efficient allocation is to the rich person.

The second critical feature of Kaldor–Hicks efficiency or wealth maximization is that the consent of all those affected can be dispensed with. Thus, in the previous example, if the milk were already the property of the poor person, devotion to wealth maximization might require taking the milk from the poor person and simply transferring it to the rich person so that it would be possessed by the person "valuing" it the most.

Obviously, although wealth maximization overcomes the inflexibility of Paretian concepts of efficiency, it does so at two costs. First, there is no guarantee that maximizing wealth maximizes any other measure of well-being including utility or happiness. In addition, the protection of individual autonomy inherent in Paretian concepts of efficiency is lost.

Richard Posner, in particular, offers an argument that this loss in autonomy may be overstated. He does so by employing the concept of *ex ante* compensation.[2] In a simple form, the argument is that many, if not most, instances in which individuals find they are "worse off" are really the result of choices the individuals made to forego courses of action that would have prevented the loss. The riskier course of action is typically the less expensive and the "compensation" may be in the form of the money saved by taking that option. Thus, the

2. Richard Posner, *The Economics of Justice* 94–95 (1980).

individual "consented to" and was compensated ahead of time for the loss that is now experienced. Judge Posner's effort to reconcile the Kaldor–Hicks or wealth maximization approach with Paretian concepts of efficiency by use of the notion of *ex ante* compensation has met with substantial criticism.[3] One issue is whether the fact that one pays less for something means they have consented to all the possible consequences. For example, if you rented an apartment in a less safe part of town, have you consented to an increased possibility of robbery?

F. EXTERNALITIES

1. NEGATIVE EXTERNALITIES AND PROPERTY RIGHTS

a. Negative Externalities

Much of law and economics is concerned with what are called externalities. Externalities are either positive or negative. A negative externality results when the activity of one person or a business imposes a cost on someone else. The most commonly used example is that of the polluting factory. The owners of the factory may use a variety of inputs for which they pay suppliers. In addition, they may pollute the water and air, making them less useful to others, but not pay for the loss to others. The critical question is whether the activity imposes on others in a negative way.

3. See e.g. Jules Coleman, "Efficiency, Utility and Wealth Maximization," 8 *Hofstra Law Review* 509, 534–540 (1980).

Although any negative impact is an externality, the concept of an externality has a more practical connotation resulting from the fundamental question of what rights a person has. If the people affected by the factory have no "right" to clear air or water, there is still technically an externality but the law does not recognize it as such. Other examples of activities that create externalities include cigarette smoking, driving recklessly, and producing defective products. As you can see, the existence of negative externalities explains a great deal of environmental, tort, and property law.

b. The Tragedy of the Commons

A concept that illustrates negative externalities and explains the need for property rights is the "tragedy of the commons."[4] The problem, as described by Garrett Hardin, involves a group of herdsmen who make use of a common area for grazing. Each makes what seems be a rational assessment of the costs and benefits of adding one animal to his herd. For each one the benefit is the profit to be earned from one additional animal. The cost, however, is a general cost of over-grazing that is spread throughout the community. In effect, the full profit is *internalized* by the herdsman but the cost is not fully internalized. Since each person engages in the same reasoning, over the long run, the "tragedy" is that the commons are destroyed. Today, of course, the tragedy can be applied to everything from global warming to the decline in

4. Garrett Hardin, "The Tragedy of the Commons" 162 *Science* 1243 (1968).

fishing stocks. The "tragedy of the commons" provides a powerful argument for the assignment of property rights. Such an assignment would mean that the costs of adding an animal to the herd would be fully internalized by the landowners.

c. The Prisoner's Dilemma

The tragedy of the commons is also useful to illustrate the advantages of cooperative behavior. In the case of the herdsmen, everyone is ultimately made worse off by pursuing what seemed to be his or her self-interest. If they could reach some sort of agreement about the use of the commons under which they gave up some of their individual freedom, they would all be likely to benefit in the long run. Cooperative behavior could substitute for a public assignment of property rights.

The most commonly used construct in law and economics to illustrate the importance of cooperation is called the "prisoner's dilemma." The problem involves two prisoners who are being held apart from each other after being arrested in connection with a crime. Separately they are questioned. If both prisoners confess they will receive sentences of five years. If neither confesses they will receive sentences of two years. Finally, if one confesses and the other does not, the confessor will be given a one year sentence and the prisoner choosing not to confess will be sentenced to 10 years.

Without cooperating, each party will assume that the other will act selfishly and try to save his own skin. The result will be that each will confess and receive a sentence of five years. The alternative of not confessing is far too risky because it could mean a 10 year sentence. Of course, the best outcome would be for both parties to do exactly that—not confess. But this is an outcome that is unlikely to come about without some ability to form an enforceable agreement.

The Prisoner's Dilemma can be easily adapted to the "tragedy of the commons." Suppose that two farmers on adjoining land draw water from the same reservoir. If both attempt to draw enough water to maximize their output, the water supply will run out before the growing season ends, and the value of their output will be $50 each. If one farmer takes voluntary conservation measures in the form of rationing her use over the growing season, the conserver will produce output worth $30 and the nonconserver will produce $70 of output. If they both take conservation measures, the water will last the entire growing season, they will each have an output of $60, and joint production will be maximized.

In the absence of something more, the parties are destined to produce $50 worth of output each for a total of $100. Just like the prisoners, the rationally self-interested act is to assume the other party will try to maximize his gain. If that is so, it is rational for the counterpart to do the same. It is also rational to adopt the selfish strategy if one assumes the other party will adopt a cooperative strategy.

There are two ways out of the dilemma. The first is to assign property rights so that each party will have the right to exclude the other from unlimited use of the water. Too much use by a party would then give rise to an "externality" and give the other party a legal basis for stopping the overuse. Actually, as discussed in the next chapter, it may not matter to whom the "right" is assigned. The other way out is for the parties to cooperate and privately to create a system of "rights."

2. POSITIVE EXTERNALITIES, FREE–RIDING AND PUBLIC GOODS

a. Positive Externalities

Positive externalities occur when the activities of an individual or a firm result in benefits, the value of which the producer is unable to internalize or enjoy. For example, suppose a homeowner has his or her property beautifully landscaped and the effect is to increase both the value of the recently landscaped property and of the entire neighborhood. Here, the benefit to the neighboring property owners would be a positive externality.

b. Free–Riding

The possibility of positive externalities gives rise to the concept of "free-riding." Free-riding takes place when individuals are able to take advantage of the benefits of the activities of others without paying for those benefits. For example, without copyright protection, a composer might find that others are able to perform his or her music without paying. Similarly, without patent protection, an inventor of a new process may find that manufacturers are making use of that process without compensating the inventor. Positive externalities and free-riding explain the existence of copyright, trademark, and patent law.

Just how pervasive free-riding problems are is an empirical question. It seems clear that not as much free-riding takes place as there are opportunities to do so. People do contribute to public broadcasting and to charities without any assurance that their contributions are really necessary for the success of the operation.[5] Interestingly, it is often hard to square these acts with the standard economic assumption that people are rational maximizers of self-interest.

c. Public Goods

Goods for which there are positive externalities and free-rider problems may not be produced in the quantities in which they would be produced if those problems did not exist. Specifically, they may not be produced at allocatively efficient levels. The problem is that even though potential buyers may desire the good, they are tempted not to buy or produce it themselves in hopes that they can free-ride off the production or purchases of others. In effect, the private market receives an incorrect and weak signal with respect to the value of these goods.

---

5. See Jeffrey Harrison, "Egoism, Altruism and Market Illusions: The Limits of Law and Economics," 33 *U.C.L.A. L. Rev.* 1309, 1338–1340 (1986).

For example, suppose my house is close to my neighbor's and, if either one of us purchased a watch dog, the dog would alert both of us to any intruder. I might not buy a watch dog because I hope my neighbor will buy one, and he might take the same approach. If so, neither of us will buy a watch dog, even though the value we place on the protection of a watch dog would more than offset the cost of buying the dog.

Economists and game theorists use a construct called the "chicken game" to illustrate the free-riding problem.[6] Like the actors in the prisoner's dilemma, the participants in the chicken game have a choice of two actions. In the watch dog example, it would be to buy or not buy a watch dog. Here each party would prefer that the other party incur the expense of the dog. If a party were positive the other party would not acquire the dog, then he would be willing to buy it because the value of the dog would outweigh its cost.

The problem in the chicken game and in the case of free-riding generally is that the market receives a false signal as to the value potential buyers attribute to a good or service. This can be illustrated in Figure 2. D_1 is the actual demand of the good for which there are positive externalities and S is the supply. D_2 shows what the demand would be if people were not making an effort to free-ride. Put differently, D_2 shows the true value of the good. The

6. Charles Goetz, Law and Economics: Case and Materials 17–19, 29–32 (1983).

actual quantity produced will be Q_1, but the allocatively efficient level of production would be Q_2.

Figure 10

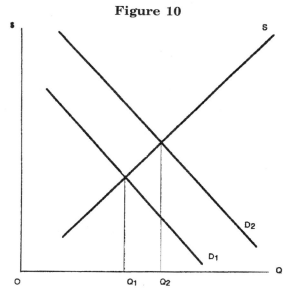

Often when the good in question is subject to these types of influences, it is provided by the government and financed by tax revenues. These types of goods are called "public goods," and the justification for government involvement is that the goods would not be produced in sufficient quantities without government action.

G. TAKINGS, EFFICIENCY AND EXTERNALITIES

An area of law in which many of the issues discussed here can be seen as coming into play is that dealing with takings. As you may know, the U.S. Constitution prohibits government takings of property unless it is for public use and just compensation is paid. Some takings are obviously that—the government takes land, for example, from someone and uses it itself or allows someone else to use it. This might be the case if a highway were constructed. In other cases, the government regulates the use of property and, in some instances, this too is regarded as a taking. In the case of the highway, the objective is to build a public good—something would likely not be produced due to free-riding. In the case of regulation, typically there is a negative externality that the state seeks to control.

When a taking occurs, compensation is required. The fact that it is required does not mean that the taking is efficient. On the other hand, even if compensation were not required, the taking might still be efficient. First take the case in which compensation is required. Suppose the state pays $20,000 for a parcel of land that has a market value of $20,000 but the owners would not have sold it for less that $25,000 because it has been in the family for years and they attach sentimental value to it. The taking here, even with compensation, is not efficient from either a Pareto or Kaldor–Hicks standpoint.

Now suppose no compensation is required but somehow we know the public values a parcel of land as part of a highway at $10,000 and the owners value it at $8,000. Here a decision to take the land and not pay would be Kaldor–Hicks efficient. This assumes that taking the land produces no other costs. Frank Michleman has made the point that living in a society in which land may be taken without compensation may have a demoralizing effect.[7] If so, this too would be a cost the state would have to consider in making a Kaldor–Hicks evaluation. Interestingly, this means a consistent policy of compensation could have the effect of lowering the cost of public projects.

It is even possible to work the idea of *ex ante* compensation into an analysis of takings law. One of the factors courts consider when determining whether a regulation amounts to a taking is "reasonable investment backed expectations." (District Intown Properties Limited Partnership v. District of Columbia, 198 F.3d 874 (D.C. Cir. 1999)). The suggestion is that the probability of being subject to regulation may be reflected in the price one pays for property. For example, if a person purchases a business that produces externalities, the likelihood of eventual regulation could be reflected in the price paid. If so, a denial of compensation would be consistent with the view that the buyers actually

7. Frank I. Michleman, "Property, Utility, and Fairness: Comments on the Ethical Foundations of 'Just Compensation' Law," 80 Harv. L. Rev. 1165 (1967)

did not possess a property right that had been taken.

H.　SOME ADDITIONAL USEFUL CONCEPTS

In addition to the terms described above, economists rely on a number of additional concepts that are useful when applying economics to law.

1.　OPPORTUNITY COST

To a large extent, economists measure the cost of one action in terms of the next best alternative. This is "opportunity cost." It is the value of the opportunity foregone. For example, suppose you are a professional basketball player earning $10 million a year. What is the opportunity cost for you in terms of the foregone employment? Maybe your next best occupation would be selling insurance and earning $100,000 per year. That is the opportunity cost of being a basketball player. If you are a full time law student, your opportunity cost is what you could earn if you were employed full time.

2.　DISCOUNTING AND PRESENT VALUE

A very important element in economic analysis relates to the impact of time on how things are valued. For example, if you were offered $10 now or $10 in a year, in all likelihood, you would like to have the money now. Money now is worth more than money in the future. In fact, suppose you were fairly certain to receive $10 in one year and you decided to sell that right to someone else right now. They might offer to buy it for $9.80. In other words, they "discount" the value of the $10 because it will not be received for some time. You might say that the "present value" of $10 to be received a year from now is $9.80.

Why is there a difference? The primary reason is risk. For one thing, the value of money may decline. If the price of goods and services increases throughout the year, $10 in a year may not buy what $10 would buy today. Even the *possibility* of inflation makes it preferable to have the money now. Second, until you actually have the money in hand, there is some probability that it will never be delivered.

Sometimes we speak informally about discounting the likelihood that something will happen in the future. More formally, discounting involves reducing the value of a future payment to a current amount using a discount or interest rate. For example, a payment of $100 payable in 12 months would have a present value of $90.90 if the discount rate applied were 10%. In law, discounting often comes into play when determining the present value of lost earnings or the present value of an extended period of medical care expenses. The idea is that the defendant or the defendant's insurance company makes one current payment that is equal to the present value of all future amounts. This amount is discounted (is less) because the plaintiff can then earn interest on that amount and will eventually receive the full amount of damages awarded.

An issue that arises is whether the discount rate should be the nominal interest rate or the "real" interest rate. You can understand the difference by thinking of the two sources of risks described above. The nominal interest rate—what a bank might quote you for a loan—includes allowances for the possibility that money paid in the future may be worth less due to inflation plus an allowance for all other risks. Obviously, when discounting, defendants favor using the nominal interest rate and plaintiff would prefer the real interest rate or no interest rate at all. The correct position from an economic perspective depends on whether plaintiffs, in determining damages that would be incurred in the future are permitted to allow for inflation.

3.   RISK AVERSION

As a general matter people will pay to avoid risks. For example, for the average person the amount paid for any kind of insurance will exceed the claims that will be made on that insurance policy over the period it is held. Otherwise, insurance companies would always run at a loss at least with respect to claims. The point is that risk itself is a source of disutility and there is a market for shifting that risk to others. Obviously there are some people who prefer risk and actually pay for it. For example, on average the casino gambler will lose more than he or she wins. The difference between winnings and loses can be seen as a payment to the casino for supplying the risk. On balance a generalized preference for risk is relatively rare.

Risk aversion is typically traced to the diminishing marginal utility for money. What this complicated phrase means is that as people have addition money each extra dollar results in less and less utility. So, if you have $100 you feel worse about wasting or losing a dollar than you would if you had $1000. To understand how this is connected to risk aversion, focus on a person who is faced with a coin flip. If it is heads, $100 will be taken away. If it is tails, he or she will receive $100. The question is whether the utility from an extra $100 is as great as the disutility from losing $100. Most people behave as though it is not.

Risk aversion comes into play when economics is applied to law at a number of points. The most important one is products liability. For example, should manufacturers be held liable for injuries to consumers even though we know they may simply raise the price of the good to all consumers by some amount? If consumers are risk averse, such a policy may make sense because they are willing to pay to have the manufacturer improve the product to pay damages if a harm does result. You can also extend the concept to criminal law. As you will see, economists write about efficient levels of crime. Granted this seems bizarre and you will read more about it in Chapter Eight. Achieving an efficient level of crime means setting the cost of committing a crime at an appropriate level. Of course those committing crimes are at risk of being caught. This risk is a cost of committing the crime and, technically, setting the cost to achieve the "right" level of crime requires allowing for this risk.

CHAPTER THREE

NORMATIVE AND BEHAVIORAL COMPLICATIONS IN THE APPLICATION OF ECONOMICS TO LAW

This Chapter is devoted to some of the controversies and complexities encountered in the study of law and economics. The first three sections deal with the behavioral assumptions economists make. The first addresses questions that arise from the economist's assumption that individuals are "rational maximizers of self-interest." It is important to establish what this term means. Whether people actually are rational and self-interested is an inquiry that is important to economics generally and perhaps especially important when economics is applied to law. From there, the Chapter goes on to address the question of whether choices and preferences are consistent. This may seem like a strange issue, but economics is generally focused on maximizing some measure of social welfare based, in part, on the choices people make. If these choices are not consistent with actual preferences, it is comparable to sending an incorrect signal to the market. The Chapter's next section considers three specific problems encountered when one attempts to use economics as the basis for policy. Including in this section is a discussion of the relatively recent emphasis on actual happiness as an economic goal. The final section of this chapter is devoted to the normative implications of applying economics to law.

A. RATIONAL MAXIMIZER OF SELF–INTEREST

Central to conventional law and economics is the assumption that individuals are rational maximizers of self-interest. These seemingly non-controversial terms can be broken into two components. Rationality would require most basically that the individuals not engage in acts that seem to be inconsistent. Often the critical matter that comes up here is the "law of transitivity." Under the law of transitivity, if an individual expresses a preference for apples over pears and pears over oranges, they would not then express a preference for oranges over apples. The importance of the rationality assumption is fairly obvious. Economics, above all else, is about getting the most out of scarce resources, and inconsistent, irrational behavior will impair the functioning of markets and render this goal impossible. The maximizing behavior assumption requires that decisions be made that advance some end. For example, if you wanted to be the richest person in the world, it would not be consistent to give money away unless you viewed it as an investment.

The self-interest assumption is more difficult to define. To some, it means to behave selfishly in the most common sense. Others, however, take the view that all rational conduct is self-interested. From this point of view, any choice that one makes is motivated by the fact that the selection is the one that "feels" better. If an option feels better then you prefer it, and to select options you prefer is to act self-interestedly. An example is a seemingly altruistic act. In the jargon of the most die-hard economists, the altruistic person gains more utility—satisfaction—from acting altruistically than from acting in a manner that would appear to be selfish. The altruistic act is explained by self-interest. The person who acts altruistically is really not uncompensated—she receives "psychic income." Psychic income attempts to explain everything but ultimately proves useless because one is still forced to distinguish amongst the different forms of self-interest. These different forms can be very important considerations when one applies economics to law.

Of the two ideas—rationality and self-interest—rationality is the more intriguing because numerous studies conducted by economists and psychologists over the last 30 years suggest that people do not behave rationally. It is important to remember that the criticism of economics is not whether the assumptions are perfectly accurate, but whether they are realistic enough that theories based on them are dependable in real world applications.

1. WEALTH AND ENDOWMENT EFFECTS

One general observation that indicates that the rationality assumption is incorrect, or at least far more complicated than traditionally assumed, is that people tend to react differently to the same gain or loss depending on their starting point. This is, in fact, one of the elements of "prospect theory," an area of research pioneered by Nobel Prize winner Daniel Kahneman and coauthor Amos Tversky.[1]

One of the central problems associated with relying on choices made or statements about the intensity of individual preferences is the wealth effect. Although the wealth effect can present itself in a number of forms, one of the more perplexing is that a person may seem to value an item or a right more when they possess it than when it is possessed by someone else. For example, suppose an individual owns a piece of property with an ocean view and, because of a deed restriction on the height of structures on a neighboring property, the view cannot be obstructed. If asked by someone what she would take to give up her right to the unobstructed view, her answer might be $50,000. On the other hand, if she did not possess that right but it was offered to her by the owner of the right to build an obstructing dwelling on the neighboring land, she might be willing to pay only $20,000. The fact that expressions of value vary depending upon whether an

1. Daniel Kaheman and Amos Tversky, "Prospect Theory: An Analysis of Decision Under Risk," 47 *Econometrica* 263 (1979).

individual is a potential buyer or seller has been empirically verified.

In some measure, the fact that individuals value things more if they own them can be traced to the fact that ownership means they actually are wealthier and, therefore, are capable of paying more for the items than if they did not own them. Or, more simply, if one already owns the item they do not actually have to have the income necessary to buy it. The wealth effect, however, goes much deeper than these possibilities. For example, it seems to hold even when the item at stake is of insignificant value. The problem this poses for law and economics is that the determination of preferences and the strength of those preferences may be contingent on whether or not the person currently owns the property. This is particularly troublesome for those who adhere to a concept of efficiency that seeks to maximize wealth where wealth is determined by how much one is said to value a particular item or right.

2. ULTIMATUM GAMES

The most interesting challenge to the rationality assumption has resulted from experiments conducted by economists and psychologists in which people do not behave as expected. The most important of these experiments is the ultimatum game, which works like this: Groups of subjects are broken into pairs. One person is given a sum of money and can give any amount of it to the other person. If the other person accepts the offer, they both keep what they have. If the other person rejects the offer, neither party receives anything. There is only one chance and the two parties do not communicate.

The rationality assumption would seem to require the first person to offer the second person very little or nothing. If he or she offers nothing, at least the second party is no worse off and would appear to have little reason to reject the offer. If the second person is offered a small amount there seems to be even less reason to reject the offer, since doing so means receiving nothing.

Repeatedly, the game results are that the first party offers more than a minimal share of the total, and the second party rejects offers of very small shares. The implications for rationality are obvious. If a person prefers more wealth to less, why reject a sum that at least builds in that direction? Put differently, if a person would bend over to pick up a dollar on the ground, why would he or she reject an offer of a dollar out of a total of $10? The answer seems to be that people value both fair treatment and others' perceptions that they are fair.

The "sense of fairness" explanation is demonstrated particularly well in a game designed by Richard Thaler. Thaler asked a group of people to assume it was a hot day at the beach and that a friend has offered to go find a beer. Part of the group was told that the beer will be bought from a fancy resort bar. Part of group was told that the beer would be bought at a run-down grocery store.[2]

2. Richard Thaler, The Winner's Curse: Paradoxes and Anomalies of Economic Life, 21–49 (1992).

Each group was then asked what was the highest price they would pay for the beer. Those who saw themselves as buying from the resort were willing to pay an average price of $2.65. The group buying from the grocery store were willing, on average, to pay $1.50.

One interpretation of the results of the experiment is that people questioned the fairness or the right of a run-down grocery store to charge as much as the resort. Put differently, those buying from the grocery store would have felt a sense of unfairness if the grocery store had required resort level prices. What appears to be happening is that individuals seem to place an independent value on coming away from an exchange with a sense of having been treated fairly.

The possible existence of an independent value for fairness is complex enough, but it becomes even more intriguing when one realizes that individuals may differ on what they perceive to be fair. This creates the possibility that two people may attribute the same utility and value to a good or service if they possess it, but might express their preferences in the market quite differently. For example, one person could find the price of an automobile acceptable while another would regard the same price as a "rip off." And, it would make sense, in this context, for sellers to discriminate between groups of buyers with differing senses of fairness.[3]

3. See generally, Ian Ayres, "Fair Driving: Gender and Race Discrimination in Retail Car Negotiations," 104 *Harv. L. Rev.* 817 (1991); Ian Ayres, "Further Evidence of Discrimination in

It is not clear that ultimatum games prove that people are irrational. A dollar found on the ground is not exactly the same thing as a dollar share of a much larger pot, and it is easy to imagine a set of preferences that would be both consistent and allow one to pick up the lost dollar and reject the offered dollar. What the games suggest is that rational people have complex preferences. If so, the implications for the application of economics to law are enormous. People who study law and economics tend to write about efficient levels of contract breach and crime based strictly on the dollar values involved. What the ultimatum games indicate is that this is an overly simplistic analysis.

The issues of what people find acceptable and why are studied by sociologists in the fields of equity theory and relative deprivation rather than by economists. These are, however, critical matters for those who apply economics to law in the hopes of using that analysis to help formulate policy. These concepts go beyond economics alone and permit one to pierce some of the mysteries of market behavior in order to make more informed decisions about the use of law.

B. CHOICES AND PREFERENCES

As mentioned above, one of the important assumptions that must be made to apply economics to law is that people reveal their preferences in the

New Car Negotiations and Estimates of Its Causes," 94 *Mich. L. Rev.* 109 (1991).

choices they make. Of course, the biggest problem with this assumption is that people with extremely strong preferences may not have the funds to express those preferences in the market. Since law responds to more than just the needs expressed in markets, this is a crucial matter to consider. Beyond that issue, it's important to be aware of a number of other factors that mean observed choices may be inconsistent with preferences.

1. PUBLIC GOODS AND FREE RIDING

You were already introduced to one of the ways in which the choices made in markets can be misleading when you read about the chicken game and public goods in Chapter Two. To review, imagine a case in which you and a pal are enrolled in the same class. You hope that your friend will attend class and share the notes with you so that you won't have to do any work. If you have to, however, you will go to class to take notes yourself. Thus, your preferences could be ordered as follows: friend goes to class and shares notes with you (#1 choice), you go to class and take notes yourself (#2), or you have no notes (#3). The problem is that to get your first choice you may have to act as though the notes are less important to you than they actually are. You engage in bluffing designed to convince your friend that the only way for her to get the notes is to go to class herself.

You can see the problem here for an economist who is trying to gauge your preferences but is not a mind-reader. For strategic reasons, your signal must be different from how you actually feel, and the "choice" or lack thereof does not reveal your preference at all.

2. THE PRISONER'S DILEMMA

A similar problem arises in the prisoner's dilemma, which you also saw in Chapter Two. Again, the problem involves two prisoners who are being held apart from each other after being arrested in connection with a crime. They are separately questioned. If both prisoners confess they will both receive a sentence of five years. If neither confesses they will receive sentences of two years. Finally, if one confesses and the other does not, the confessor will be given a one-year sentence and the prisoner choosing not to confess will be sentenced to 10 years. The ideal strategy is for both prisoners to not confess because this means only two years of prison each. The big drawback to this strategy is that the other prisoner may then elect to confess and the non-confessor gets 10 years. As a result, each prisoner will attempt to save themselves and confess.

The way to get to the ideal outcome is for the prisoners to make an enforceable agreement—something the rules of the game exclude—or to cooperate. There is, in fact, a great deal of evidence that people do learn to cooperate, especially after repeated tries, in order to get to the best outcome. The problem for those who rely on choices to reveal preferences is that, unless the observer understands the game, the action adopted to achieve the best outcome will appear to be inconsistent with what is really desired.

3.   THE POSSIBILITY OF COUNTER–PREFERENTIAL CHOICE

The possibility of choices revealing preferences becomes even more remote if people are capable of counter-preferential choices. Nobel Award winning economist Amartya Sen suggests this possibility when he distinguishes sympathy from commitment. To understand this difference, suppose you become a vegetarian even though you love the taste of meat. Maybe you empathize with the animals' suffering, or perhaps you believe that all animals are sentient beings and deserve to have rights, one of which is to not be eaten. The standard analysis that your choice in the market reveals something about your taste for eating meat would miss the fact that you actually do like the taste of meat and might buy similarly-tasting products. More importantly, it misses a complexity in the choice-making process that could be especially useful to understand when economics is applied to law.

4.   FALSE CONSCIOUSNESS

A failure to match choices with preferences, according to some, can result from the inability of an individual to know or express what is in his best interest. This is best understood if one uses the notion of coercion as a baseline. A person who chooses to give up his wallet instead of both giving it up and being beaten has, in a sense, expressed a preference. Still, we tend not to give much credence to that choice as something the law should legitimize. Moving from that point, the question becomes: when should the choices made be regarded as free? When are the factors influencing a choice legitimate and when do they prevent someone from expressing his "true" preference? These are obviously open-ended questions without answers that will satisfy everyone. They are critical though, because choices that do not reveal "true" preferences can hardly be said to be consistent with efficient outcomes.[4]

Other than distinguishing choices that would be made if one were "free" to choose from those resulting from illegitimate influences, questions can arise when people seem unable to control their choices. For example, an alcoholic may prefer not to be an alcoholic and at the same time consume a great deal of alcohol. A similar case is the heavy smoker who also buys nicotine patches in an effort to give up smoking. Again, since economics is so crucially linked with preferences and the expression of preferences, it is a problem when there is a gap between expressions and actual preferences.

5. FRAMING PROBLEMS

The problem of determining preferences is also complicated by the fact that people seem to give

4. See Cass Sunstein, "Legal Interference With Private Preferences," 53 *U. Chi. L. Rev.* 1129 (1986).

inconsistent answers to questions that are substantively the same depending on how those questions are framed. In one famous example, individuals were asked to assume that a disease outbreak in the United States was expected to kill 600 people.[5] They were then asked to choose between two programs stated as follows: "If program A is adopted, 200 people will be saved. If program B is adopted, there is a one-third probability that 600 people will be saved, and a two-thirds probability that no people will be saved." Stated this way, there was a strong preference for program A.

The choice was then presented as follows: "If program C is adopted, 400 people will die. If program D is adopted, there is a one-third probability that nobody will die, and a two-thirds probability that 600 people will die." This time choice D was heavily favored. The problem is that programs A and C are identical as are choices B and D. The difference is in the way the choice is perceived.

C. PREFERENCES, VALUES, AND LEXICAL ORDERING

One of the assumptions that make conventional economics "work" is that all sources of utility or pleasure are similar in that the type of utility they generate can be reduced to a common denominator.[6] For example, if someone took your auto-

5. See Daniel Kahneman and Amos Tversky, "Framing Decisions and the Psychology of Choice," 211 *Science* 453 (1981).

6. Nicolas Georgescu–Roegen, "Choice Expectation and Measurability," 68 *Q. J. Econ.* 503 (1954).

graphed copy of Kingsley Amis' *Lucky Jim* it might be a terrible loss. Under the conventional thinking, no matter how great your loss in utility, you could somehow be compensated and restored—perhaps by receiving a carton of Rod McKuen poetry books—to your original level of utility or happiness.

Of course, under this way of thinking, money is used for compensation because it can be exchanged for all sorts of worldly goods and services. Moreover, everything is ultimately for sale. After all, if you could be compensated for any involuntary loss, presumably you could be compensated at just a slightly higher rate and freely give up whatever is at stake. For a price, your arm is for sale as well as your children. In a more familiar legal context, it could mean that, if the price is high enough, you will break a promise, or breach a contract, drive recklessly through a playground, or enslave someone.

But what if you are guided by principle: You will not allow someone to break your leg at any price, no amount of money will entice you into driving recklessly through a playground, and you refuse to break the knees of, say, a competing figure skater no matter how much you are offered. When these things come up, the assumption that everything can be reduced to simple utility does not hold. Moreover, it is least likely to hold when the "goods" involved are associated with some moral obligation and oft times with law.

It is easy to say that in these examples, you are simply not offered enough, or you are acting irrationally. Another explanation is that some sources of utility are lexically or lexicographically ordered.[7] An example of lexical ordering is a dictionary. In a dictionary any word beginning with the letter "a" comes before words beginning with the letter "b." Even a word beginning with "b" and followed by an infinite number of "a's" cannot be placed ahead of a word beginning with an "a," even if that "a" is followed by a whole host of "z's."

Like words in the dictionary, some values are, no doubt, ranked in such a way that they are not interchangeable with values or sources of utility that exist at a different level. This means concepts like "compensation" and "incentive" may be more complex than conventional economics seems to allow. This is particularly important in the application of economics to law because law is about so many of these values.

The possibility of the existence of different types of values can be especially important at a very practical level. In order to understand why, it is important to understand that economists usually start from the point of view that a person's tastes and preferences are fixed. The term here is that they are "exogenously" determined. This would be important if one wanted to examine the impact of a price change on the sales of orange juice. It is only possible to isolate the effect of the price change if the taste for orange juice remains constant whatever the price. In other words, even though the price

7.   John Rawls, *A Theory of Justice* 42–43 (1971).

change will affect the amount of orange juice purchased, it must not affect how much people enjoy orange juice.

This requirement presents a problem when economics is applied to law. For example, instead of orange juice, suppose one wanted to determine the impact of higher fines on speeding. The idea, of course, is that higher fines will decrease speeding. The problem is that the increase in fines may actually effect how people feel about speeding. That is, a higher fine may signify societal disapproval and actually have an impact on the individual's "taste" for speeding. More technically, law may act as an endogenous variable, not simply an exogenous one.[8] This means that the "markets" that are the subject of law and economics are probably far more complex than the ones to which conventional analysis is applied.

To give you an idea of how this makes the economic analysis of law more complex than the economic analysis of more conventional markets, consider the behavioral assumptions specified by one leading law and economics scholar. The author states the usual assumption underlying his analysis, that individuals are rational maximizes of self-interest. He then explains that this means they do not obey the law out of a sense of duty.[9] This is not

8. See Kenneth G. Dau–Schmidt, "An Economic Analysis of the Criminal Law as a Preference Shaping Policy," 1990 *Duke L. J.* 1; Jeffrey L. Harrison, "Class, Personality, Contract and Unconscionability," 35 *William and Mary L. Rev.* 445 (1994).

9. Robert Cooter, "Prices and Sanctions," 84 *Colum. L. Rev.* 1523, 1527 (1984).

atypical, and there is nothing inherently wrong with making assumptions. It does, however, give one a sense of how the economic analysis of law may be limited. For example, people who obey the law because it is the law or who change their behavior when something becomes illegal—and not as a result of a cost-benefit analysis—may be left out of the economist's theory.

D. NORMATIVE QUESTIONS IN THE APPLICATION OF LAW TO ECONOMICS

Overriding the concerns about whether people behave as they are assumed to behave by economics is the question of whether the highly normative field of law should be guided by economic analysis. If this were the case, a number of outcomes would run counter to what most people regard as fair or even sensible. For example, law and economics give rise to the concept of the efficient breach of contract and efficient levels of crime. It also means that it may be efficient to allow the market to operate to satisfy tastes—including racist, sexist, and homophobic—that the majority of society finds offensive. (Do you see why the same activities are not efficient if enough people are offended?) This is because economics makes no distinction among various sources of utility. Thus, the efficient outcome may be offensive to many and a normative decision must be made about the importance of efficiency.

Probably the factor that is most worrisome about the application of economics to law is the use of price as a rationing mechanism. In other words, markets respond not to needs—no matter how consistent with utility—but to the amounts people are willing and able to spend. This is a concern at two levels. The first are choices made with respect to what is produced and not produced. For example, some people spend money on yachts, mansions, and elaborate vacations while others cannot afford to buy enough food to live a minimally healthy life. Some people spend $300,000 on college educations while others grow up under conditions that mean they are unlikely to attend college at all, or even finish high school. What seems to be missing is a connection between what money is spent on (and the goods and services produced) and an overriding measure of fairness, justice, or happiness

The second level of concern is with the allocation of wealth and income. The question is whether one's happiness and utility should be a function of his or her ability to produce the goods and services that others want and are able to pay for. Here again there are a couple of complexities. First, some people are excellent at producing things that bring a great deal of happiness to others. This does not mean that those people who would be better off are able to pay. Thus, even some of the most productive people, in terms useful goods and services, are not rewarded. Second, suppose you were content with a system that rewards people on what they produce that others can pay for. Since they produce what others can pay for, they, in turn, are able to spend more themselves. The problem with this is that, in reality, the ability to spend is not necessarily a function of the ability to produce. Much of what is spent by a great number of people is not earned by them at all. This notion obviously covers instances of inherited wealth but can also extend to inherited intellectual and physical talents. Thus, it can come down to whether it is fair or just for economic well-being to be determined by the traits and wealth of one's parents.

E. WHAT ABOUT HAPPINESS?

You have already seen one reason why some notions of efficiency are not the same as maximizing actual well-being: there is a separation between resource allocation based on willingness and ability to pay and one based on the utility that would be derived. Of course, no one knows and it appears to be impossible to determine what a utility-based allocation would look like. Another issue that comes up with respect to efficiency is that the usual measures are determined by observed choices. For example, in the case of Pareto efficiency, if two people choose to make an exchange and no one is worse off, we view it as an increase in social welfare. The problem is that we assume they are better off because of the choice made and no one follows up to see if they are actually better off. Put differently, there is no assessment of whether they are actually happier because conventional notions of efficiency are based on expectations, not on outcomes. This not to say there is always a difference but, as you know from personal experience, often a choice can lead to a disappointing result.

The disconnect between observed choices and actual well-being has fueled an enormous amount of research into the question of actual happiness. Economists and law professors have begun to ask the question of whether there can be an efficiency standard based on what actually happens. In fact, some have devised elaborate tests to assess how people feel at any one moment while going through an experience. The results suggest that a happiness standard for efficiency may be a difficult one to achieve but some of the implications of the possibility are quite important.

Consider this example. Some research indicates that people tend over the long run to settle into a set level of happiness. When a good thing happens, they are happier for a period and then return to their original level of happiness. Or, when a bad thing happens, they are less happy and then also return to the original level of happiness. This seems to occur even if they suffer a severe injury or the loss of a loved one. One possibility here is that damages for pain and suffering after and accident are routinely too high. You will understand this argument better after reading about tort remedies but even now you can understand at least the argument that people do not suffer as much as they may think they will when the harm occurs.

This example, however, along with many others, reflects the controversies that can come up when happiness is the focus of the analysis. For example, one argument against the idea that people return to their prior level of happiness is that they simply begin to relate to different standard, one that is viewed as "I am pretty happy, given the circumstances." In effect, the alter their expectations an measure their happiness against new expectations.

Another happiness controversy is: What matters, how one feels or how one actually is. This is the difference between subjective well-being and actual or objective well-being. A heavy smoker may feel happy as can be while, as an objective matter, he is not all that well off. Questions also arise as to when happiness matters. What we know is that when events occur people may experience one level of happiness or even misery but later on feel quite differently. For example, you may go through an experience and at the time, if you were asked, you might reply that it is horrible. (Maybe like the first year of law school.) A few years later you may have only fond memories and feel a great sense of accomplishment.

What all this suggests is that the conventional economic analysis has many limitations. It is largely based on expectations expressed in the market. This means it focuses on those who are able to participate in the market. In addition, we know their decisions may be influenced by things that divert them from maximizing their utility. Moreover, even a very well-informed person may make a choice that leaves him or her feeling worse off. The problem is that most, but not all, of these limitations are difficult to address in a way that is consistently dependable and agreeable to all. The most important thing this means for you as a person who is studying law and economics is to be mindful of these limits.

CHAPTER FOUR

THE COASE THEOREM AND RELATED PROPERTY ISSUES

A. THE COASE THEOREM

Nothing is more central to the study of law and economics or more responsible for its growth than the Coase Theorem.[1] The Coase Theorem says that, in many instances, the assignment of rights by courts or legal authorities may have little to do with who eventually possesses those rights. In the words of Mark Kelman, "the market, like an untameable river, will knock out attempts to alter its mighty course."[2]

Although the Theorem has implications for a wide variety of areas of substantive law, it is most easily explained and understood in the context of competing uses for resources. A case that lends itself to a Coasian analysis is *Fontainebleau Hotel Corp. v. Forty–Five Twenty–Five, Inc.*, 114 So.2d 357 (Fla.App.1959). The dispute revolved around the

[1]. Ronald Coase, "The Problem of Social Cost," 3 *J. L. & Econ.* 1 (1960).

[2]. Mark Kelman, "Consumption Theory, Production Theory, and Ideology in the Coase Theorem," 52 *So. Cal. L. Rev.* 669, 675 (1979).

right of the Fountainbleau hotel in Miami Beach to build a fourteen-story addition. The problem with the addition was that its shadow would fall over the cabana, swimming pool, and sunbathing areas of a neighboring hotel, the Eden Roc. The Eden Roc sought to enjoin the construction of the addition and eventually lost. In more technical terms, the shadow could be viewed as a negative externality—a cost imposed on the Eden Roc by the Fountainbleau's construction project. As it turned out, the Eden Roc was denied injunctive relief; the right to build the addition, even though it blocked the sun, was assigned by the court to the Fountainbleau.

1. ALLOCATIVE IMPLICATIONS

The question from a Coasian perspective is whether it really matters how the court decided the issue. Obviously the "right" to build had some value in terms of the present value of the expected profit the Fountainbleau would earn from the addition. Suppose this value was $1,000,000. Suppose also that the Eden Roc executives had studied the matter and determined that the present value of the profits lost due to the fact that a sunless resort hotel is less desirable to tourists is $1,100,000. At that point, it would have made sense for the managers of the Fountainbleau and Eden Roc to determine whether they could have made an exchange that left them both better off—in a Pareto Superior position. Obviously, any price in excess of $1,000,000 would have made the Fountainbleu better off and any price less than $1,100,000 would have improved the position of the Eden Roc. Thus, at least at this initial level of analysis, the right to build should have been sold to the Eden Roc and the initial assignment would not have withstood the influence of market.

The critical element of the Coase Theorem is that the outcome in terms of which hotel eventually owns the right to build or to prevent building is not affected by the initial assignment of that right. Thus, had the Florida court decided that the Eden Roc did have the right to enjoin the construction of the shadow-casting addition, presumably, the parties involved would once again engage in their valuation process. The Fountainbleau would be unwilling to pay any more than $1,000,000 for the Eden Roc's "right" to enjoin construction, and the Eden Roc would not take anything less that $1,100,000 for that right. Here again, the addition would not be built.

It is important to see how the Coase Theorem applies to the typical case involving a factory which, in its production process, pollutes either the air or the water in a nearby river. In both instances, the pollution, like the shadow cast by the Fountainbleau's addition, could be viewed as an externality. The question the Coase Theorem answers is whether the amount of this pollution really will be affected by whether or not the polluting factory has a right to pollute. What the Theorem tells us is that, however the right is initially assigned, the eventual use of the water will be left to market forces and the level of pollution will be the same.

It is important not to lose sight of the breadth of the implications of the Coase Theorem. The dispute between the Eden Roc and Fountainbleau illustrates the Theorem in very simple terms. Coase's proposition was initially illustrated by competing users of land, a cattle raiser with straying cattle and a farmer whose crops were endangered by the straying cattle. This type of example allows one to focus on the workings of the Theorem in a context in which marginal analysis—the mainstay of microeconomics—is easily visualized. In this famous example, the relevant comparison was between the value of each additional steer and the annual crop loss per additional steer. Again, regardless of the initial assignment, one would expect the land to be put to the use for which it generates the greatest profit. In this example, where the output of each user can be divided into individual units, it is likely to mean the land will be divided in some fashion between cattle raising and farming.

The Theorem can also be viewed in the context of a standard contract law topic. Suppose Bud agrees to sell his 1957 Chevy to Bette. They agree on a price of $10,000. The most Bette would have paid is $12,000. In other words the benefit of the bargain to Bette is $2,000. Now Jack comes along and offers Bud $15,000 for the car. Bud would like to breach but would have to pay Bette $5,000 in liquidated damages if he does. In effect, he is no better off breaching and selling the car to Jack than he would be if he delivered it to Bette. Obviously, Jack values the car the most of the trio. The problem is whether the market will find a way around the fact that Bette is entitled to the car or $5,000 and steer it into Jack's hands. Here Bud would be willing to buy the right to breach for up to $3,000 and Bette would be willing to sell it for something in excess of $2,000. Presumably they will make the exchange and the car will be resold to Jack. As for the liquidated damages, Bud can just threaten to perform (which only gets Bette a $2,000 surplus) anytime Bette presses the issue of the liquidated damages clause.

2. ASSIGNMENT OF RIGHTS AND DISTRIBUTIVE EFFECTS

The Coase Theorem focuses on allocative effects. In its simplest form, it can be viewed as saying that an initial assignment that is allocatively inefficient—assigned to the party who does not attribute the greatest value to the right—will be "corrected" by the market. This hardly means the assignment by the court, legislature, or administrative body is irrelevant. That assignment can have huge distributive effects. For example, assigning the right to build to the Fountainbleau, meant that the Fountainbleau would keep the right or be enriched by someone who valued it more. Put differently, the assignment may not determine the ultimate allocation of various rights, but it will have an impact on the distribution of wealth.

Oft-times courts seem to react to the distributive implications even when the parties seem capable of bargaining around the initial allocation. For example, in a contracts case, *McKinnon v. Benedict*, 157 N.W.2d 665 (Wis.1968), the court was faced with the issue of whether to enjoin the land development efforts of one landowner at the request of a neighboring landowner. The parties evidently had significant personal contact, and it seems clear that the parties could reallocate the development rights should the relative values attributed to those rights by the parties warrant. The court denied the injunction, favoring the party it characterized as having limited financial means and limited business experience. The decision had the effect of enhancing the wealth of the disadvantaged party and creating a situation in which the wealthier party would be required to purchase the defendant's right to develop the property rather than have it granted to him by the court.

This particular example may give the reader pause because it seems clear that had the injunction been issued, the party with the limited resources would not have been able to buy the right to develop from the other landowner. From the standpoint of conventional economic analysis, the inability to pay is really indistinguishable from the unwillingness to pay. The conclusion would still be that the relatively poor landowner did not sufficiently value the right. If this is disconcerting, conventional economists would remind the reader that if the land were sufficiently profitable when developed, the poor landowner would be able to find investors quite willing to loan him the money to buy the development rights from the landowner to whom the injunction was granted.

An even more direct interest in allowing for both allocative and distributive effects is found in *Spur Industries, Inc. v. Del E. Webb Development Co.*, 494 P.2d 700 (Ariz.1972). Spur operated a feed lot in an isolated area. Over the years, land near the feedlot was developed for residential purposes, resulting eventually in complaints that the feedlot was a nuisance due to the insects and odors it caused. Del Webb, a developer, successfully sought an order permanently enjoining Spur from operating the feed lot. The court granted the injunction. From a strictly allocative perspective, there would appear to be little reason for the court to go any further. The court, however, seemingly desirous of altering what it viewed as an unfair distributive outcome, ordered the developer to pay Spur for the expenses of relocating.

3.   TRANSACTION COSTS

The Fountainbleau and Eden Roc dispute is an easy example of how the Coase Theorem might work. A problem, which Professor Coase readily recognized, is that virtually all exchanges have a cost. These costs are called transaction costs. It is important to note that a transaction cost is not the price of an item or a right. Instead, it is the cost of the transaction itself. These costs include search

costs, information costs, the costs of meetings, negotiations, and any other costs incurred to make the
primary exchange occur. If these costs exceed the
gain from the exchange itself, the exchange will not
take place.

In the Fountainbleau example, the gain from the
exchange would be $100,000. That is, the right to
the sunlight is worth $100,000 more to the Eden
Roc than the right to build is to the Fountainbleau.
Thus, it would make economic sense, assuming no
one is made worse off by the exchange, for the right
to eventually find its way into the possession of the
Eden Roc. Suppose, however, that the transaction
involved substantial attorneys' fees and air fares in
order to gather the interested parties together. If
the transaction costs exceed $100,000, which in this
case they very well might, the surplus or profit
created by the exchange will be offset by the costs of
the exchange. Thus, transaction costs, like the friction encountered in a physics experiment, may keep
us from observing what would actually happen if
the market were completely fluid. In short, in many
instances, the market will not overcome an initial,
possibly inefficient, assignment.

Two additional facets of the transaction costs
problem are important to note. The first concerns
situations in which the possible exchange does not
involve single entities on both sides of the bargaining table but, on at least one side, there are
multiple parties. Here the difficulty of achieving
an exchange is made more severe by the costs of
contacting a number of individuals and reaching

agreement among them as to an acceptable selling or buying price. This coordination problem exists even if the parties are perfectly willing to cooperate. Another possibility—that they are not so willing to cooperate—is discussed below.

The second factor is the implication of time limitations. For example, the well-known case of *Ploof v. Putnam*, 71 A. 188 (Vt. 1908) involved the efforts by an individual sailing with his family who was caught in a violent storm. When he tied up at the defendant's dock, the defendant untied his mooring lines and his boat was cast adrift. Ultimately the court assigned the right to the party in distress to use the dock of the landowner. In this type of situation, any misallocation would be difficult to overcome. Here the costs of the transaction may not be prohibitive in the abstract but, when they must be expended in a very short period, they become prohibitive.

4. BARGAINING PROBLEMS

The Coase Theorem has its best chance of actually "working" when the parties do not have significant "market power." In this context, "market power" means the ability to hold out for more favorable terms without fearing that the other party will easily turn to another seller or buyer. The bargaining problem can arise in two distinct contexts.

The first and most extreme example of when "market power" can be a problem is when there is only one buyer and one seller. This is called a bilateral monopoly. First, consider the basic Fountainbleau example in its simplest form—the single owner of the Fountainbleau bargaining with the owner of the Eden Roc. In the example presented earlier, the building right was worth $100,000 more to the owner of the Eden Roc than to the owner of the Fountainbleau. The least the Fountainbleau would take for this right was $1,000,000 and the most the Eden Roc would offer was $1,100,000. The parties must, however, determine an actual sales price. Presumably, they will both use a variety of bargaining strategies in order to get the most favorable price possible. In other words, they will each try to get the largest share possible of the gain created by the exchange. As they parry back and forth in an effort to gain the upper hand, it may be that the time for a mutually beneficial exchange will simply run out.

Whether the delays associated with bilateral monopoly that mean the exchange may not take place are fairly termed transaction costs in Coasian terms is not clear. They may be viewed as a form of transaction cost or it may be that the Coase Theorem involves an assumption that the bargaining parties will cooperate in order to consummate the exchange. In either case, there seems to be general agreement that the bargaining problem creates the same kind of "friction" as traditional transaction costs.[3]

3. See Robert Cooter, "The Cost of Coase," 11 *J. Leg. Stud.* 1 (1982).

Much the same problem arises if the hypothetical is revised so that the Eden Roc is owned by a single individual, but the Fountainbleau is owned by several individuals, all of whom must agree in order for the exchange to be consummated. The most obvious difficulty this presents is an array of variations on traditional transaction costs. A larger number of individuals means increased difficulties of coordination, contract drafting, etc. In addition, each seller or buyer will have the potential power to veto the exchange. In effect, each owner has monopoly power with respect to her ownership rights. Here again, the absence of a competitive market may mean that some individuals hold out for a disproportionate share of the proceeds from the sale. Of course, this may entail a fair amount of strategic behavior in the form of bluffing. The general problem is the same as that which exists between the buyer and seller in that the holdout has the power to undermine what would otherwise be an exchange that would leave all parties better off.

In addition to the problems associated with strategic behavior in bargaining, there may be another obstacle to the free exchange. Referring again to the Eden Roc example, it is clear that under a traditional analysis any price between $1,000,000 and $1,100,000 will leave both parties in a better position than the one in which they started. One would think that they would realize that it is more important to come to an agreement that improves the lot of both parties than it is to hold out for the very best bargain. Under this line of reasoning, once all the haggling and bluffing is over, the parties would agree to something. The additional problem that may arise here is that both parties may approach the bargaining with expectations about what a "fair" division of the surplus made possible by the exchange would be. These expectations may result from an inflated sense of entitlement resulting from social class or a simple desire to save face. If one or both of the parties takes the view that they will take none of the surplus before they will settle for what is seen as an inadequate share, the deal may still fall through despite their best efforts. This "equity" barrier is probably of greater importance when the bargaining takes on an interpersonal character.[4]

B. THE WEALTH EFFECT

One of the most frequently discussed criticisms of the Coase Theorem and of the economic analysis of law generally is the "wealth effect." To understand the importance of the wealth effect, one must recall that what the Coase Theorem guarantees is that, in a transaction-cost-free context, resources and rights will end up in the hands of those who value them most. The wealth effect introduces an element of circularity into the theory by suggesting that the one who values something most is, all other things being equal, the person who already possesses what-

4.   Jeffrey Harrison, "Trends and Traces: A Preliminary Evaluation of Economic Analysis in Contract Law," 1988 *Ann. Survey of Am. L.* 73, 96.

ever is at stake. It also suggests a bias in favor of the *status quo* as far as resource allocation goes.

What this means in the Eden Roc example is that, if the right had been assigned to the Eden Roc and the Fountainbleau was enjoined from constructing its addition, the bias introduced in the system is that the right will not be transferred. Conversely, if the right is granted to the Fountainbleau, as was the case, the bias introduced favors the right remaining with the Fountainbleau.

In its most fundamental form, the actual ownership of an asset affects the ability of a party to pay. In actuality, factors that have only a minimal effect on wealth or no effect also seem to create the same kind of inertia that the traditional wealth effect produces. One of best examples of how "wealth-like effects" can work at insignificant levels of wealth was illustrated in an experiment in which individuals, upon entering a room, were given either a lottery ticket or $3.00.[5] After the nature of the lottery was explained, they were given an opportunity to exchange their lottery tickets for $3.00 or to exchange their $3.00 for a lottery ticket. The majority of participants, whether they were initially given lottery tickets or given $3.00, elected to keep what they had. In essence, the mere possession of one item instead of another seemed to give rise to some form of inertia that precluded an exchange. The

5. Jack Knetch & J. A. Sinden, "Willingness to Pay and Compensation Demanded: Experimental Evidence of an Unexpected Distortion in Measures of Value," 99 *Q. J. Econ.* 507 (1984).

value one attributed to $3.00 or to the lottery ticket was determined solely by whether he or she had been handed $3.00 or a lottery ticket in the first place.

An illustration of inertia resulting in a wealth-effect type of influence is the change in the mobility of professional baseball players before and after free-agency.[6] Until relatively recently, due to agreements among the owners of professional sports teams, a player would be drafted by one team and generally would stay with that team unless traded to another team. In effect, the right to the player's services belonged to the team owner. The services of that player would have a certain value to that team and the player could be sold or traded to another owner who valued those services more than the original owner.

Under a free-agency system, which allows the players to sell their services, one would expect the level of player mobility to remain the same. In other words, players would still end up playing for teams that attributed to them the highest value based on revenue-generating potential. In actuality, in the era of free-agency, players have turned out to be significantly more mobile as owners bid for their services. Since it is unlikely that actual revenue-generating potential increased, it appears that owners valued the players' services more when they owned the rights to those services. Another explanation for the inertia under the former system is that owners found it far easier to refuse offers made

6. See M. Kelman, *supra* note 2, at 682–685.

for the rights to their players than to actually incur an out-of-pocket expense of the same amount in order to obtain a player.

It is not clear whether the wealth effect and effects having the same manifestations really undermine the Coase Theorem. At one level, the Theorem seems to hold. As a technical matter, the eventual allocation does end up being to the party who attributes the greatest value to the right or item in question. On the other hand, the person who that happens to be and the allocatively efficient outcome are in some sense predetermined by the fortuity of the initial allocation. A different initial allocation may mean a different distribution would be allocatively efficient. In a sense, *who* really values something the most is indeterminate.

One additional and very intriguing problem further complicates the issue of valid expression of value. As you have seen, valuation may be affected by ownership. Now add to this the possibility that one can be wrong about that ownership. In other words, whatever wealth effect there is may be based on an incorrect premise. For example, one recent study found that terminable-at-will employees believe they cannot be terminated arbitrarily when, in fact, they can be.[7] The question to untangle is what to make of any expressions the workers may make with respect to the value of those rights.

7.   Pauline T. Kim, "Bargaining with Imperfect Information: A Study of Worker Perceptions of Legal Protection in an At–Will World," 85 *Cornell L. Rev.* 105 (1997).

C. REACTIONS TO TRANSACTION COSTS

1. DUPLICATING FRICTION– FREE TRANSACTIONS

An important issue that arises in the context of the Coase Theorem is whether a court should take note of the presence or absence of transaction costs in its delineation of legal rights. There are a number of possibilities. The most commonly discussed possibility, typically attributed to Judge Richard Posner, is that the court should assign the right as the parties would have if they were not hampered by transaction costs.

For example, take a case like *Boomer v. Atlantic Cement Company*, 257 N.E.2d 870 (N.Y.1970), a casebook favorite dealing with the subject of nuisance. The dirt, smoke and vibration associated with the operation of defendant's cement factory resulted in $185,000 in damages to the eight plaintiffs who requested an injunction. The cement plant represented a $45 million investment and presumably had a current value well in excess of $185,000.

In Coase Theorem terms, there would seem to be little long-run allocative impact from any decision the court made. Supposedly, if it had granted the injunction, the factory owners would have purchased the right to continue polluting from the land-owners. Transaction costs might have been quite low, and certainly low enough not to cancel out the gain from an exchange in which the landowners value the right at $185,000 and the factory values it at several million dollars. With eight sellers, however, the possibility of hold-out problems exist and if the injunction were granted, the factory could not operate. In addition, if the number of plaintiffs were increased, there would be an even greater possibility that the exchange would not take place. One solution is to simply assign the right to the party that values it the most—in this case the owners of the cement factory. After all, the reasoning goes, this is what the parties would have done if they could. In the case, the court did, but it also granted damages to the landowners.

The solution to the transaction costs problem of granting the right to the party who would have purchased it in a friction-free market is subject to both practical and moral questions. From the point of view of simple practicality, it is not clear exactly how a court or any rights-allocating body is supposed to gauge, consistently and accurately, the value of the right to the respective parties. While the Posner solution seems to envision some kind of giant auction, that is not what happens, and courts are left to their usual means of attempting to assess value. This means reliance on objective as opposed to subjective values and the possibility that the court will simply get it wrong.

A more difficult issue is whether courts *should* try to replicate the allocations that would occur in the market. It should be recalled that one possibly comforting implication of the Coase Theorem is that both parties would agree to any reallocation of rights. In other words, since both parties consent to the exchange, it seems they have made a Pareto superior move as long as others were not negatively affected. Of course, this is all subject to the limitations discussed in Chapter Three with respect to the disconnection between choices and preferences.

Can a court replicate the same outcome? Probably not. Returning once again to the Fountainbleau case suppose the numbers are the same as above— the right to build and block the sunlight is worth $1,000,000 to the Fountainbleau and access to sunlight is worth $1,100,000 to the Eden Roc. Due to transaction costs, suppose further that it is clear that once the assignment is made, the parties will not be able to exchange the right. If the court chooses to assign the right to the party who would have ended up with it in a transaction-costs free environment, it would be assigned to the Eden Roc. In the context of the case, the court would have granted the Eden Roc's request for an injunction. Such an assignment would seem to be consistent with wealth-maximizing or Kaldor–Hicks standards of efficiency. After all, even if one wanted to view the decision as involving a reallocation from the Fountainbleau to the Eden Roc, the gain for the Eden Roc would exceed the loss to the Fountainbleau.

On the other hand, the allocation will not be consistent with Pareto superiority. Again, a Pareto superior move requires that the position of at least one party be improved and that no parties be made worse off. In the example, the Eden Roc will be no worse off as it always claimed the right to un-blocked sunlight. The Fountainbleau, however, must be viewed as being worse off. It may be true that the right to sunlight/right to build dispute had not been previously settled and that neither party had a clear foundation for viewing its version of the right as a settled part of its property. Still, until the decision, it did view itself as either owning the right or, at least, having some probability of owning the right. Indeed, this undetermined interest probably could have been sold—with a suitable discount. Certainly, neither party would abandon its claim without compensation. Thus, the court's allocation worsens the position of the Fountainbleau. Without consent and with one party being made worse off, the moral appeal of judicial assignment is weak-ened.

There is a subtle and suspect reason for arguing that the court's policy of mimicking the market does not leave the Fountainbleau worse off. Pre-sumably, the amount paid by each party for its property included embedded within it an allowance for the fact that property rights, particularly with respect to future events and assignments, are inher-ently uncertain. One of these areas of uncertainty would be one's right to unrestricted access to the sun or the right to build. In the case of the Founta-inbleau, the argument would be that the owners would have been willing to pay more when the site was initially purchased if the title to the land in-cluded a known right to build as high as they wished. The argument is that the Fountainbleau "consented" ahead of time to the risk of losing access to the sun. In addition, the owners were compensated for the loss by means of the lower price paid for the property. This is known as *ex ante* compensation. Again, whether this is consent in any meaningful way is questionable.

These situations can be distinguished from another in which it may be possible to achieve both wealth maximization and Pareto superiority. Suppose the right in question was oil drilling rights off the coast of Miami Beach and that neither party had expected that such activity would become legal. Now when the parties bid and the right is assigned to the highest bidder that party is better off. Moreover, unless there is some ultimate adverse impact on the losing party's business or BP is in charge, it is difficult to see how it is made worse off. In effect, the creation and assignment of a new right does not necessarily leave the losing bidder in any worse position than it would have been in had the new right not evolved.

The issue of how to react to transaction costs has one more wrinkle. Suppose you take the view that, for one reason or another, a court should not attempt to mimic the market in high transaction cost contexts, even if it can do so accurately. You are, however, perfectly willing to allow people to voluntarily exchange rights once a court has assigned them. The problem here is that the only thing determining whether an efficient allocation takes place is the existence of transaction costs. Unless there is some moral significance to the existence of these costs, the position that you and many others have adopted seems to have no morally principled underpinnings because it reduces to a view that efficiency is desired when transaction costs are low and not as important when they are high.

2. ASYMMETRICAL TRANSACTION COSTS

As already noted, determining which party attributes greater value to a right is not likely to be an easy task. Thus, even if one is devoted to wealth-maximization as a legitimate goal of courts and legislators, there is no clear formula that determines how to achieve that goal. Guido Calabresi, and perhaps others, has offered a kind of back-up strategy that indirectly would achieve the wealth maximization goal. This strategy calls for assigning the right to the party from whom it could be transferred less expensively.[8]

For example, suppose both the Eden Roc and Fountainbleau attributed significant value to access to sunlight, but there was a problem in ascertaining their relative valuations. If we knew that a transfer from the Eden Roc would involve lower transaction costs than a transfer from the Fountainbleau, the proper strategy would be to assign the right to the Eden Roc. If this turns out to an incorrect assignment, the chances that there will be a market correction are higher than if the incorrect assignment were made to the Fountainbleau.

8. Guido Calabresi, *The Costs of Accidents* 150–152 (1970).

D. PROTECTING ENTITLEMENTS

Although it may be possible for parties to bargain and engage in exchange when the rights at issue are not perfectly defined, most would argue that the Coase Theorem is far more likely to work when the ownership of various rights or entitlements is clear. The question that remains open is exactly how these entitlements are to be protected. In an important 1972 article, "Property Rules, Liability Rules, and Inalienability: One View of the Cathedral," Professor Guido Calabresi and A. Douglas Melamed outlined the options and the justifications for each of three possibilities.[9]

The proposition set forth by Calabresi and Melamed is that entitlements can be protected by liability rules, property rules or a rule of inalienability. Liability rules are used when a person is permitted to invade the rights of another and then compensate him or her. Typical of this would be an accident in which the person at fault is required to compensate the victim for personal or property damage.

A property rule, on the other hand, is one under which a party must have permission from the affected party before taking or using the other party's entitlement. Finally, in some cases, the rule is that the entitlement cannot be sold or otherwise exchanged, making it a rule of inalienability.

9. Guido Calabresi & A. Douglas Melamed, "Property Rules, Liability Rules and Inalienability: One View of the Cathedral," 85 *Harv. L. Rev.* 1086 (1972).

For law and economics purposes, the important question is when it makes sense to apply these various means of protecting entitlements. As a general matter, when transaction costs are likely to be high, a liability rule has much to recommend it. For example, returning to *Boomer v. Atlantic Cement Company,* suppose the entitlement was that the homeowners had the right to be free from the dirt, smoke and vibration caused by the cement factory. Suppose further that, as the case states, the damage to the cement factory of being required to shut down would far exceed the damage to property owners if it were permitted to continue operating. In a transaction-costs-free environment, it would not matter if the court had "mistakenly" applied a property rule and enjoined the factory from operating. In that context, the factory could easily buy out the rights of the landowners.

It is possible, however, that rather than a smooth exchange, there might be significant transaction costs. Or, as suggested above, the landowners, any one of whom could submarine the whole deal, just cannot agree to sell their right to have the factory's activity enjoined. Here, the idea of permitting the factory to pollute and to pay the victims for their losses has appeal, especially to those who are interested in traditional notions of efficiency. As it turned out, the court basically applied a liability rule by granting an injunction but ordering it vacated once the factory compensated the landowners.

The same sort of logic applies to accidents. Obviously, in the case of negligence, it would be impossible for the person causing the damage to negotiate with the victim beforehand. Presumably, the injurer does not know the victim or even anticipate the accident. Transaction costs are virtually limitless and liability rules are thus employed in these kinds of cases. Calabresi and Melamed make the point that requiring the parties to negotiate in advance for permission would really require a great deal of potential accident-causing activity to stop altogether.

As attractive as liability rules are—due to the relative ease with which entitlements can be transferred, there are three drawbacks, all of which are absent if one relies on a property rule instead. First, use of a liability rule permits one to take the property of another without her consent. Even though there is compensation after the fact, and even if the compensation seems fair, those who value consent as an independent interest—perhaps superseding economic interests—will find the liability rule objectionable.

Second, liability rules are risky when it comes to recognizing the subjective valuations of individuals. Suppose someone dearly loves his home, in part for sentimental reasons. Perhaps it has been the family home for generations. If the home is then accidentally destroyed through the acts of another, the victim may find he is only paid the fair market value for the home. This amount does not account for his attachment and would not have been acceptable compensation in a market transaction. The problem here is not just that the victim has not been adequately compensated, but that the "exchange" itself has not led to any version of efficiency. If the victim would not have consented to an exchange for a price equal to the damages he or she is awarded, the "exchange" is neither Pareto superior nor wealth-maximizing.

The problem of properly protecting subjective values helps explain why interference with the rights of others is addressed not by simple compensation but by criminal penalties. If everyone simply had to pay the fair market value for damages caused or for items taken (assuming they are caught), property rules would be changed to liability rules. Yet, as Calabresi and Melamed point out, liability rules may understate the value to the victim of what was taken and invite inefficient "transfers." Hence, when the transfer could have been negotiated— transaction costs are low—it makes sense to employ a property rule and add on a penalty for those who try to substitute a liability rule.

A third objection to the use of liability rules is based on distributive consequences. Suppose in the typical polluting factory case, like *Boomer v. Atlantic Cement,* the fair market value of the damage to the landowner is $50,000 and the value to the factory of continued operations is $100,000. Suppose further that the landowner is entitled to be free of pollution. If a liability rule is employed, the factory will continue to pollute and simply compensate the landowner. The landowner would receive $50,000. In effect, the factory is permitted to pay only $50,000 for a right or resource (the air) to which it attributes a value of $100,000. Put in contracts terms, the benefit of the bargain is $50,000 and all of that benefit is captured by the factory. The landowner, in effect, is required to sell and the factory is permitted to buy the entitlement for the landowner's reservation price—the lowest price that would have been acceptable in a market exchange. The problem is that the "forced sale" does not permit the landowner to acquire at least some portion of the gain or surplus created by the exchange. Although this is irrelevant as a matter of allocative efficiency, it does have obvious distributive implications.

In some instances, entitlements are "protected" to such an extent that the owners are not permitted to sell them. Some examples are votes, organs and sex. Although this is of little consequence to those who would not sell under any circumstances, in some instances it is clear that the rule interferes with the preferences of potential sellers. This leads to the question of how it can be efficient or even just to interfere with the expression of individuals in the market. As a general matter, rules that prohibit the exchange of one's entitlements are typically justified by the fact that some exchanges are morally repugnant. Put in economic terms, one could say that those exchanges have negative— perhaps only psychological—effects on those who are not parties to the exchange. In addition, there are paternalistic justifications based on the belief that the parties to the exchange really do not know what is best for them. This too can be put in economic terms by claiming that the preference that might otherwise be expressed by the party is one that, sooner or later, she would regret. Consequently, it is not ultimately utility-maximizing.

CHAPTER FIVE

THE ECONOMICS OF ENFORCING PROMISES

Of the areas of law to which economic analysis has been applied the best "fit" is probably found in contracts, torts, antitrust, and government regulation. The application of economics to contract law tends to be relatively easy to understand since both the Coase Theorem and the concept of Pareto superiority envision some form of exchange. This Chapter begins with the basic economic theory linking contract formation with increases in efficiency. It then addresses a number of contract law issues that can be approached from an economic perspective. Contract remedies are examined in the final section. In all cases, the discussion centers on whether or not contract doctrine can be squared with economic interests. Concluding that they can, however, does not necessarily mean that contract doctrine is the product of economic reasoning. In addition, this Chapter considers gratuitous promises and the doctrine of promissory estoppel. Here the economic arguments are not as clear cut as they are in the case of conventional contracts.

A. THE ECONOMICS OF EXCHANGE

In order to understand the economics of contract formation, it is necessary to grasp the concept of an indifference curve. An indifference curve illustrates all the combinations of two products that would leave an individual feeling equally well off. For example, in Figure 1, numbers of sweaters is plotted along the vertical axis and numbers of oranges is plotted along the horizontal axis. The curve labeled with an "I" might illustrate all the combinations of oranges and sweaters that leave Juan feeling the same in terms of his utility. In other words, Juan has no preference for any point on curve I over any other point.

Figure 1

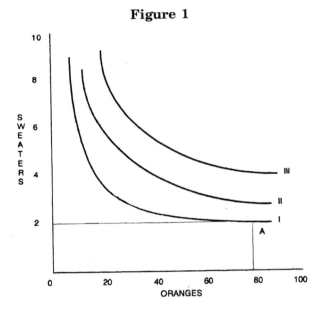

The graph also includes a number of other indifference curves; together they constitute an indifference map. As the curves move out from the origin, each curve signifies a higher level of utility. Thus, although Juan is indifferent to the points on any one curve, he would like to be on the curve farthest from the origin. In fact, what is really going on here is that this graph has a third dimension projecting out from the page, and the third dimension plots utility. Farther out from the origin is actually farther up from the page.

On curve I, point A is a combination of eighty oranges and two sweaters. Let's suppose that this is

Juan's stock of goods at the moment. The notions of contract and exchange require that another participant be introduced into the model. Let's say Figure 2 illustrates the utility map of Lolita. Again, each curve indicates the combinations of sweaters and oranges that result in the same level of utility for Lolita. Further suppose that Lolita is currently in possession of 20 oranges and 8 sweaters. This would be point A on utility curve I. Given the uneven distribution of sweaters and oranges, Juan and Lolita may be potential traders.

Figure 2

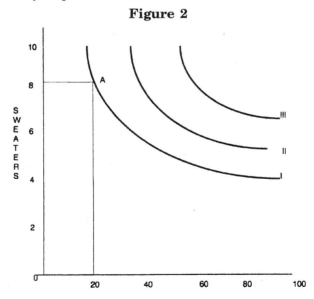

To illustrate the theory of why and how the trading might occur, it is necessary to convert the two sets of indifference curves into what is called an

Edgeworth Box. The Edgeworth Box for Juan and Lolita is Figure 3. Although it looks a bit confusing, all that has happened is that the origin for Lolita's indifference map is no longer the lower left corner of the graph, but is now at the upper right corner. Thus, for Juan, utility increases as he moves upward and to the right, and for Lolita, utility increases as she moves downward and to the left. Point A is now common to both parties. For Juan, it is still 80 oranges and 2 sweaters, and for Lolita it is still 20 oranges and 8 sweaters.

Figure 3

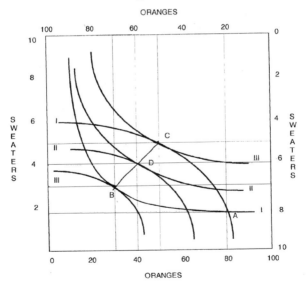

It is important to remember that each party would like to move as far from his or her origin as possible. In the context of this mini economy, they can achieve this by exchanging sweaters for oranges. But there are obviously limits on what "price" each will be willing to pay for what the other is offering. For example, consider point B. This is on utility curve I for Juan and curve III for Lolita. To achieve this outcome, Juan would have to give up 50 oranges in order to get one sweater from Lolita, leaving him with 30 oranges and 3 sweaters. Lolita would be giving up one sweater for 50 oranges, leaving her with 7 sweaters and 70 oranges. Because this would put Lolita on indifference curve III, she would probably be delighted with the exchange. On the other hand, Juan would not be delighted or anything other than indifferent because he remains at the same level of utility. At point B, all the gains from the exchange would have accrued to Lolita.

Comparable to point B is point C, which is on indifference curve III for Juan and indifference curve I for Lolita. Here Juan exchanges 30 oranges for 3 sweaters and each party ends up with 50 oranges and 5 sweaters. Juan is on a higher indifference curve and Lolita is on her original curve.

Movements to point B or point C would both be to Pareto superior states because one party will be better off and no one will be worse off. These are extreme points, however, in that they involve cases in which the parties are willing to make an exchange that does not improve his or her position. Certainly, neither party would settle for terms that would result in movement to an indifference curve that would be lower than curve I, and movement to any curve above curve I is an improvement. Thus, all the points between Juan's indifference curve I and Lolita's indifference curve I are Pareto superior to point A. This oblong area between the curves is referred to as the "lens."

It is important to remember that both parties want to move to levels of indifference that are as far from the origins of their indifference maps as possible. This produces some particularly attractive points. These are the points at which their curves are tangent. In Figure 3, a line is drawn through the points of tangency between Juan's and Lolita's indifference curves. This is called the "contract curve." Points B and C form the extremes of the contract curve. Point D, at which Juan gives up 40 oranges for 2 sweaters, is also on the contract curve.

As already noted, any movement from point A to a point within the lens is a movement to a Pareto superior state. What is different about the contract curve as opposed to other points within the lens is that once the parties agree to an exchange along the contract curve, they have arrived at a Pareto optimal point. In other words, once on the contract curve, they cannot change the distribution of sweaters and oranges without making one of them worse off. This can be tested at point D, where Juan has 40 oranges and 4 sweaters and Lolita has 60 oranges and 6 sweaters. There is no way to move from this point to another distribution without one of the parties moving to a lower indifference curve.

The price that contracting parties agree upon is really a decision about which point on the contract curve will be selected. In the typical bargaining context, each party will prefer a point as close to the origin of the other party as possible. The issue of "price," or the point on the curve they select, directly implicates the distributive consequences of the contract. Simply arriving at a point on the curve increases general welfare and the utility of both parties. The actual point on the curve determines how the gain from the exchange will be divided between the parties. Thus, the Edgeworth Box allows one to consider both the allocative and distributive implications of the exchange. As will be discussed below, most of contract law, when it is viewed in economic terms, can be seen as responding to allocative or distributive issues. In fact, as the pages that follow illustrate, most of standard contract doctrine, ranging from offer and acceptance to consideration and competency, can be explained by an economic rationale. Before turning to those questions, however, a few more basics need to be addressed.

B. WHY DOES CONTRACT LAW EXIST?

While the Edgeworth Box and the derivation of the contract curve explain why exchange is important, those constructs do not directly address the function of contract law. More specifically, why should executory contracts be enforced and what mechanisms should be used to further that end?

To be more specific, all the gains from the exchange just described between Lolita and Juan could be achieved if Juan showed up at a designated spot with his oranges and Lolita showed up with her sweaters and they swapped. In essence, the contract would be formed and executed simultaneously. In fact, if the parties made a point to thoroughly inspect the goods they were exchanging and adjusted the price to account for any uncertainty about the quality of the goods, formal contract law would seem to have little importance.

The problem is that the oranges for sweaters exchange is very primitive—it assumes a face-to-face transaction in which the entire contract is executed on the spot and the parties are able to make an assessment of what they are getting and what they are giving up. In reality, things are much more complex. For example, a general contractor may not be willing to bid on a large construction project unless he can be assured that numerous subcontractors will perform at specified times in the future. Similarly, if one's performance is to be financed with the payment received from the other party, simultaneous face-to-face exchange is not possible. Thus, a building contractor may need progress payments that are received before the contractor can perform.

In theory, virtually all of these problems could be and sometimes are overcome through the use of bonding arrangements and escrow agents. Of course, the bonding agreement and the contract with the escrow agent may themselves give rise to complexities that cannot be overcome by a face-to-face simultaneous exchange. In short, in the absence of contract law, the transaction costs of many day-to-day exchanges would be extraordinarily high. Consequently, exchanges that would be allocatively efficient may not take place. The existence of contract law lowers these costs and permits them to take place. As long as the cost of administering contract law is less than the gain from the exchange and less than efforts to create "private" contract law, it makes economic sense to have a body of law devoted to contracts.

The importance of the transaction cost lowering process is best understood by focusing on the principal reason for making contracts. In large measure, contracts are means of privately allocating risks. For example, if Angie hires Brad to paint her house for $10,000, she is assuming the risk that no one will do an equivalent job for less and that she will not find another opportunity for spending $10,000 that she would find more attractive. Similarly, Brad is assuming the risk that someone will not offer him an opportunity that he would find more attractive and that the cost of the project will not exceed $10,000.

Of course, the risk allocation features of contracts are far more extensive than this example. In large commercial contracts that stretch over several years, the parties can be seen as purchasing insurance from each other. For example, a public utility may buy guaranteed deliveries of coal at a guaranteed price from a producer. That producer, perhaps on the verge of a substantial capital outlay, is looking for a hedge against a precipitous drop in the demand for and price of coal. In this type of instance, the private risk allocation may take the form of a requirements contract. The point is that when performance takes place over an extended period of time, a private system of enforcing contracts becomes even more expensive and a public, and in particular, a uniform system of enforcement is even more attractive.

C. THE SPECIFIC ECONOMIC FUNCTIONS OF CONTRACT LAW

Given that the economic function of contract law is to facilitate exchange by overcoming transaction costs, it may seem odd that so much of substantive contract law is devoted to rules about what must happen in order for a contract to be enforceable. These specific rules concern issues ranging from the capacity of the parties to formalistic notions of offer, acceptance, and consideration. Taken together, the rules of contract law seem to perform a number of economic functions. The first is to enforce only those agreements that are likely to result in increases in efficiency. The second function is to keep the cost of administering contract law as low as possible.

A third function is to allocate risks that are not expressly allocated by the parties. In this respect, contract law serves a gap-filling function. Gap filling pervades contract law but is dealt with most expressly when considering issues of ambiguity, breach, the proper remedy, and whether one party's non-performance will be excused. Even the mainstay lost profits case, *Hadley v. Baxendale*, 1854 WL 7208 (Eng.1854) is a study in determining how the parties allocated the risk of consequential damages. From an economic point of view, it makes sense to allocate that risk to the party who can control the event or insure against it more economically.

Finally, it seems clear that much of contract law is devoted to concerns about the distributive consequences of the bargains people make. Courts, applying contract law, often find ways to excuse parties from contracts that are deemed to be unfair. In this sense, contract law plays the role of setting limits on what is permissible bargaining behavior and encourages conformity with socially acceptable bargaining norms. This is probably the most controversial function of contract law, in part because there is great disparity in views about whether contract law should be used for this purpose and whether it is an effective means of addressing social injustice.

Often a court is faced with a question in which achieving one goal is inconsistent with achieving another. This tension between goals occurs most frequently when the court must choose between efficiency goals and distributive goals.

D. THE ECONOMICS OF CONTRACT FORMATION

When one thinks of contract formation, a number of questions are raised:

1. Do the parties have capacity to contract?

2. Was assent the result of duress or undue influence?

3. Is there an offer?

4. Is there an acceptance?

5. Is there consideration?

6. Must the contract be in writing?

These questions can be seen as a means of determining whether both parties have truly consented to the exchange. Although there are no guarantees that actual utility or happiness will be increased if the parties have consented, there is at least a reasonable likelihood that consent and Pareto superiority go hand-in-hand. All of the questions associated with contract formation can be traced to a desire for clear signals that the parties have, in fact, made an agreement.

1. CAPACITY

At one level of analysis, the basic rules about capacity—whether applied to minors, those who are inebriated, or those who are cognitively or volitionally impaired—seem straightforward. Decisions made by those who are unable to understand what they are doing or unable to control those actions may not lead to Pareto superior outcomes. The decision that the party lacks capacity is really one that says that the perception of increased well-being is likely to be the result of a cognitive distortion.

While these limitations on contracts can be viewed as having an "objective" economic basis, the truth is that standards for capacity can vary from era to era. Decisions about who is capable of forming a binding contract are, therefore, often political decisions about the limits of enforceable consent. Moreover, any examination of a sample of capacity cases leads one to believe that the economic concerns are not about efficiency as much as they are about distributive outcomes.

Still, some of the more specific rules pertaining to capacity and avoidability can be reconciled with conventional economic interests. For example, the *Restatement (Second) of Contracts*, section 15, takes the position that a party may void a contract on the basis of volitional impairment or intoxication only if the other contracting party had reason to know of the impairment or intoxication. On the other hand, the power of minors to void contracts is not similarly limited. In terms of risk allocation, the contracting minor is less likely to be "stuck" with a contract he wants out of than someone who forms a contract while intoxicated.

The greater risk incurred by the intoxicated party is best explained by the judgments society makes about people who drink too much. In economic terms, there is a disincentive to become intoxicated.

From a non-moralistic economic point of view, forming a contract that turns out, in hindsight, not to be to one's liking is a little like making a "mistake" or being involved in an accident. In the case of intoxication, the person who is arguably in the better position to avoid the mistake is given an incentive to do so. Of course, if the other party has reason to know of the intoxication, he or she is in as good or better position to avoid the accident and then the contract is voidable by the intoxicated party.

In the case of minors there is no similar morality-based distinction. In a sense, those who contract with minors, with few exceptions, are "strictly liable." In other words, the adult assumes the risk that if other contracting party is a minor it is avoidable. Still, the underlying economic rationale is same as it is in other capacity cases: Minors are viewed as unlikely to make contracts that result in Pareto Superior outcomes. The balance shifts when the minor contracts for "necessaries." Two factors are involved. First, in the case of essential items, a disincentive to contract with minors actually raises the search costs to the minor seeking to obtain essential items. Second, the purchase of necessaries is less likely to be based on a whim.

The capacity question in contracts raises concerns about paternalism and interference with autonomy and liberty. To some extent, these concerns may be offset by the fact that most of the rules about capacity make contracts voidable, not void. On the other hand, there are economic reasons why the importance of this distinction can be over-estimated. The fact that individuals lacking capacity can step out of contracts at their prerogative greatly increases the risk and, therefore, the cost of dealing with those lacking capacity. Since this discourages people from contracting with those who may be impaired, the actual outcome, in terms of choice, autonomy, and numbers of utility-increasing contracts may be about the same as it would be if the contracts were simply void.

As suggested above, distributive concerns are probably behind a great deal of the law that has evolved with respect to capacity. In other words, even if it could be shown that the contracts formed by those who lack capacity have resulted in Pareto superior outcomes, the contract law of capacity would still be applied to protect those who have not shared fairly in the surplus created by the exchange. In particular, concerns about overreaching and advantage-taking are obviously at the heart of rules allowing minors or those who are mentally impaired to void contracts.

This is no more pointedly illustrated than *Ortelere v. Teachers' Retirement Board*, 250 N.E.2d 460 (N.Y.1969), in which a retired teacher made a retirement benefit election. Her choices were a lower payment that would extend through her life or her husband's, whichever was longer, or a higher payment through her lifetime alone. She died two months after electing the higher payment, and her election, upon being challenged by her husband, was found to be voidable. The decision is hard to view as being driven by concerns about efficiency. Instead, the decision was whether the pension fund should benefit, as a result of Ortelere's decision, when her husband would then be deprived of an extended period of benefits.

2. DURESS

Duress and undue influence are also doctrines that permit individuals to avoid contracts. Here again, the issue goes to the nature or the *quality* of consent at the point of contract formation. From the standpoint of economic analysis, duress and related doctrines address both allocative efficiency and distributive outcomes. The concepts are difficult to grapple with because there is no bright-line test to be applied as in the case of the contracting party's age.

One of the factors complicating duress is that, once the party has made a decision while under duress, that decision may very well achieve Pareto superiority. Taking the simplest example, even the party who enters into a contract at gunpoint can be viewed as moving to a Pareto superior position, given the circumstances. Thus, the process of defining duress is really one of determining which decisions achieving Pareto superior outcomes are legitimate and which ones are the result of illegitimate pressure.

Section 175 of the *Restatement (Second) of Contracts* makes an effort to narrow the focus by defining duress as the use of an improper threat that leaves the victim "no reasonable alternative." The *Restatement* further defines what would be improper but, except for the examples of when the threat would amount to a crime or a tort, the language is very imprecise. Robert Nozick suggests that duress may be viewed as a situation in which the party is offered an option that he would prefer not to have heard about at all.[1] This makes a great deal of sense; the party who would have preferred not to have heard about the new choices finds his new set of options Pareto inferior to his prior state. In essence, he has been made worse off without compensation. It is hard to then "bootstrap" this into the type of exchange that leads to a legitimate form of Pareto superiority.

The *Restatement (Second)*, section 175, distinguishes between instances in which the threatening party is the other contracting party and when she is not. As one would expect, the contract is more easily avoided when the coercing party is a party to the contract. This reduces the incentive to make an improper threat and allocates the risk that one's threat may be deemed improper to the party in the best position to control the threatening behavior. The allocation of the risk is reversed when the party contracting with the victim has no reason to know of the duress and has given value or has relied on the transaction. It makes economic sense to allocate the risk in this manner because the coerced party is in possession of information that he

1. For a discussion and criticism see Mark Kelman, "Choices and Utility," 1979 *Wisc. L. Rev.* 769, 789–790.

is under duress and, by notifying the other party, could preserve his right to avoid the contract.

Use of the doctrine of duress is explained as much by distributive goals as it is by goals linked to allocative efficiency and risk allocation. In fact, under section 176(2) of the *Restatement (Second)*, bargains that are uneven are viewed as candidates for the duress label, which then creates in the "victim" the right to void the contract. A closer look at the contract doctrines that foster distributive ends is reserved for Section C.

3.   OFFER AND ACCEPTANCE AND OTHER FORMALITIES

Offer and acceptance are symbols of consent. Thus, requiring them to be present is consistent with the desire to enforce efficiency-producing agreements. In addition, to the extent that the law requires a fairly high level of specificity and a lack of ambivalence for a communication to qualify as an offer, the effect is to lower the costs of administering a system of contract law. The same is true with respect to the traditional "mirror image" rule in the case of acceptances.

In highly complex commercial transactions, rigid adherence to the "mirror image" rule could impede the formation of contracts. In effect, the transaction costs of finding a point in the negotiation at which all parties are in complete agreement with respect to every term in the contract could be quite high. Section 2–207 of the Uniform Commercial Code, which permits contracts to be formed in the absence of complete consistency between offer and acceptance, avoids some of these transaction costs. The consequence is that efficiency-producing exchanges are not thwarted by formal requirements. On the other hand and only partly in jest, whatever benefits may flow from section 2–207, might be offset by the disutility students and others suffer while trying to master it.

One of the standard rules of contract law is that the acceptance must be in the exact form designated in the offer. This leads to the question of the appropriate type of response to an offer that is ambiguous with respect to the means of acceptance. For efficiency purposes, the risk of any confusion should be borne by the party who has created the ambiguity. This is basically consistent with the common law view as reflected by section 32 of the *Restatement (Second)*, which permits the offeree to accept by promising or by performing.

Another area in which softening the formal requirements may very well be consistent with economic efficiency is the creation of a limited number of instances in which silence may be construed as acceptance. It is important in this context to remember that, from an economic perspective, one purpose of offer and acceptance is to avoid the enforcement of "contracts" to which the parties did not consent. When it is clear that the offeror has good reason to believe that silence by the offeree signifies assent, there is no reason to insist on an express acceptance. This is generally in accord with section 69 of the *Restatement (Second)*, which lists the circumstances under which silence may be viewed as acceptance or that the risk that silence may be mistakenly taken as acceptance should be allocated to the offeree.

One more contract law standard that is susceptible to economic justification is the statute of frauds, which requires some contracts to be evidenced by a written memorandum. A writing has probative value with respect to consent. Moreover, to the extent any contract specifications are included in the writing, the cost of administering a system of contract law is decreased.

4. THE CONSIDERATION REQUIREMENT

A black letter rule of contract law is that a promise must be supported by consideration in order to be binding. The consideration requirement is essentially that the promise or performance of one party be in exchange for the promise or performance of a counterpart. One implication for the economics of contract law is fairly obvious. The notion of "exchange" has an important symbolic value in terms of signifying consent. But it is equally clear that the rules pertaining to consideration reflect some ambivalence about its importance. Inconsistent responses to the consideration requirement may be the result of the tension between competing economic goals of contract law. This is illustrated by looking more closely at three specific areas.

a. Adequacy of Consideration

The baseline rule is that, as long as there is consideration, the matter of "adequacy" of consideration is not at issue. This is the so-called "peppercorn" theory of consideration. The explanation for this, in economic terms, is that an assessment of relative amounts of consideration involves making an "interpersonal comparison of utility." In effect, to intervene when consideration appears to be lopsided amounts to an effort to compare the increase in utility experienced by one party with the increase in utility experienced by the other party. Such comparisons cannot be made. Consequently, once there is consent as signified by offer, acceptance and some kind of exchange, it makes no economic sense to attempt further inquiry. This particular view is consistent with viewing contract law as having the primary function of supporting Pareto superior exchanges.

The problem is that this rigid view of consideration gives way very often when courts address distributive goals. Thus, an uneven exchange can be viewed as evidence of duress or can be an element of unconscionability. In some instances, the distributive matter is handled by simply declaring that there was no consideration when in fact there was. A good example is *Newman and Snell's State Bank v. Hunter*, 220 N.W. 665 (Mich.1928), in which the bank sold to a widow the promissory note of her deceased husband. The collateral for the note was in the form of the stock of an insolvent corporation. The widow received the actual note—certainly the equivalent of a peppercorn and quite likely the source of comfort. Yet the court held that there was an absence of consideration due to the fact that the note did not have monetary value.

b.   Nominal Consideration

Another area in which this ambivalence is revealed is in the treatment of nominal consideration. The issue here is: what happens if the parties, conscious of the consideration requirement, observe the formality of reciting consideration? The earlier view as reflected by the first *Restatement of Contracts* was that nominal consideration was sufficient. This view was probably driven more by rigid adherence to the peppercorn theory than by any intuitive notion of the efficiency derived from enforcement of gratuitous promises. It made sense from the point of view of economic efficiency since both parties consented to a process they thought would create a binding obligation. Moreover, as discussed below, there are other economic reasons for enforcing gratuitous promises. The comments to section 71 of the *Restatement (Second) of Contracts* permit courts to pierce the formality of the arrangement and to make a finding that nominal consideration is not consideration at all. When all the other indicia of consent are present, it is hard to square this rule with economic efficiency.

c.   Contract Modification

As noted above, consideration performs the important function of signifying assent. This explains the long-standing rule that a contract modification is not binding in the absence of consideration. The rationale is that it makes little sense for a rational party, who is entitled to a certain level of performance by another, to pay more for the same performance. A modification without consideration, one might reason, is a sure sign that the modification was made under duress and does not increase the well-being of both parties. Both the Uniform Commercial Code and the *Restatement (Second) of Contracts* protect against coerced modification. However, under certain circumstances, both the *Restatement (Second)* and the Uniform Commercial Code permit modifications without consideration. They implicitly recognize that in the context of a contractual relationship, especially in light of the likelihood of repeated transactions, it may be in the rational self-interest of both parties to allow variations from the strict terms of the contract.[2] Efforts to anticipate and contractually treat every possible contingency would drive transaction costs up.

E. CONTRACT LAW AND DISTRIBUTIVE GOALS

As noted at the outset of this Chapter, there is a fair amount of tension in contract law between efficiency goals and distributive goals. To put the issue in its usual terms, efficiency goals are those that are aimed at increasing utility or wealth with-

[2]. This is consistent with the findings of an empirical study undertaken by Russell J. Weintraub, *see* "A Study of Contract Practice and Policy," 1992 *Wis. L. Rev.* 1.

out regard for whom is actually made better off. Distributive goals focus on which individuals or classes of individuals are better off. There is a continuous debate about whether contract law should be concerned with distributive issues at all. Those who oppose this use of contract law, if they favor redistribution at all, would prefer the use of taxes and transfer payments to achieve those ends. Despite these philosophical differences, it is clear that much of contract law responds to distributive goals.

In terms of the contract curve in Figure 3, there are two situations that raise distributive concerns. The first deals with advantage-taking that is so extreme that one of the parties does not end up with an exchange that places him or her within the lens. This seems most likely to occur when one of the parties lacks the capacity to contract. In these cases, one party is made worse off by the contract and the outcome is Pareto inferior.

A different type of problem can arise when the parties bargain to a point on the contract curve. If the bargain struck lies at the extreme end of the curve, it indicates that one party has gained most of the surplus created by the exchange. In these instances, a refusal to enforce the contract has the effect of "undoing" what was a movement to a Pareto superior position. While such decisions may only mean that future bargains occur on different terms, there is also the danger that future efficiency-producing bargains will not occur at all. This presents the classic clash between allocative efficiency and distributive justice.

Another type of case involves instances in which the parties both seem to move to a position within the lens and perhaps on the contract curve, but after the fact it is determined that one of the parties is not better off at all. That party either regrets making the contract or something happens to make either the gain from the contract less valuable or performance more onerous. In the latter group of cases, the various doctrines that excuse non-performance come into play.

Many different theories are used by the courts to deal with these distributive concerns. Sometimes the distributive outcomes of contracts affect the way a court reacts to a formation question. The most obvious examples are the use of capacity, duress, and misrepresentation as means of upsetting bargains. But, as illustrated above, distributive concerns can also affect the way a court views the issue of whether a promise is supported by consideration. Beyond these justifications lie even less clear notions like unequal bargaining power, unconscionability, and contracts of adhesion. The precise theory is probably not as important as the effects of contract law decisions that seem to have a distributive purpose. The primary concerns are that contracts that benefit both parties will not be enforced and that there will be long-term implications affecting individuals who are not parties to the contract. These issues can be seen more clearly in the context of two common problems.

1. EXCULPATORY PROVISIONS

A typical case involving an exculpatory provision is *O'Callaghan v. Waller & Beckwith Realty Co.*, 155 N.E.2d 545 (Ill.1958) which concerned the enforceability of an exculpatory clause in the lease of an apartment. The implications of either a judicial or legislative determination that such a provision is unenforceable can be illustrated graphically. In Figure 4, D represents the demand for housing. S_1 represents the supply of housing. In the market depicted here, the equilibrium price will be P_1 and the quantity of rental housing available will be Q_1. Presumably the exchange of P_1 dollars for housing increases the welfare of both lessors and tenants. Lessors prefer P_1 dollars to possession of the housing unit, and the tenants prefer housing to keeping the money or spending it on something else.

Figure 4

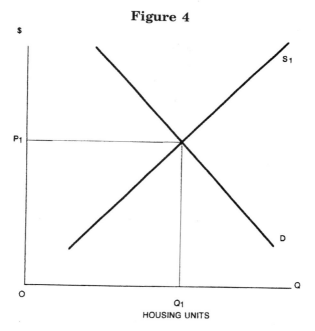

HOUSING UNITS

It will be recalled from Chapter Two that supply is also the marginal cost of production. A decision that the exculpatory provision will not be enforced is really a decision that tenants should get more for their rent payments. It can be viewed as an effort to transfer wealth from the lessors to tenants. If it is determined that exculpatory provisions are not enforceable, the cost of providing housing will presumably increase as lessors improve the housing or increase their insurance coverage. In theory, this will mean that the supply of housing will decrease— the supply curve for housing will shift upward and to the left. This is depicted in Figure 5 in which S_2 is the supply of housing after the lessors purchase insurance. At least in theory, the result of this change in the law is an increase in the price of housing and a decrease in the amount rented.

Figure 5

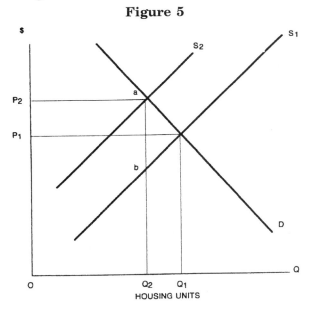

One way of viewing what has happened is to say that the efforts to make tenants better off has backfired in that some tenants—possibly those with the lowest incomes—have been priced out of the market and are worse off than they would have been if the exculpatory clause had been enforced. In addition, although those tenants remaining in the market are getting more favorable lease terms, they are paying higher rent. It is even possible that they preferred the old lease at the lower price to the new one at the higher price, so they too are worse off. Indeed, one might argue that had they wanted the newly provided protection, they could have purchased insurance.

There is another side of this story, though. First, as the graph illustrates, the increase in rent from P_1 to P_2 is not equal to the increase in the cost of supplying housing, which is the distance between a and b. It is possible that some of the increase is, therefore, actually absorbed by the lessors. As discussed in Chapter Two, whether the lessors absorb the cost will depend on market conditions. If the market is relatively competitive, lessors will have a difficult time passing the increased cost to tenants. On the other hand, if the market is not competitive, most of the increased cost will be passed along. This can be understood quite easily by supposing that the market has but one lessor—tenants must rent from that lessor or go without housing. In this instance, tenants will have little choice but to pay for nearly all of the cost increase. The phrase often used to describe contracts made when these are the market conditions is "contract of adhesion," which suggests that one of the parties was faced with a "take it or leave it" contract. In effect, there were no other parties with whom that person could have contracted on more favorable terms.

The rental apartment/exculpatory clause example calls for pushing the analysis one more step. So far, the discussion has been based on the assumption that a ruling that exculpatory provisions are unenforceable has an impact only on the supply side of the market. It is possible to view such a ruling as one that requires all apartments offered for lease to be of a higher quality. And, if all apartments were otherwise exactly as they were before, but now are of higher quality, demand may increase.

Figure 6 illustrates how this might work. The X axis shows numbers of apartments. From Chapter Two, we know that demand shows the amount people are willing and able to buy at each price. Conversely, it shows the price at which each quantity will be taken off the market. Thus, if the basic unit for sale increases in quality, one would expect the amount people are willing to pay to increase as well. This means that the demand curve would increase—shift upward and to the right. In the Figure this is depicted by a shift from D_1 to D_2. Precisely what this means in terms of the eventual price, quantity, and distributive effect depends on how much demand and supply shift and how elastic these curves are. In Figure 6, the eventual decrease in quantity, to Q_3, is less than if there had been no demand side reaction to the change in quality.

Figure 6

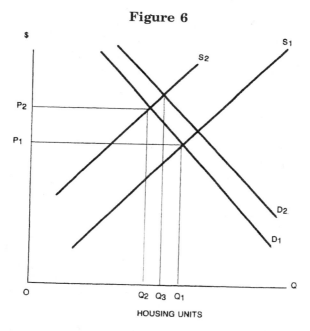

HOUSING UNITS

There is one more application of economic analysis that is relevant here. As already indicated, the supply curve will shift upward by the amount of increase in the cost of providing housing. The demand curve will shift upward by the amount of extra value tenants attribute to the "improved" housing. If the shift upward in demand exceeds the shift upward in supply, the change in the rule with respect to exculpatory clauses can be viewed as being allocatively efficient in that the increased value to buyers exceeds the cost of producing the improvement. In a smoothly working market, lessors would have recognized that the value of improvements exceeded their cost and exculpatory provisions would have disappeared without judicial or legislative help. There are many reasons why this might not happen. The primary one is the existence of transaction costs.

2.   UNCONSCIONABILITY

Unconscionability is usually said to have a procedural and substantive component.[3] The notion of a procedural component means that there was something amiss in the contract-formation process. It could be something like fraud, but it could also be something as simple as overly aggressive sales practices or using small print or confusing language for terms that turn out to be especially disadvantageous to one of the parties. The substantive component has to do with the actual balance of the exchange.

The procedural element allows the court to examine whether the process of achieving mutual assent should, as a policy matter, be viewed as legitimate. The substantive element is a way of assessing whether any possible procedural problems really resulted in any "harm." Even though courts are quite reluctant to label a bargain unconscionable, it is likely that the theory is not just reserved for Pareto inferior outcomes. It seems also to be used when the bargain is so uneven that it violates norms of fairness.

3. Arthur A. Leff, "Unconscionability and the Code—The Emperor's New Clause," 115 *U. Pa. L. Rev.* 485 (1967).

Probably the most analyzed unconscionability case is *Williams v. Walker–Thomas Furniture*, 350 F.2d 445 (D.C.Cir.1965). Williams made a series of purchases from Walker–Thomas. Her contract included what is called a cross-collaterization or add-on clause. In effect, when she made a purchase, all of the items that she had previously purchased on credit and that were not paid off became part of the collateral for the current purchase. When she defaulted, Walker–Thomas attempted to repossess a number of previously purchased items. The issue was whether the clause could be regarded as unconscionable.

A decision that an add-on clause like that in *Williams v. Walker–Thomas* is unconscionable can be seen as having a number of effects. The first and perhaps most obvious effect is to require the seller to be more forthcoming about what the buyer is giving up. If this occurs, Williams is in a better position to assess the full price and determine whether she is still willing to buy the item. In more technical terms, her information costs are lowered. In effect, Williams is in a better position to recognize more clearly what is being demanded of her and any surprises about the consequences of signing the contract are eliminated.

Other effects are not so favorable for Williams. The price paid, along with the add-on clause, are both part of the consideration package offered by Williams. It may be that she is better able to pay in the form of the add-on clause than in the form of its cash equivalent. If Williams is not permitted to pay with the "currency" of the add-on clause, she may not be able to afford the item at all.

At a more basic level, decisions about unconscionability can be seen as simply creating limits on the prices that can be charged by some merchants to some classes of buyers. As with exculpatory provisions, whether there is any long-run beneficial distributive effect is much debated. Those who oppose what amount to price ceilings seem to make two arguments. First, assume the high price really does permit the merchant to earn a very high profit. If the market system is working, the high profit will attract new sellers into the market. Supply will increase and prices will fall. The "problem" takes care of itself.

Second, it may be that the high price simply reflects the cost of doing business. In the case of *Walker–Thomas*, the argument might be that the store is in a crime-ridden neighborhood and that a disproportionate number of its customers are bad credit risks. Consequently, the risk and, therefore, the cost of doing business is high. The add-on clause is necessary. This follows from the fact that a small down payment is all that is possible and the item sold immediately depreciates so that it is worth less than the amount owed. If the add-on clause reflects a cost of doing business and the firm is not making huge profits, the consequence of deeming the term unconscionable may be that the firm closes down. And, so the argument goes, the effort to achieve a different distributive outcome ends up leaving both buyers and sellers worse off.

These worst-case scenarios can be countered by other observations. First, take the case in which the firm is earning high or "economic" profits. There is no guarantee that these profits will lure new sellers into the market. Information costs and a general lack of responsiveness in investment resources may delay or prevent such a movement. Thus, whether today's high prices are necessary so that consumers will ultimately be better off is at least an empirical question. Moreover, the notion that it is somehow fair for today's buyers to take the brunt of high prices so that consumers in the future can have lower prices is subject to debate. Finally, there is the question of just how much the price ceiling will actually retard new entry. It is true that high profits are likely to attract new entrants. But what about lower profits and long lines of consumers willing to pay the lower price? Presumably, when the price ceiling is imposed, the quantity demanded will increase. The existing firm will either serve all those who want to buy at the lower price or it will find there are lines of consumers forming each day. Potential entrants, seeing the numbers of people who are willing to purchase at the lower price, may find entrance into the market quite attractive.

Aside from arguments that price ceilings will retard new entry, there are arguments that the ceiling will cause the existing seller to sell less. Put in more basic terms, if a price ceiling is imposed, sellers will move to a lower quantity supplied on their supply curves. Figure 7 illustrates the typical concerns. In the Figure, D is demand and S is supply. The equilibrium price is P_1 and the equilibrium quantity is Q_1. If the price ceiling is set at P_2, the quantity demanded will be Q_2 and the quantity supplied will be Q_3. Thus, sales in the market will drop from Q_1 to Q_3. Those who are able to purchase the good will get it at the regulated price and are presumably better off than they were at the original price. From the standpoint of economics, however, those who are now unable to buy the good are obviously not better off.

Figure 7

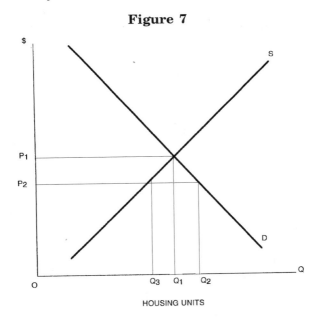

HOUSING UNITS

On the other hand, the analysis in Figure 7 holds only under special circumstances. Suppose instead that sellers have some market power and are not selling at prices equal to cost. In fact, what if the firm really is making a huge profit on each sale? As long as the price ceiling is high enough to cover the marginal cost of each sale, there seems to be little reason not to sell at least as much as was being sold before and perhaps even more.

To understand why, examine Figure 8, which is reproduced, with some additions, from the discussion of imperfect competition in Chapter 2. As will be recalled, the firm will select the quantity where marginal revenue (MR) and marginal cost (MC) intersect. Under ordinary circumstances, this will mean the quantity will be Q_1 and the price will be P_1. Suppose that a price ceiling is imposed at P_2. Obviously, everyone who was willing to pay above P_2 is still willing to purchase the item. From the firm's point of view, the relationship between its demand curve and marginal revenue curve is now beside the point. In other words, for all those people who were willing to pay above P_2, it will charge P_2. Since it does not have to lower the price to sell additional units to this group of buyers, the horizontal line at P_2 is really its new marginal revenue curve. This is true out to the intersection of the horizontal line at P_2 with the demand curve. At that point, the firm will have to lower the price to sell more and the original marginal revenue curve comes into play. This means the marginal revenue curve drops down, or is discontinuous, at point C.

Figure 8

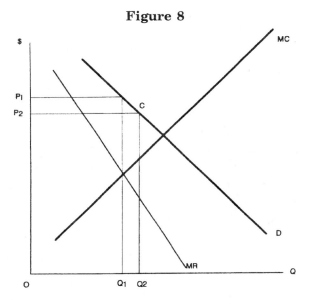

Now, following the standard of producing as long as marginal revenue exceeds marginal cost, the firm will produce out to Q_2. In effect, the price ceiling means that more is sold at a lower price. Here the distributive impact is that money that was once going to the seller is kept by the buyers. This is not to say there is increased efficiency. From a Paretian standpoint, even though buyers are better off, sellers are worse off and there is no way to gauge how things balance out. Still, the graph illustrates that, under some market conditions, efforts to redistribute in favor of buyers does not mean that they will necessarily be worse off after the effort.[4]

4. Discussions of inequities in contract law often focus on buyers who have been taken advantage of by sellers. It is good to

One final note is in order with respect to all efforts to use contract law for distributive goals. For the most part, conventional economic analysis has adopted a very narrow perspective and examined only whether those in the market are better or worse off. This is appealing and, perhaps, the most appropriate perspective to take. It misses, however, the impact of perceived market inequities on those who are not direct participants. In reality, if economists are to remain true to their own analysis, any discomfort outsiders feel about advantage-taking by others or any increased sense of well-being they experience when the perceived injustice is eliminated must be included in the calculation.

F.   CONTRACT REMEDIES

One of the favorite areas of discussion for those applying economic analysis to contract law is remedies. All of the economic issues raised by contract remedies cannot be treated in an exhaustive manner here. Instead, several matters that are particularly susceptible to economic analysis are considered.

1.   THE EFFICIENT BREACH

When economic analysis is brought to bear on contract remedies, the starting place is the so-called efficient breach. The idea is that contract remedies should be set so that a party will breach when it is

keep in mind that sellers too can be vulnerable. A good example is sellers of labor in certain labor markets.

"efficient" to do so. Efficiency in this context can refer to both Pareto superiority and wealth maximization, although Pareto superiority is more difficult to achieve.

The key to insuring that a breach will be efficient is to protect the expectancy of the non-breaching party. That is, the damages for breach must put the non-breaching party in the position, utility-wise, that he would have been in but for the breach. It is important that the damages do not improve the position of the non-breaching party.

A typical example goes like this. Suppose Jackson has a rare set of recordings of Grateful Dead live performances, all signed by Jerry Garcia. He values the recordings at $3,000. Paula, a big fan of the Dead, values the recordings at $5,000. Jackson agrees to sell the recordings to Paula for $4,000. This means Paula gets a consumer surplus or benefit of the bargain of $1,000. In economic terms, both parties are better off and, unless someone is worse off, this reallocation is Pareto superior.

Before Jackson delivers the recordings to Paula, suppose Georgette comes along and offers Jackson $6,000 for the recordings. Thus, Georgette attributes more value to the recordings than either Paula or Jackson. In fact, if Georgette had come along before Paula, a deal would have been struck that would have meant that Georgette would have ended up with the recordings at a price between $3,000 and $6,000.

The key to the efficient breach is to set the remedy so that it just gives Paula her expectancy. In this example, it would mean that she gets the benefit of her bargain, which is $1,000. If Jackson knows this when he meets Georgette, he will know that he should not breach unless Georgette is willing to pay at least $5,000. For example, suppose Georgette and Jackson arrive at a price of $5,500. This means that Georgette gets the recordings that she values at $6,000 for $5,500 and her position is improved. Paula will be paid $1,000 and be in a position that is the equivalent of what she expected. Jackson, after paying Paula $1,000, receives $4,500, which improves his position.

In theory, the remedy that protects Paula's expectancy, but does no more than that, facilitates movement to a Pareto superior outcome. Contrast this with a policy that allows for punitive damages. For example, suppose the remedy is expectancy times three. Paula would be entitled to damages of $3000. The goal would be to discourage promise-breaking. As a consequence, Georgette would not end up with the recordings even though she values them at $6,000 and Paula only values them at $5,000. In fact, in the hypothetical, Georgette would have to pay Jackson over $7,000 for it to be worthwhile for Jackson to breach his contract with Paula. From this standpoint, the "efficient breach" would appear to be thwarted.

One should not take the notion of the efficient breach too seriously. First of all, the model assumes a very simple set of facts. If information costs were not prohibitive, an efficient reallocation could occur in the absence of a breach; for example, Jackson sells to Paula and then Paula sells to Georgette. Second, the model includes the assumption that one is able to determine the non-breaching party's expectancy or the monetary equivalent of performance. This is crucial because, if the expectancy is set at too low an amount, the breach will take place and the non-breaching party will be worse off. If the amount is too high, the breach may not take place even though everyone might have been better off if it had.

A related problem is that the model requires reliance on an objective standard for the determination of the non-breaching party's expectancy. This is fine unless the non-breaching party attributes value to the expected performance that is different from the market value. Thus, in the example, perhaps Paula values the collection at $7,000, but the market value which is used to determine damages is set by different people. In short, the efficient breach model can subordinate the autonomy and preferences of the actual individuals involved. From the standpoint of efficiency, it may mean that Paula is worse off and the outcome, although possibly wealth maximizing, is not Pareto superior.

Finally, the efficient breach model seems to assume that the original contracting parties are unable to communicate with each other. For example, suppose the rule is that contract damages are triple expectancy. In the context of the Grateful Dead hypothetical, Paula values the recordings at $5,000 and would be entitled to $3,000 (3 x $1,000) if Jackson breaches. We know that Paula was only expecting to be better off by $1,000 and that Georgette values the recordings at $6,000.

Using a Coasian analysis, Paula is entitled to the recordings or to $3,000 in damages. The question is whether Jackson can, in effect, buy back the rights to the recordings from Paula. His leverage, if Paula insists on performance, would be to simply deliver the recordings, giving Paula only the $1,000 benefit of the bargain. Paula might decline Jackson's offer of $1,000, but any amount he is willing to pay in excess of $1,000 will put her in a better position than his performance. Jackson's top offer to Paula will be determined by what he thinks he can get from Georgette. The point is, as devoted Coasians have no doubt already noted, even if the legal rule about damages is "inefficient," the parties will have an opportunity to bargain around the rule to an efficient allocation. Of course, high transaction costs may impede this bargaining.

Those who are interested in the distributive implications of various legal rules may find the over-protection of Paula's expectancy through the triple expectancy rule attractive for other reasons. Under the conventional rule of protecting no more than expectancy, Paula is protected from being made worse off but she does not share in the gain from the sale to Georgette. When Georgette enters, there is an opportunity for a gain that, but for the fact that performance has not taken place, would have gone to Paula. The over-expectancy measure allows

Paula to share in part of this gain. If you take the view that the collection was, effectively, Paula's already, you may feel Paula deserves some part of the profit attributed to the breach. On the other hand, if it is the hard work of Jackson that created the opportunity presented by Georgette, allowing Jackson to keep the gain makes economic sense.

2.   SPECIFIC PERFORMANCE

Problems with expectancy as the baseline contract remedy lead naturally to considerations of specific performance. After all, specific performance can be regarded as "literal expectancy" in that it means that the non-breaching party does not run the risk of receiving an inadequate payment in the form of damages.

The primary drawback of specific performance is that it typically requires greater judicial resources to administer than the payment of money. For example, the complexity of what is adequate performance may make it very difficult for a court to determine when the breaching party has adequately performed. Thus, specific performance is most attractive from an economic standpoint when judicial supervision is relatively easy and what constitutes "performance" can be defined.

One issue that arises is whether specific performance may stand in the way of the efficient breach. For example, if Jackson is required by a court to turn over the Grateful Dead collection to Paula and the transaction costs associated with Paula and

Georgette finding each other are high, the efficient breach would appear to be thwarted.

Two very good cases that can be adapted to illustrate both the advantages of specific performance in terms of assuring the non-breaching party of receiving expectancy and the fact that specific performance may not retard an efficient reallocation are *Groves v. John Wunder Co.*, 286 N.W. 235 (Minn.1939) and *Peevyhouse v. Garland Coal & Min. Co.*, 382 P.2d 109 (Okla.1962). One or both of these cases are in almost every contract law casebook because they are instances in which the cost of performing the contract greatly exceeds the objective value of that performance. The problem is one of determining which of these two possible measures of expectancy to use.

In *Garland Coal*, as part of its agreement to strip-mine coal from the Peevyhouse property, Garland agreed to restore the land to its original condition, which it failed to do. The cost of performance was $29,000. The performance would have enhanced the market value of the property by less than $300. From an objective market-based standpoint, the Peevyhouses could be given expectancy of less than $300. On the other hand, they may have subjectively valued having the land restored at a figure much higher than that—maybe $29,000 or more.

The problem is that, if the actual preferences of the Peevyhouses are to count, there is no way to accurately set a figure for damages that will assure an efficient breach. One approach is to actually test their subjective valuation by granting specific performance. In Coasian terms, they would be entitled to have the land restored. Of course, this entitlement could be transferred to Garland Coal.

Suppose, in fact, that it is worth $5,000 to the Peevyhouses to have the land restored. Obviously, it is worth up to $29,000 to Garland Coal to avoid restoring the land. The parties would agree on some figure between $5,000 and $29,000, and the land will not be restored. In fact, as long as the cost of restoration exceeds the value to the Peevyhouses of having the land restored, chances are they will settle the case and the land will not be restored. In short, specific performance, at least in theory, would seem to be an effective way of making sure that expectancy is protected and an efficient resource allocation occurs.

A drawback to specific performance as a means to facilitating the efficient breach lies in the fact that it is dependent on an agreement between the parties. One complication is that the agreement must take place in the context of what is called bilateral monopoly. Bilateral monopoly is a structure under which there is only one buyer and one seller of a particular good—or in this case, a right. Since neither party can threaten to buy from or sell to a competitor, the parties have a strong incentive to engage in the types of strategic behavior that may impede and ultimately preclude a bargain.

The attraction of a judicially determined damage award is that it avoids the bilateral monopoly problem. In effect, the Peevyhouses are *forced* to sell their "right" to restoration at a price which may or may not fully protect their expectancy. Economists disagree about how important the bilateral monopoly problem is and, by implication, the merits of routinely granting specific performance.

3. LIQUIDATED DAMAGES

A fair amount of literature in law and economics and contract law is devoted to the issue of enforcement of liquidated damages clauses. The typical common law reluctance to enforce these clauses is generally viewed with disfavor. The consensus seems to be that a liquidated damage clause, even one in excess of what the likely damages may turn out to be, can be a useful way for one party to assure the other party of her dependability. Moreover, the liquidated damages clause is but one of the negotiated terms. Perhaps one party agreed to pay a higher price because the other agreed to what seems to be excessive liquidated damages. The point is that not to enforce the clause upsets the balance the parties have established.

At first glance, the common law position of disfavoring liquidated damage clauses because they may have the effect of a penalty seems to fit nicely with the theory of the efficient breach. Specifically, a clause setting damages at a level that would exceed the expectancy damages of the non-breaching party would deter the potentially breaching party.

The Grateful Dead example introduced above shows that this threat is not really very great. In that example, assume that the parties stipulated to damages of $4,000 should Jackson not deliver the recordings to Paula. In this instance, Jackson will not breach and sell the recordings unless he can avoid the liquidated damages. In effect, Paula is in the same position as someone who has been granted specific performance. She would prefer a payment of anything in excess of $1,000 to performance by Jackson. Knowing that Georgette is willing to pay $6,000 for the recordings, Jackson will be willing to offer Paula up to $2,000 to buy his way out of the liquidated damages provision.

It may be that Paula will simply hold out for the performance or for liquidated damages. But this seems unlikely. Jackson's leverage, should Paula decide to hold out, would be the threat of performance. This would only make Paula $1,000 better off, while allowing Jackson not to perform would be more valuable to her. In effect, Paula is likely to sell her "right" to liquidated damages for a price between $1,000 and $2,000, and the recordings will find their way into Georgette's hands. The point is that the so-called penalty will not lead to a different allocative outcome than would a proper determination of Paula's expectancy.

The liquidated damages example does reintroduce the problem of bilateral monopoly. In effect, Paula is the only one who can sell her right to liquidated damages, and Jackson is the only one in the market for that right. On the other hand, liquidated damages and the process of bargaining around the "penalty" raise the probability that Paula will have an opportunity to share in the profit made by Jackson when he sells the recordings to Georgette.

4. THE LOST VOLUME SELLER

An issue in contract damages that has been subject to economic analysis both in the literature and in judicial opinions is the matter of the "lost volume" seller. Typically, the issue arises in the sale of goods when the buyer breaches and the seller is able to resell the goods intended for the buyer at little or no loss. A good example of the problem and a sophisticated economically-based response is found in *R.E. Davis Chemical Corp. v. Diasonics, Inc.*, 826 F.2d 678 (7th Cir.1987), in which the seller contracted to sell medical diagnostic equipment. When the buyer breached, the seller was able to sell the same equipment to another customer. From one point of view, the seller was not damaged by the breach since the resale was for the same price as the original sale. This might be the case if one applies section 2–706 of the Uniform Commercial Code. Or, even if there was not a resale, as long as the contract price and the market price were the same, one could argue that under section 2–708(1) of the Code, the seller was not damaged.

On the other hand, if the seller could have made the original sale as well as the second sale, the breach has resulted in lost volume. On first impression, the logical answer seems to be that in order to put the seller in the position it would have been in but for the breach, it is necessary to measure damages as the profit lost from the first sale. This appears to be what is permitted under section 2–708(2) of the Code.

A number of questions arise in determining whether a seller is actually a lost volume seller. These questions are derived from the basic price theory introduced in Chapter Two. In particular, according to economic theory, most firms select a unique level of output to sell. This is called the profit-maximizing level. Figure 9 illustrates this proposition. A firm will produce and sell units as long as the extra or marginal revenue (MR) from selling that item exceeds the marginal cost (MC). Thus, in the graph, the seller will produce seven units and sell them for $10.00.

Figure 9

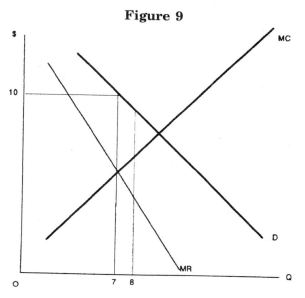

Under the lost volume analysis, the seventh unit is sold, the buyer breaches and then a new buyer agrees to buy unit seven. In order to claim that the breach has resulted in "lost volume," the seller would have to claim that even had the breach not occurred, he would have been willing to sell unit eight. The problem, as the graph indicates, is that unit eight would not have been produced and sold because the marginal cost of its production would have exceeded its marginal revenue.

In *Diasonics*, the court responded to the problem by ruling that the seller making a lost volume claim would be required to show that it had the productive capacity to produce the extra unit and that the unit could have been sold at a profit. Even if the "lost volume" sale would have been possible and profitable, the question of *how* profitable should be examined. Since marginal revenue slopes downward and marginal cost upward, the profit lost due to the lost volume unit may be less than the profit resulting from the sale of other units.

G.   BREACH AND EXCUSES FOR NON-PERFORMANCE

The issue of risk allocation in contract law is probably most starkly evident when the parties disagree about whether one of them has complied with the terms of the contract. In other words, has there been a breach? Closely related are the instances in which a party has admittedly not performed the contract but asks that its non-performance be excused as a result of mutual mistake, impossibility, frustration of purpose, or commercial impracticability.

1.   BREACH

In many instances, in which the issue of breach arises the analysis is straight-forward. In effect, the party who breaches has not shouldered all the risks that it had agreed to assume under the contract. Very often, however, the matter of how the risks and burdens were allocated by the parties is not clear. Here contract law is called on to interpret the contract and allocate these risks.

The range of ways this issue can present itself is enormous, but the basic economic approach tends to be one that assigns the risk of a lack of clarity to the party who might be viewed as having been in a better position to clarify things when the contract was formed. Take the casebook standard, *Frigaliment Importing Co. v. B.N.S. International Sales Corp.*, 190 F.Supp. 116 (S.D.N.Y. 1960), in which Judge Friendly states the issue as "What is chicken?" The defendant argued for a broad definition that would permit it to fulfill the contract by shipping older, lower quality birds while the plaintiff claimed that the younger birds were intended. An economic approach to the issue would suggest that the party intending a narrower and more expensive definition of chicken should bear the burden of ensuring the that this point is clarified when the contract is made. And Judge Friendly's opinion is consistent with this approach.

Closely related is the reliance of the U.C.C. and the common law on gap-filler or contract default terms. For example, references to course of performance, course of dealing, or trade usage amount to the establishment of "norms," and the party wishing to deviate from the norm typically bears the risk of proving that the parties have agreed to that deviation. Similar in effect is the interpretation of the terms of requirement contracts and exclusive dealing arrangements. The problem, in the case of a requirements contract, for example, is that the quantity term is left open. Thus, the buyer may be tempted to vary the amount "required" by unexpectedly large amounts or for reasons the seller would find objectionable. Here the U.C.C. refers to "actual requirements as may occur in good faith" and sets norms equal to stated amounts or prior requirements. In essence, the party wishing to deviate from these norms assumes the risk of clarifying this in the contract. This approach has economic appeal because the party wishing to deviate from the norm is also the party most likely to possess the information about the need for deviation and is in the best position to avoid disagreement down the line.

One of the more intriguing interpretation problems arises when there is a shirking problem. Shirking can be an issue when the interests of the parties are aligned but not completely. Take the example of listing a house with a real estate agent. The agent may get a fixed percentage of the selling price. The realtor's net gain will be that fixed percentage minus any amount expended in his or her selling efforts. Obviously, the interests of the homeowner and the agent coincide with respect to the selling price. The problem is that the owner's preference is for the agent to expend maximum effort to sell the home while the agent must balance the selling costs against the income from the sale. The agent's reluctance to make as much effort as the owner would prefer can be interpreted as "shirking" and amount to a breach. The issue is complicated because, at the outset, both parties know that their interests do not exactly coincide. In many instances, they will specify exactly what is expected of the agent. When this does not occur, the courts are again left to fill in the gap with a default or norm-like position. This amounts to what the parties would have reasonably expected. The party wishing to deviate has the burden of establishing that both parties knew or should have known that the norm would not govern.

2.   EXCUSES FOR NON–PERFORMANCE

The issue of excuse is very similar in theme to the question of how far the liability of a breaching party extends when the breach has resulted in special or consequential damages. In fact, the "lost profits" damages issue and all of the "excuse" doctrines are amenable to the same basic analysis. When a party makes a contract, he naturally hopes that nothing will happen to make performance more difficult than planned or render the outcome valueless. It is clear that if events do spoil matters, the performing party is generally expected to perform nonetheless. For the courts to take any other view would undercut the basic risk allocation and insurance function of the contract.

It is clear that at some point, though, the party will be excused.[5] Sometimes, but rarely, this occurs when *one* party has made the mistake. It is more likely when both parties have made the mistake. When a party is excused, he or she is regarded as not having assumed the risk of the event making performance more onerous or less desirable. The real economic function of contract law in these

5.   In the context of damages this could be seen as being excused from paying for the full consequences of one's breach.

instances is to allocate the risk in a manner that will signal which class or classes of parties will be required to assume the risk in the future. In other words, the decision has little connection with "efficiency" with respect to the two parties currently in the dispute. (For them, the effects of the decision are distributive.) Instead, these cases can be viewed as tools through which courts can direct parties toward risk allocation in the future. This requires that the party assuming the risk be the party who is in the best position to avoid the harm from the event or to insure against it at the lowest cost.

a. Unilateral Cases

A typically unilateral mistake case involves information asymmetry. One party knows that a item is more valuable than the person selling it thinks it is. Think of yourself as walking through a yard sale and seeing a collectable poster worth $1000 that is marked $.50. The sale is made and the seller asks to be excused because of her mistake about the value of the poster. The most widely accepted explanation for not excusing performance is one first offered by Anthony Kronman.[6] In the example, the buyer may have invested in his education as an art expert. In addition, that expertise led to the recovery of a poster that might end up in a land fill or a teenager's room where it is unappreciated. Allowing the seller to claim there was an excuse would mean the buyer is unable to internalize the benefits of the

6. Anthony T. Kronman, Mistake, Disclosure, Information, and the Law of Contracts, 7 *J. Legal Stud.* 1 (1978)

investment and less of that kind of investment may be made in the future.

You can view the theory more generally. Investments in human capital often have important allocative effects in terms of bringing a resource into a market where it is most or, at least, more valued. This could apply to the art expert described above as well as to the geologist who buys land from a farmer because his studies suggest there may be oil beneath the land. If every disappointed buyer or seller who says he would not have made the exchange had he know the truth were permitted to avoid the contract, a great deal of this investment may not occur and the positive allocative effects lost.

The theory has a couple of important limitations. One is that not all information that allows one to find and redirect resources is the result of an investment. Kronman notes this and would permit avoidance when the information is casually acquired. Avoidance in these cases does not result in lower investments. A second problem is that there is no reason to believe that investments in information are not also made to advance distributive ends. In the poster example, the art expert may get up at the crack of dawn and visit all the yard sales knowing that the poster will be discovered by someone and he just wants to be first. In this case, nothing positive occurs from an allocative point of view. And, investments made strictly to affect distributive ends can be regarded as a form of waste—resources are used but nothing new is produced.[7]

b.   Bilateral Cases

Bilateral cases go under a number categories—mutual mistake, impossibility, frustration of purpose, commercial impracticability—but the basic analysis is the same. In an interesting 1977 article, Richard Posner and Andrew Rosenfield[8] suggested a methodology for determining the proper risk allocation in these cases. They explain that the party who is better able to avoid the risk or insure against it is the one who would have assumed the risk at the time of contracting had the issue arisen. For example, suppose that Elton and Brittany are preparing to sign a contract that will require Brittany to use her boat to carry Elton's llamas from Costa Rica to Miami. Under the terms of the contract, Brittany is to leave Costa Rica on June 15th and arrive in Miami on July 15th. Just before signing the contract, they both realize that it is hurricane season in the Caribbean and there is a 10% chance of a delay due to a hurricane. Brittany asks to insert a clause that excuses her for delays due to hurricanes. Elton, of course, resists.

The real issue is how much Elton will pay Brittany if the clause is left out and what is the least Brittany will take. Brittany may realize that if the

7.   See Jeffrey L. Harrison, Rethinking Mistake and Nondisclosure in Contract Law, 17 *George Mason L. Rev.* 335 (2010).

8.   Richard Posner & Andrew Rosenfield, "Impossibility and Related Doctrines in Contract Law: An Economic Analysis," 6 *J. Leg. Stud.* 83 (1977).

clause is left out, her only alternative will be to charter Sonny's airplane and have the llamas delivered at an extra cost of $1,000. Elton may calculate that the delay will cost him $2,000 and the best deal he can find on an air charter is $1,500. At this point, Brittany will take no less than $100 to leave the clause out. This is the expected cost to her, calculated by multiplying the probability of a hurricane times the cost if the hurricane does materialize. Elton is willing to pay up to $150. In all likelihood, the clause will be left out and Elton will pay something between $100 and $150 to Brittany.

Under the Posner/Rosenfield model, this means that had they not anticipated the hurricane problem and one did delay Brittany's performance, she would be liable for Elton's losses. Brittany's non-performance would not be excused. Posner and Rosenfield favor a rule that would only rarely excuse performance, apparently based on the notion that parties promising to do something are generally in the best position to anticipate what sorts of events might hamper performance or, in the case of frustration of purpose, render the received performance valueless.

Again, it should be noted that this model does not achieve any sort of efficiency between Elton and Brittany. Only the most tenuous notions of consent and Pareto superiority would support a view that the parties had somehow agreed to this allocation. This "crystal ball" approach is best at providing some direction to parties in the future, who then allocate resources in such a way that the harm from the event is minimized. In a very real sense, it is comparable to allocating the risk of an accident to the party who could have avoided it or insured against it less expensively.

One important corollary of this approach is that there should be no effort to split the loss between the parties once the loss occurs. The argument is that dividing the extra cost would just lower the incentive for the party in the best position to assume the risk to actually take risk-avoidance steps. Once again, however, distributive concerns do come into play and some courts find ways of dividing the losses.

H.   GRATUITOUS PROMISES

As noted earlier, the consideration requirement itself lowers the costs of determining whether parties did agree to an exchange. In the 20th Century courts increasingly enforced gratuitous promises. In other words, the consideration requirement was put aside in some cases. There are solid economic arguments in favor of this trend. Once again, though, the support found in economic theory for enforcement of gratuitous promises does not mean that courts pursuing this course are driven by economic concerns.

Reasoning by law and economics scholars supporting the enforcement of gratuitous promises is based on possible increases in efficiency. There is some tension here, however, in that a system of contract law that includes a subset of rules that support enforcing gratuitous promises can be costly to administer. To some extent, reliance by the promisee as required by section 90 of both the first *Restatement* and the *Restatement (Second)* lowers these costs. This is especially true when the reliance takes the form of an action, such as incurring out-of-pocket expenses, that seems unreasonable unless the action was induced by the promise.

Before describing some of the recent economic arguments in favor of enforcement of gratuitous promises, it is useful to note what actually occurs when gratuitous promises are enforced. Before development of promissory estoppel and section 90, the promisor remained, in effect, the "owner" of the promise. It created no particular entitlement in the promisee and, except for instances in which courts were willing to tinker with consideration and equitable estoppel, the promise could be withdrawn with impunity. The judicial evolution in this area has the effect of reallocating this right in favor of the promisee and creating a duty in the promisor.

It is tempting to think that this change can be justified by reasoning that the maker of a promise that is later broken is at "fault." In tort-sounding terms, one could say the maker of the promise puts the promisee at risk by making a promise upon which the promisee relies. Carrying the tort analogy one step further, however, if it were commonly known that gratuitous promises were not enforced, one would have to regard the relying party as contributorily negligent. Consequently, from an efficient risk-allocation point of view, it is not clear that gratuitous promises should be enforced. Thus, the reallocation of the promissory "right" cannot be based simply on the notion that broken promises may harm promisees. Something more is needed.

The question of whether the trend toward enforcement of these promises is consistent with economic efficiency is made more intriguing by the fact that it is not as simple as asking whether this reallocation of the promissory "right" means that it ends up in the hands of the parties who attribute the greatest value to it. This is because it is possible that both promisees and promisors may prefer that the right be allocated differently. If so, this may be one of those instances in which seeming to take a right from one party and give it to another may result in a Pareto superior outcome.

Before considering why, the issue can be narrowed a bit further. Assuming the parties are rational and self-interested in the conventional sense, the utility of the promisor will increase when the promise is made. (Otherwise why make it?) Assuming the probability that the promise will be kept is greater than zero, the promisee is also made better off. At least one party is better off, no one is worse off, and the Pareto standard is satisfied. This still leaves open the question of whether it makes any economic sense for the law to increase the *probability* of performance so that the promisee does not have to rely solely on the trustworthiness of the promisor. Put differently, is there a good reason for making promises, more generally, the "property" of the promisee?

Richard Posner offers an economic justification for enforcing the promise.[9] An example goes as follows. Suppose I honestly desire to give my friend a gift of $100 per week for the next 52 weeks. If I simply make the promise and my friend then discounts the promise due to the fact that gratuitous promises are not enforceable and I may change my mind, the actual perceived benefit to my friend may be less than $100 per week. Thus, by enforcing the promise, the value to my friend increases without any increase in cost to me.

Another way of looking at it is to assume I understand the discounting my friend will do, and I still want to give a gift that will be the equivalent of $100 per week. In order to actually give a perceived benefit of $100 per week, I may have to promise $125 per week. In other words, the promise will be more expensive to me. On the other hand, if my friend and I both know that the promise will be enforced, the promise of $100 per week will be worth its stated value or something fairly close. In short, the gift becomes less expensive to me and stays at the $100 per week value for my friend. The outcome is that promisors may prefer a rule that holds them to their promises.

In both versions of this example, it is important to note that the promisor does give up something that presumably has some value: the right to change her mind. Thus, for the change in the rule to lead to a Pareto superior outcome, the value of

9. Richard Posner, "Gratuitous Promises in Economics and Law," 6 *J. Leg. Stud.* 411 (1977).

the "right" to break promises must be exceeded by the gains to promisors resulting from making their promises more valuable. Of course, even if the rule change is not consistent with Pareto superiority, it may still be wealth-maximizing.

The efficiency-increasing effects of enforcing gratuitous promises also extend to the ways in which promisees may react to promises. Professors Scott and Goetz offer a useful way of viewing the ways in which increasing the dependability of these promises may increase efficiency.[10] Again, a simple example is instructive. Suppose I wish to make a gift of $5,000 to my friend in six months' time. I have two choices. I can make a promise now to give the gift in six months, or I can simply wait six months and give him the $5,000 as a surprise. Certainly, in either case, the gift will move my friend to a higher indifference curve than if there had not been a gift. But two things seem clear. The person who knows ahead of time about the future gift will alter not just spending patterns in the future but current spending patterns in anticipation of the gift. Thus, the friend is likely to move to a higher indifference curve if the gift is known about in advance. Goetz and Scott call this ability to anticipate and move to a higher indifference curve "beneficial reliance" and view it as "the principal social rationale of promising."

10. Charles Goetz and Robert Scott, "Enforcing Promises: An Examination of the Basis of Contract," 89 *Yale L. J.* 1261 (1980).

The second matter that seems clear is that, the higher the probability the gift will be given, the greater the degree of reliance on the gift and the greater the level of beneficial reliance. In other words, the higher the likelihood that the money will be paid, the more comfortable the promisee will be about altering current spending patterns on the basis of the promise.

These arguments do not really address a slightly different issue. Even if we are decide to enforce promises made without consideration, what form should the promises take? There could be a rule, like that in many countries, that the lack of consideration is not a problem but that the promise must be in a formal writing. It is possible that this would mean obtaining many of the advantages of enforcing gratuitous promises but doing so at a lower cost of administration.

CHAPTER SIX

ECONOMICS OF TORT LAW

This Chapter focuses on unintentional torts.[1] As a general statement, an economic approach to tort law is one that seeks to minimize the costs of accidents. It does this by allocating the costs of accidents to the party or parties who are in the best position to avoid the accidents at the lowest cost. In theory, that person makes a decision about whether the benefits of the activity outweigh those costs.

By limiting its focus to "accidents," this Chapter does not consider the economics of intentional torts, including such torts as defamation or "tortous interference with business relationships." In addition, by emphasizing economics, this Chapter does not directly take on the weighty issues of what tort system is ultimately "just" and whether tort remedies should have as their main objective the "correction" of a "wrong."[2]

In terms of approach, there are good reasons for examining the economics of tort law from a different perspective than that applied in the case of contracts. Contract law is structured so that each

1. The organization of this Chapter is based on David Barnes and Lynn Stout, *Law and Economics: Cases and Materials*, Chapter 3 (1993).

2. See Jules Coleman, *Risks and Wrongs* (1992).

doctrine can be examined separately from the others and then combined to achieve an overall picture. An economic analysis of tort law requires a more integrated approach. In the pages that follow, the simple core elements will be discussed and then levels of complexity added.

This analysis begins with a description of the ideal outcome of tort law from the perspective of economic efficiency. The negligence standard is then considered, along with the Hand formula. Discussions of comparative negligence, strict liability, and damages follow. In all instances, the question is the extent to which economic goals are achieved.

A. THE COSTS OF ACCIDENTS AND THE ECONOMICS OF TORT LAW

When considering the economics of tort law, the touchstone scholarly work is Guido Calabresi's *The Costs of Accidents*.[3] Professor Calabresi identifies three types of costs that result from accidents. Primary costs are those associated with the harm to the injured party. This would include such things as the cost of medical care and lost earning capacity. Secondary costs, according to Calabresi, are "the societal costs resulting from accidents." Tertiary costs are those associated with administering the tort system.

Of these three categories, the second is the most difficult to understand. This category deals not with the absolute dollar losses associated with accidents,

3. Guido Calabresi, *The Costs of Accidents* (1970).

but as Jules Coleman puts it, with the "costs of bearing the costs of accidents."[4] For example, a $1,000 loss spread across 1000 individuals may result in less "dislocation" than if it were borne by a single person. Similarly, a wealthy person may suffer less utility from a $1000 loss that a poor person would.

Minimizing one cost may not be consistent with minimizing another cost. For example, a system that always accurately assigns the primary costs of accidents to those who cause accidents may be expensive to administer. Similarly, some efforts to reduce secondary accident costs may mean the party causing the accident does not feel the full impact of the harm done and may not take cost-justified steps to avoid the same accident in the future.

Although this list of costs is a useful way to envision the harms generated by accidents, the economic approach to tort law does not call for the minimization of these costs. For example, at some point the cost of avoiding accidents would be greater than the harm that would be caused by those accidents. Thus, the economic goal is to minimize the sum of the costs of accidents and the costs of efforts to prevent accidents. This is consistent with the notion of allocative efficiency discussed in Chapter Two. As long as the benefits of accident avoidance exceed the costs of prevention, it makes sense to invest in prevention. At some point, however, avoidance efforts will be more costly than the costs of the accident itself. The continued use of re-

4.   Jules Coleman, *supra* note 2, at 204.

sources to avoid accidents in these instances would be allocatively inefficient. The seemingly harsh conventional economic truth is that there may be an efficient level of accidents resulting not just in property damage but in personal injury and death.

Also implicated in the economic goals of tort law is a factor similar to productive efficiency.[5] Not only is the economist interested in avoiding those accidents that result in more damage than the cost of avoiding them, but the avoidance steps, when warranted, should be the least costly available. Thus, the economic approach to accidents seeks to make certain that the right quantity of avoidance is "produced" at the lowest possible cost.

B. LIABILITY, THE ASSIGNMENT OF RIGHTS AND EXTERNALITIES

Production of the right amount of accident avoidance at the lowest possible cost fits within the basic construct of the Coase Theorem. As an example, suppose a common hazard is that shoppers in grocery stores slip and fall on milk that has been spilled around the dairy department. In the language of tort law, the question is whether the operator of the store has a "duty" to keep spills off the floor. This right can be viewed as an entitlement or property right and, from an economic perspective, it should wind up in the possession of the party who values it most.

5. See Chapter Three.

If the right in this example is "owned" by shoppers, the store will owe a duty to the shoppers and will be liable for "breaching" this duty if spills are allowed to occur and consumers slip on them. If the right is owned by the operators of grocery stores, they do not owe a duty to shoppers and are not liable in the typical "slip and fall" incident.

The question posed for determining the efficient assignment of this right or duty would be: Who would pay more for it? Presumably, rational consumers with perfect information would bid either an amount up to the probability that they will slip times the "damage" if the slip occurs or the cost of avoiding the slip, whichever is lower. For example, suppose the probability of a slip and damaging fall is 1 in 1,000 for each visit to the store and the resulting injury, on average, is valued at $1,000. Also assume that by renting slip-proof slippers at the grocery store door for fifty cents each shopper can avoid the harm. Given these options, the consumer would pay up to fifty cents to own the right to be free of slippery floors and have the duty assigned to the store operator. If there were 1,000 shoppers a day, a cooperative of shoppers, assuming no free-riding, would bid up to $500.

On the other hand, assume the store could completely avoid the spill hazard by posting a person with a mop at each end of the dairy department. The cost per day would be $100. Or, the average cost per shopper-visit would be ten cents per day.

If an auction could take place, it is clear that shoppers would outbid store operators for the right. The consumers would bid up to $500 per day to have the duty assigned to the store owner. The store operator would bid only up to $100 per day for the right that would permit him to ignore the milk spills and escape liability. In other words, if the right could be allocated through the market, it would end up being *owned* by consumers. And, the duty would be *owed* by the lowest cost avoider of the accident—store operators.

Of course, the ownership of the duty in this type of case will be determined by a court. The assignment of liability may be assigned to the shoppers or to store owners. Under the Coase Theorem, in the absence of transaction costs, this initial assignment will not affect the eventual ownership of the right. In the above example, suppose the court assigned rights so that grocery stores would not be liable for slips. Since stores value the right to milky floors at $100, and shoppers the right to milk-free floors at $500, the shoppers would buy the milk-free-floor right at something between $100 and $500. The store would then guarantee that there would be no milk spills on the floor. Avoidance would take place, and it would take place at the lowest cost.

Obviously, in this example transaction costs would probably make such an exchange impossible. One thousand shoppers who do not know each other would have to combine and enter into some kind of binding contract with the store owner. There would be huge coordination expenses as well as free-rider problems. In many other instances, the parties are simply unable to bargain over these "rights" because there is not enough time. All of these limitations on the ability of parties to privately establish "duties of care" mean that it is critical, from an economic perspective, for the court to make the "correct" assignment in the first place.

Determining the "correct" assignment is complicated by the many factors discussed in Chapter Four. In addition, as will be discussed in detail in the pages that follow, damages for violating the rights of another in a torts context are the "prices" one has to pay. In effect, an involuntary exchange takes place. In the context of contracts and voluntary exchanges we can have some confidence that Pareto superior outcomes are achieved. The involuntary exchanges of tort law, under "liability rules," offer no such assurances. Although one can argue that the injurer is better off because he has consented to the exchange by choosing the riskier course of action, this is stretching the limits of the type of consent that would be consistent with Pareto superiority. In addition, the compensation of the injured party may not put that party in a position, utility-wise, that is the equivalent of his pre-accident state. This compensation will be determined by objective indicators, not by the actual value attributed by the victim to the harm that is done. The danger from a Pareto standpoint is that the injured party will be undercompensated.[6] Although the

6. Over-compensation may also occur which raises problems discussed below in Section H.3.

availability of punitive damages and damages for pain and suffering may offset this and provide for adequate compensation, the goal of punitive damages, in particular, is not compensation. Consequently, a match between damages and subjective losses will still be happenstance.

C. THE NEGLIGENCE STANDARD

1. THE HAND FORMULA

In order to achieve the goal of minimizing the sum of accident costs and their prevention, it is important that the right signal be sent to those who make decisions about whether to invest in accident prevention. This "signaling" is captured at the most basic level by the Hand formula as explained in the well-known case, *United States v. Carroll Towing Co.*, 159 F.2d 169 (2d Cir.1947). Judge Hand saw the issue of liability as being the function of three variables: the probability of the harm (P), the amount of harm should it occur (L) and the cost of prevention (B). P multiplied by L is the "expected harm." Thus, under the Hand formula, when PL exceeds B, a party is regarded as negligent. Conversely, if the expected harm is less than the cost of prevention, the party is not negligent.

Inherent in the Hand formula is a "pricing" effect that creates certain incentives. In theory, any actor has a choice of taking steps to avoid an accident or not. The Hand formula informs the actors of the price of each of those choices. When the prices are compared, presumably the rational actor will select the lower-priced option. For example, if the cost of avoidance is less than the expected harm, the choice would be to avoid the accident. The result of a "wrong" choice is that the injurer will be required to pay for the damages caused. Of course, it is also possible to make the wrong choice when PL is less than B. In these cases, the level of care is inefficiently high but there is no legal wrong. The overly cautious person does, however, internalize the cost of too much care.

At this basic level, the Hand formula focuses only on the behavior of the defendant. A finding that the defendant passed on an opportunity to take cost-justified preventive action does not mean that the defendant is the best cost avoider. Thus, a finding of liability under the negligence standard falls short of providing the proper signal if the other party can avoid the accident at a lower cost.

2.   DISTRIBUTIVE CONSEQUENCES

In virtually all instances of assigning rights, duties or entitlements, the effects are both allocative as well as distributive. To be more specific, the impact of the assignment of the right, even to the party that values it the most, is in no way "neutral." Thus, in the simple example of the potentially slippery dairy department, an assignment of the right to the shoppers to be free of the danger of spilled milk gives them something of value and has a distributive consequence. They become "richer," while the requirement that the store either pay for the accident or prevent it results in a decrease in the wealth of store owners. This is not to say, however, that some of this cost may not be shifted back to shoppers. The actual ultimate distributive effect can depend on a variety of factors in addition to the initial assignment.[7]

D. REFINING THE NEGLIGENCE MODEL: CONTRIBUTORY NEGLIGENCE

1. THE CONVENTIONAL DOCTRINE

Typically, the negligence standard is considered in the context of various defenses, including the possibility that the injured party has also acted negligently. The traditional approach in such instances could be to apply Hand formula to the injured party. The question would be whether the injured party's accident-avoidance costs were lower than the expected harm of the accident.

In the slippery dairy department example, all shoppers could rent slip-proof slippers for fifty cents each time they visited the grocery store. The expected harm per shopper of $1.00 would exceed the shoppers' cost of avoidance and, from the standpoint of the Hand formula, the shoppers would be regarded as negligent. Thus, the conventional common law doctrine would allow what amounted to a defense if the injurer failed the Hand formula test as long as it was shown that PL exceeded B for the injured party also.

7. For more on this see Chapter Three.

2. RECONCILING CONTRIBUTORY NEGLIGENCE AND EFFICIENCY

The example of the slippery dairy section and the possibility of renting slip-proof slippers illustrates one of the economic problems of the standard contributory negligence formulation. Each shopper can avoid the expected harm of $1.00 for fifty cents. The store operators can avoid the harm for ten cents per shopper. Both parties could avoid the expected harm at a lower cost than the expected harm. Consequently, adhering to the rule of contributory negligence will result in the harm being avoided by the parties—shoppers—who can efficiently do so but who are not the "best cost avoiders." In a sense, they are not the most productively efficient. Such an assignment would be inconsistent with the overall goal of minimizing the sum of the costs of accidents and their prevention.

Richard Posner makes the point that this inefficiency will not occur if the proper standard is applied. In the above example, he would say that, given that the store owners can avoid the care at ten cents per shopper, the shoppers will not be motivated to take care as long as the law defines due care as "the level of care that is optimal if the other party is taking due care."[8] A technical problem with Judge Posner's theory is that it defines due care in terms of due care. What he seems to mean is that each

8. Richard Posner, The Economic Analysis of Law 173 (6th ed. 2003) (emphasis deleted).

party is entitled to act as though the other party is acting in the matter that is most efficient from the standpoint of minimizing the primary cost of the accident. Thus, the shoppers, even though their B is less than PL, are permitted to act as though the store's B is also less than PL by an even greater margin and that the store has acted accordingly. According to Judge Posner, this is the way the courts define due care.[9]

This leads to the issue of whether a party who is likely to be harmed by the negligent conduct of another party must take steps to avoid the harm. First, it is useful to note that an injured party who has no basis to know of the injuring party's conduct will be able to recover even if he could have efficiently taken preventive action. In this situation, even though avoidance may be relatively inexpensive, the B in the Hand formula could be viewed as being quite high since the burden would involve not just the effort to avoid the harm but the costs of discovering that the other party has acted in a careless fashion.

On the other hand, if the victim knows or has reason to know of the other party's negligent conduct, the question is whether she can blithely bypass avoiding the accident confident that the injurer will be liable. In terms of the shoppers and the store, can the shoppers walk through obvious spilt

---

9. Judge Posner has been challenged on this. See David W. Barnes & Rosemary McCool, "Reasonable Care in Tort Law: The Duty to Take Corrective Precaution," 36 *Ariz. L. Rev.* 357 (1994).

milk and hold the store liable if they slip? Judge Posner evidently thinks that they can because they are permitted to act as though the store owners have acted efficiently.

From a common sense point of view, it seems clear that the victim should be required to take action to avoid the harm. This is consistent with the Hand formula if one views the issue in a compressed time frame because, once the hazard is known, the possibly large search costs are no longer part of the burden. This outcome is also consistent with section 466 of the *Restatement (Second) of Torts*, which states that a plaintiff is contributorily negligent when exposing himself "to danger created by the defendant's negligence, of which danger the plaintiff knows or has reason to know." The requirement that the victim react to the negligent behavior of the injuring party does not necessarily mean that the victim is the best cost avoider. Thus, the inconsistency of the negligence/contributory negligence standard with the cost minimization goal remains.

Another refinement of the negligence standard that seems designed to avoid inefficient outcomes resulting from strict adherence to contributory negligence is the doctrine of "last clear chance." Last clear chance is different from the possibilities discussed above in that it permits a negligent victim to shift liability back to the injurer by showing that the injurer was, *at the time of the accident*, able to avoid the accident at a cost that was lower than the expected harm. Again, the critical variable in terms of the Hand formula is B, the burden. At the time of the accident the burden on the victim may be quite high. Since P and L are the same for both parties, the proper risk allocation is to the injurer, who can efficiently avoid the harm.

E. REDEFINING THE NEGLIGENCE STANDARD: COMPARATIVE NEGLIGENCE

The adoption of comparative negligence in one form or another by most states represents an effort to alter the perceived inequity resulting from the "all or nothing" outcomes of strict application of negligence and contributory negligence standards. Whatever the equities inherent in comparative negligence, it may or may not be an improvement over contributory negligence in terms of providing the best cost avoider with the maximum incentive to avoid the harm.

There are a variety of comparative negligence regimes. Under the most common, loss is apportioned among the parties according to how fault is allocated among them. Under this system, the injured party's recovery is reduced, but not necessarily eliminated, because of negligence. In effect, it is apportioned. Under a less common approach, the negligent injured person may recover so long as the negligence of the injurer is gross when compared to that of the injured party. Under this approach, loss is not apportioned, so it has the all-or-nothing characteristic of traditional contributory negligence.

These two forms of comparative negligence are discussed in turn.

1. APPORTIONED COMPARATIVE NEGLIGENCE

In order to illustrate the possible economic consequences of comparative negligence, it is useful to start with a simple example. In the case of the slippery dairy department, suppose the floor actually was wet from some recently spilled milk and that a shopper who was running through the department slipped and was injured to the extent of $200,000. A possible outcome in a comparative negligence state might be that the store is viewed as being 60 percent responsible, while the injured party is viewed as being 40 percent responsible. See *Scott v. Alpha Beta Company*, 163 Cal.Rptr. 544 (App.1980). The plaintiff would recover $120,000. In other words, the recovery is reduced by the portion of the plaintiff's contribution to the harm.

The obvious difference between contributory negligence and comparative negligence is that, under the former, one party *or* the other will be motivated to avoid the harm. Under comparative negligence, both parties will have some incentive to avoid the harm. The problem from an economic standpoint is that the parties may both attempt to avoid the harm when the efforts of either one would be sufficient. This may mean there is an over-investment in avoidance. Another possibility is that the incentive to avoid the harm is reduced to the point that neither party takes preventive action, even though the prevention of the accident is cost-justified.

For example, suppose an accident that will result in a $1,000 loss can be prevented by a $50 expenditure by the defendant or a $100 expenditure by the plaintiff.[10] Under an apportioned approach to comparative negligence, the defendant will be viewed as bearing two-thirds of the responsibility for the accident and the plaintiff's responsibility will be one-third. Each party's share is equal to the ratio of the other party's individual avoidance costs to the sum of the avoidance costs. Based on these numbers, the defendant would be responsible for $666.66 of the loss and the plaintiff $333.33. Thus, they would both be motivated to take the preventive steps for a total cost of $150, even though the accident could be avoided at a cost of only $50. On the other hand, each party may anticipate that the other will find it in his or her economic interest to avoid the accident. If so, neither party will avoid the accident, and the $1,000 loss will occur.

This is not to say that comparative negligence will always result in over-investment or under-investment in accident prevention. For example, suppose an accident costs $15,000 and has a 1% chance of occurring.[11] Further suppose that the cost of avoidance to the injurer is $1.00 and the cost of avoidance to the victim is $100. In this case, the

10. This explanation is found in *Golden v. McCurry*, 392 So.2d 815 (Ala.1980), cited by Barnes and Stout, supra note 1.

11. This example is from David Barnes and Lynn Stout, *supra* note 1, at 122.

expected cost of the accident to the injurer would be the probability of the accident times the cost of the accident times the ratio of the victim's avoidance cost to the sum of the avoidance costs. This would be $148.51, and the injurer would be motivated to take the precautionary action at a cost of $1.00. Using the same calculation, the expected cost to the victim would be $1.49, and the victim would not be motivated to take precautionary action.

Using the same numbers, however, and applying a strict contributory negligence standard, the burden to the victim of avoidance—$100—would be less than PL, which would be $150, and the victim would be motivated to spend $100 to avoid an accident that the injurer could have avoided at just $1.00.

Whether comparative negligence is inefficient depends on the numbers. The critical factor seems to be the avoidance costs of both parties relative to the risk. David Barnes and Lynn Stout divide the possibilities into three groups.[12] When avoidance costs for both parties are high relative to the risk, neither party is as likely to avoid the accident. On the other hand, when both parties' avoidance costs are relatively low as compared to the loss, both parties are likely to take action. These are the instances in which comparative negligence may lead to inefficient outcomes. On the other hand, as the numerical illustration shows, when one party's avoidance costs are high and the other's low relative to the loss, the lower cost avoider—whether injurer or

12. See David Barnes and Lynn Stout, *supra* note 1, at 123.

victim—will be motivated to take precautionary action.

2. UNAPPORTIONED COMPARATIVE NEGLIGENCE

Although both contributory negligence and comparative negligence can lead to inefficient outcomes, there are variations that increase the likelihood that the best cost avoider will take preventive steps. Although not applicable currently in any state, a rule that would consistently incorporate the equitable considerations of comparative negligence with the goal of motivating the best cost avoider to take the precautions necessary to avoid an accident is called the *Galena* rule.[13]

Under *Galena,* the injuring party is fully liable even though the victim is also negligent if the injuring party's negligence is gross relative to the victim's negligence. As long as the comparative costs of accident avoidance are used to determine the relative negligence of the parties, the proper economic signal should be sent to motivate the best cost avoider to take the precautionary action. The key feature of the rule, when compared to comparative negligence, is that liability is not split and the party who is the lower cost avoider will have the maximum incentive to avoid the accident.

Another effort to steer a path between contributory negligence and comparative negligence is the South Dakota Comparative Negligence Statute

13.   See Id., at 123–124.

which does not bar recovery by a contributorily negligent plaintiff as long as the plaintiff's negligence was "slight in comparison with the negligence of the defendant." Although recovery is not barred, it is reduced by the amount of the plaintiff's negligence. The economic effect of the rule should be that a defendant, who is the best cost avoider, will not escape liability when the plaintiff has also been negligent. Conversely, by barring a plaintiff's recovery whose negligence is more than "slight" when compared to that of the defendant, the efficient economic message should be sent to plaintiffs.

F. ASSUMPTION OF THE RISK

Assumption of the risk bars the recovery of a plaintiff in much the same manner as contributory negligence. In one form, "primary assumption of the risk," the injurer is engaged in a possibly dangerous activity, but the costs of eliminating the risk may be quite high. For example, there is a danger that spectators at a golf tournament will be bonked on the head by stray golf balls. It can really hurt and a golf glove signed by a player may not make up for the pain. Nevertheless, completely avoiding the risk, B, is probably higher than PL; the injurer is not negligent. The victim can be said to have assumed the risk.

In another form, "secondary assumption of the risk," the plaintiff's actions are dangerous because of a situation created by the injurer. In the slippery floor example, it could mean that the plaintiff walked across the floor knowing that it was slick with spilled milk. Secondary assumption of the risk can be evaluated in the same manner as contributory negligence in that it may operate as a complete bar to a plaintiff even though the defendant was the best cost avoider. The idea is that, having witnessed the negligence of the defendant, the plaintiff cannot ignore an easy and inexpensive opportunity to avoid the harm.

G. STRICT LIABILITY

Strict liability means that a party is liable for damage caused by her activity even if there is no showing of negligence. Although this may seem to undermine efforts to achieve economic efficiency, presumably those parties who are more likely to be in control of the activity will be the ones held strictly liable. Furthermore, streamlining the fault-finding process can reduce the tertiary costs of accidents.

The decision that a party will be strictly liable for the damages resulting from an activity amounts to an assignment of a right to others to be free of the consequences of that activity or to be compensated. In effect, the harm to the others is treated as an externality that the liable party is forced to "internalize."[14] Either the harm to the injured party from the activity or the investment the injuring party makes to avoid the harm becomes a cost of production whether or not the injuring party has acted

14. For an extended discussion see Chapter Three.

negligently. Presumably the strictly liable party will pick the lower of these two. Since one choice is to pay for the harm caused, it is important to note that making a party strictly liable does not mean the harm is avoided.

1.   EFFICIENCY AND STRICT LIABILITY

One of the obvious dangers of strict liability in terms of efficiency is that the liable party may not be the best cost avoider. There are two versions of this possibility. The first occurs when an accident that should be prevented from the standpoint of the Hand formula will not be prevented. In these instances, the liable party will find that PL does not exceed B and, therefore, will not take preventive action. It may be that the opposite is true for the victim and that PL will exceed B, but since the victim will be compensated by the injuring party, there will be insufficient motivation to take cost-justified preventive action. Of course, this would not be the case if contributory negligence were a defense to strict liability. Such a defense makes sense except that it then undermines one of the attractions of strict liability, the reduction of tertiary or administrative expenses.

The second possibility is that the accident will be avoided, but not by the best cost avoider. This will occur when the B exceeds the PL for both the injurer and the victim, but the B to the victim is less than the B to the injurer. In such a case, the injurer will act to avoid the accident, although it would have been less costly for the victim to do so. This inefficiency, like those described in the preceding paragraph, can be overcome by the proper application of defenses to strict liability, some of which are discussed below. In any case, if these inefficiencies are relatively rare, or relatively low-cost, the savings in tertiary costs of strict liability may still lower the overall cost of accidents.

One major consequence of applying strict liability is that it forces the party who will be liable to consider not only the standard of care but the level of activity.[15] For example, under a negligence system, a person who engages in a certain activity, like blasting, only has to be concerned with damages as a result of negligent blasting. Thus, the number of times blasting takes place would be influenced only by the likelihood that increased numbers mean increased probability that negligence will occur. On the other hand, because strict liability means all damage caused is chargeable to the blasting party, those damages will be treated like any other cost of blasting. They will increase with the amount of blasting, whether carefully or negligently conducted. Thus, the party is concerned not just with the level of care but with the level of the activity.

This distinction has particularly important implications from the standpoint of allocative efficiency. It will be recalled from Chapter Two that production is at an allocatively efficient level when the amount people are willing to pay for a product is

15. Steve Shavell, *"Strict Liability Verses Negligence,"* 9 J. Legal. Stud. 1 (1980).

equal to its marginal cost of production. Imagine a situation in which there is some damage to a nearby residential neighborhood every time a potential defendant engages in blasting. Further, suppose that under a negligence standard, the blaster would not be liable, no matter how much blasting was done and no matter how much damage accumulated unless it could be shown that the cost of prevention was less than the expected accident costs. This produces an allocative inefficiency because the cost of blasting will not be recognized as a cost of production. This is depicted in Figure 1 which shows the demand and supply for a good. S_1 is the supply under the negligence standard. The quantity produced would be Q_1 and the price would be P_1.

Figure 1

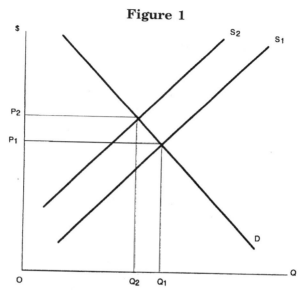

On the other hand, if the blaster pays for all
damage whether the result of negligence or not, the
amount of blasting becomes critical and the damage
caused by the activity itself—not just when it is
conducted in a negligent manner—is treated like
any other cost of production. In Figure 1, S_2 represents the supply of the product under strict liability.
It is lower than S_1 by the amount of the damage
caused by blasting. The quantity now is reduced to
Q_2 and the new price is P_2. This is a price that
reflects the cost of production including the external costs of blasting and is, therefore, consistent
with allocative efficiency.

Much the same analysis can be applied in the case
of products liability. The harm resulting from the

use of a product can be viewed as an external cost of its production. Liability requires the manufacturer to internalize that cost. The effect of this internalization, as Figure 1 illustrates, would be to increase the cost of production and the price of the item while lowering output.

As in other instances of strict liability, there is no guarantee that the products actually will be safer than they would be under a negligence standard. The manufacturer will presumably engage in the same cost-benefit analysis implicit in the Hand formula and take those measures that are less expensive than the expected costs to those who are injured by the product. Similarly, there is nothing to insure that the manufacturer is the best cost avoider. It is true, however, that when the dangerousness is a result of design or manufacturing defects, the manufacturer seems likely to be in a better position to discover most problems and may enjoy significant economies of scale in correcting those problems. In other words, although it is ultimately an empirical question, it probably makes sense to begin with the assumption that in most instances manufacturers are in the best position to minimize primary accident costs resulting from product defects.

2. RISK–AVERSION AND LOSS SPREADING

Strict liability is also often seen as a method of minimizing secondary accident costs. It will be recalled that secondary accident costs are the actual burdens felt by society as a result of accidents. The notion of secondary accident costs can be linked to the view that people are generally risk-averse in that they would pay more to avoid a loss than the amount of the actual expected loss. For example, a risk-averse individual would pay $1.01 to avoid a one in a thousand chance of incurring a $1,000 loss. A risk neutral person would be willing to pay only $1.00.

One can translate this to the question of products liability by asking whether consumers would prefer to pay a dollar to avoid the loss resulting from the use of a product with a possibly dangerous characteristic or pay a dollar less and know there is a one in a thousand chance that they will suffer a $1,000 injury due to the product. If they prefer the former, then secondary accident costs can be lowered through the use of strict products liability. This would be the case even if primary accident costs were not minimized. In other words, even if the manufacturer were not the best cost avoider, secondary and tertiary accident costs may be reduced by holding the manufacturer strictly liable.

The logic supporting the position that individuals are generally risk-averse and that secondary accident costs can be reduced by spreading losses through the use of strict liability is based on the belief that money has diminishing marginal utility. This means that, as a person has additional money, the utility derived from each additional dollar eventually declines. Conversely, as each dollar is taken away the disutility experienced increases. Thus, the total disutility as a result of 5,000 people suffering $1 losses can be less than that if one person to suffers a $5,000 loss.

The diminishing marginal utility possibility means that wealthier or "deeper pocket" parties should feel the sting of the cost of an accident less than any individual customers. Thus, the argument can be made that secondary accident costs can be reduced by holding the wealthier party—perhaps a corporation—liable for product defects. It is important to note that this theory is built on the supposition that overall preferences for money are about the same. Suppose instead that wealthy people value small sums more than people who are not wealthy. For example, it is possible that a person earning $50,000 per year finds it easier to part with $5.00 than a person earning $300,000 per year. Both parties may be subject to the diminishing marginal utility for money. On the other hand, the wealthier party's generalized preference for money may be higher than that of the middle-class person. If so, the basis for believing that the secondary costs of accidents can be lowered by loss spreading is weakened.

There are other concerns about the consequence of assigning liability to manufacturers as a means of either spreading the loss or assigning it to the wealthier party. The problem is that it is not clear who ends up ultimately paying for the accident costs. In addition, assigning it to the firm may have undesired effects. Figure 2 can be used to illustrate the problem. The demand curve for the product is D. The supply curve before strict products liability is S_1. The price is P_1 and the quantity produced is equal to Q_1.

Figure 2

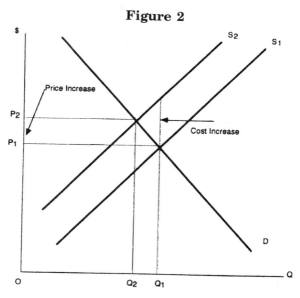

After strict products liability, the firm internalizes the cost of either accidents or preventive measures and the new supply curve is S_2. The actual cost per unit has increased by the vertical distance between S_1 and S_2. The price increase, however, is from P_1 to P_2. In other words, the price increase is less than the increase in production costs. This means that the cost increase is shared between consumers and the firm.

How the additional cost is divided between buyers and the firm is determined by the elasticities of demand and supply. The concept of elasticity is discussed in detail in Chapter Two, but for the purposes at hand it is enough to recall that elasticity measures the degree of responsiveness of buyers or sellers to changes in price. As a simple example, consider Figures 3 and 4. In Figure 3, demand is very inelastic, meaning that buyers are not very responsive to price changes. In Figure 4 on the other hand, consumers are relatively responsive to price.

Figure 3

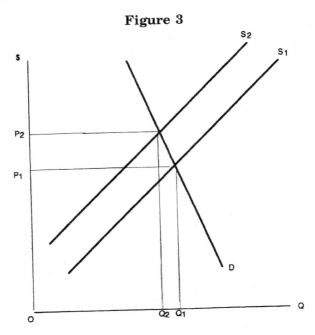

In the graphs, the initial supply curves (S_1) are identical, and the price for the item is P_1. The supply curves (S_2) after strict products liability are also identical. In other words, they have shifted up by the same vertical distance. In both instances, there is a new price (P_2). In Figure 3, however, the new price is higher than the new price in Figure 4. This makes sense because the consumers in the market illustrated in Figure 3 are not very responsive to price and are, therefore, willing to absorb most of the cost increase. The Figure 4 consumers, on the other hand, are responsive to price and the firm finds that it is unable to pass along most of the cost increase in the form of higher prices.

Figure 4

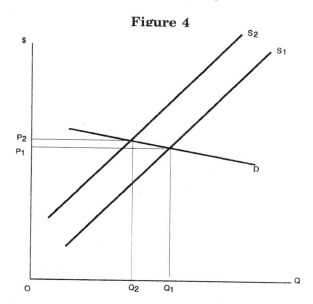

What this suggests is that strict products liability may have an impact on the costs and ultimately the profitability of firms. Of course, profitability is important to shareholders. Furthermore, a firm that is less profitable than others may not be able to attract investors as readily as more profitable firms. At the extreme, the solvency of the firm may be threatened. Consequently, the employment of those working for the firm will also be affected. The point is that the issue of strict products liability is more complex than simply spreading losses or assigning losses to the deepest pocket.

3. DUTY TO RESCUE

The "duty to rescue" is discussed here because the general rule that individuals are not liable for declining to undertake even relatively easy rescues can be seen as applying strict liability to those who are imperiled. Even seen in this light, it is difficult to square the absence of a duty to rescue with economic efficiency. The problem can be seen by thinking in terms of the Hand Formula again. In the case of the easy rescue, B is going to be quite small when compared to PL. Thus, it would seem to be efficient, at least from the standpoint of primary accident costs, to hold those liable who do not offer assistance when the burden would be small.

Arguments can be made that appear to reconcile the lack of a duty with economic efficiency. There are valid points to be made, but, even so, some of the arguments have a make-weight feel to them.

For example, Richard Posner makes the point that a duty to rescue would impose a cost on being in a position in which a rescue might be necessary and, therefore, reduce the number of would-be rescuers.[16] Similarly, he argues that a duty to rescue would eliminate the psychic income received by altruists who are likely to engage in rescues. Again the result may be fewer rescues.

Although all these arguments may be valid, it is still hard to understand how a duty to engage in easy rescues would actually decrease the number of rescues and, therefore, increase primary accident costs. The costs that may well increase if there were a duty to rescue are tertiary costs. Determining when the duty arises and when it has been abided by would be difficult and inexact.

Although the lack of a duty to rescue can probably best be explained by reference to something other than a purely economic rationale, the policy does make some economic sense. The absence of a duty to rescue is like holding parties who find themselves in need of a rescue strictly liable. For example, if you swim in deep water you are, in a sense, liable for any misfortune not caused by others. This forces you to internalize the full cost of your decision so that it is more efficient. The opposite possibility would be one in which people standing on the shore would all be liable if they did not come to your rescue. This enables you to shift some

16. Richard Posner, *Economic Analysis of Law* 190–191 (6th ed. 2003).

of the cost of your decision to others. In effect, your swimming would create an externality.

4.   DEFENSES TO STRICT LIABILITY

As with negligence, there are defenses available to those defendants who would otherwise be strictly liable. From an economic standpoint, the use of these defenses can be a problem. Their introduction may lower primary accident costs, but cause tertiary costs to increase and offset any gains. This possible offsetting effect can be lowered if the defense is clear in terms of its applicability. In the case of all defenses, the important economic question is whether the availability of the defense will increase the probability that the best cost avoider will take preventive action.

a.   Unforeseeable Misuse

Although there are good economic arguments for holding manufacturers strictly liable for the sale of defective products, a problem arises when the product is used in a manner that is not reasonably anticipated by the manufacturer. In terms of the Hand Formula, one could say that the probability of the accident is extremely low or that the burden to the manufacturer of attempting to anticipate and respond to all the possible ways in which a product might be misused is quite high. The party who misuses the product would find it less burdensome and is, therefore, more likely to be the best cost avoider.

The focus in "unforeseeable" misuse cases is not so much on misuse as it is on whether manufacturers could have reasonably anticipated the misuse and designed the product in such a way that the resulting harm could have been avoided. For example, crashing a car into another car can be viewed as a misuse of the car, but it is also something manufacturers can readily anticipate and respond to by designing and manufacturing crash-worthy cars. On the other hand, the use of the car's radiator as a food processor is not a misuse that a manufacturer would be expected to anticipate. It is important to keep in mind that even finding a manufacturer liable for "foreseeable" misuses does not mean that preventive action will be taken. As in all instances of strict liability, the liable will decide whether the burdens of making the modifications are justified by the expected liability.

b. Unreasonable Assumption of Risk

The defense of "assumption of the risk" arises when the plaintiff knows of a particular danger associated with using the product but chooses to use it anyway. Timing appears to be a factor in these cases; the product may actually be defective, but the manufacturer escapes liability because, at the time of the use of the product, the plaintiff was the best cost avoider. This approach makes economic sense when the product is not generally defective but may be dangerous for a specific use and the plaintiff is both aware of that shortcoming and chooses to use the product in a manner that tests its limitations.

Any defense may decrease a manufacturer's incentive to redesign the product. This may not be of great consequence for a couple of reasons. First, even holding the manufacturer liable may not mean that accidents are avoided in instances in which the costs of redesign are high. Second, the cost of redesign, even if justified by the expected accident costs, may not be the least expensive method of avoiding the accident. In other words, the manufacturer may not be the best cost avoider.

c. Contributory and Comparative Negligence

A possible defense to strict liability would be to permit the defendant to show the plaintiff was negligent. If this were a complete bar to the plaintiff's recovery, there is no guarantee that primary accident costs would be minimized. The problem is that, even though the plaintiff might be negligent, the defendant may be the best cost avoider. By allowing this defense, the defendant would not receive the proper economic signal and would not have the incentive to avoid the accident.

Another possibility is to apportion the damages between the parties with the plaintiff's recovery reduced by the extent to which he contributed to the accident. Such an approach has appeal since, if the plaintiff's actions contributed to the harm, it may be incorrect to regard the full amount of the harm as an externality of the manufacturer's activity. On the other hand, as demonstrated in the context of comparative negligence, dividing the losses between the parties may lead to over or under investment in prevention. Thus, if the objective is to minimize primary accident costs, it makes sense to treat the party who is the best cost avoider as liable for the full amount of the loss even if the other party could have also avoided or decreased the harm.

H. DAMAGES

As suggested throughout this Chapter, the tort system can be viewed as an effort to minimize accident costs, including efforts to prevent them, by providing the proper market incentives. Like any market, the critical link to achieving efficient outcomes is that the price charged—in this case the price for negligent behavior—be accurate. Accuracy in this instance means that the damages paid by the defendant actually reflect the costs of the behavior. Three specific issues that arise to complicate the pricing problem are the collateral source rule, future losses, and punitive damages.

1. THE COLLATERAL SOURCE RULE

Under the collateral source rule, a plaintiff who recovers from a source collateral to the injurer, like a medical insurer, can still recover in full from the injurer. This creates the possibility that the plaintiff will be over-compensated. One response to over-compensation is not to require the defendant to compensate the plaintiff when the plaintiff recovers from another source. The question from the point of view of economics is which is less desirable: over-compensation of plaintiffs or under-internalization by defendants which may result inefficient levels of care by defendants.

In the case of insurance, these possibilities are unlikely if the insurer has the benefit of a subrogation clause. This means that the plaintiff will collect only once and the insurance company will be reimbursed for any payment it has made. The market signal sent to the defendant should be the correct one from the point of view of minimizing primary accident costs.

2.   FUTURE LOSSES

One of the most common problems that arise in arriving at the right pricing signal is the calculation of future losses. For example, if the harm reduces the earning power of the injured party, how are these future losses to be expressed in current dollar damages? One possibility, of course, is simply to add up all the lost future income. Thus, if the injured party's earning power is reduced by $100 per year for 10 years, one could award $1,000 in damages. There are, however, a number of complicating factors.

First, although it is possible for the earning power of the plaintiff to be reduced by a constant level of $100 per year, in a more typical case we would expect someone to become more productive as she becomes more experienced. Thus, estimates of future earnings need to be adjusted for increases in income resulting from increases in productivity.

Second, even if the losses are constant at $100 per year for 10 years, awarding the plaintiff $1,000 will result in over-compensation. The plaintiff would have earned the $100 in the *future*, so the award should take this into account. Unless it is, the plaintiff could invest the $1,000 awarded and end up with more compensation than $100 a year. From the point of view of the proper "pricing" for purposes of allocative efficiency, the price of the activity determined to be negligent would be too high.

Third, income may also be higher in the future due to inflation. If the injured party really is to live as well after the injury as before, then the dollars received today as damages must not lose their buying power as time passes. In the absence of an accident, it is likely that the plaintiff would receive something like "cost of living" wage increases in order to at least hold her real buying power at some constant level. This suggests that the damages must also be adjusted up to allow for inflation.

Of these complications, the first is probably the least controversial. If the plaintiff were likely to experience higher income due to increases in productivity, then the loss of this potential is a legitimate part of the damage. This does not mean that showing these losses will be easy as a practical matter.

The second and third problems are related and here there is some controversy. In theory, the plaintiff should be given just enough in damages to compensate for the losses in income. Thus, rather than simply add up the losses, the goal is to give the plaintiff enough as a single payment that, when invested, will produce the desired future income stream. This means that the actual loss in the future is discounted or lowered to an amount that will result in the appropriate level of income. Technically, the future income is discounted to a present value. For example, if the going interest rate is 10%, the present value of a $100 installment due at the end of the first year would be approximately $90. This is because the $90 would grow to $100 by the end of the year.

The actual formula for the discounting process and calculating present value is:

$$\text{Future income in year } n/(1 + r)^n$$

where r is the interest rate and n is the year in which the income would have been received. Since the denominator of this fraction becomes larger as n increases, it is logical and obvious that income to be received in the more distant future is discounted more heavily.

In the context of discounting to present value, a number of issues arise. The first is whether the discounting should take place at all. One of the arguments for bypassing discounting is that the process is speculative with respect to the interest rate. In addition, if one first adjusts the future income stream up in order to allow for inflation and then discounts to present value, the two steps seem to offset each other. In fact, matters are simplified by assuming that the two effects cancel each other out. If the assumption that the discount rate and the rate of inflation offset each other is wrong, it is almost certainly because the discount rate exceeds the rate of inflation. This means that plaintiffs would be over-compensated. Although the "price" is then inaccurate with respect to primary accident costs, the approach has some appeal due to the fact that it can lower tertiary costs.

If one does not subscribe to the offset approach, then the issue becomes what discount rate to use and how to account for inflation. To understand why these issues are related, it is useful to examine the components of the interest rate. Part of the reason people charge interest is because the dollars they will be paid back in the future may be worth less than today's dollars due to inflation. The rest of the interest rate, calculated by subtracting the rate of inflation from the interest rate, is called the "real interest rate."

This means that, in theory, to adjust expected future income upward to allow for inflation and then to discount it by the full interest rate is a partially offsetting process. One approach to the discounting issue is to bypass any inflation adjustment and then discount by the real interest rate. This does not mean that there is a real interest rate that everyone can agree upon. While the real interest rate cannot be pinned down with precision, it is probably in the range of 1.5 to 3 percent.

Another issue is what to use as the discount rate. It is popular to say the discount rate should be the amount that could be earned in a safe investment, like long-term government securities. The theory is that the victim should be put in a position to take the damage award and invest it at a very low risk and receive income that would have been received but for the accident. The problem here is that the plaintiff's future income stream was probably not as risk-free as the payment from a government security. For example, the income of a jockey, or even a physician in an era of health care reform, can be quite unpredictable. Thus the argument has been made that the discount rate must be adjusted upward to allow for the risk associated with the expected future income streams.

3. HEDONIC LOSSES

Hedonic losses are those associated with losing the pleasures of life. These losses are not linked to actual expenses or lost income. For example, if you like fishing but an accident renders you unable to fish, the loss is hedonic. The idea of hedonic losses can be extended to victims who are killed. In theory, all harm caused by an accident should be internalized by the injuring party and the loss of enjoyment in life should be part of the calculation. The matter gets complicated and controversial when it involves the determination of what a victim's life was worth to him or her.

Economists can approach the issue by reasoning that goes like this. Suppose you have an option of buying a side air bag for your car and it costs $200. You buy the airbag. The chances you will be killed in a car wreck if you have the air bag is .00003. If you do not have the airbag, the chance is .00004. A way of looking at this is that .00001 of your life is worth at least $200. If .00001 is worth at least $200, then your entire life is worth at least ($200 times 100,000) $20 million. The methodology is questionable because it relies on decisions that may not have been fully informed and treats the value of an entire life as though it is divisible.

Recently, damages for hedonic losses have come under scrutiny by psychologist and economists who are interested in measuring happiness. Some of their studies suggest that people who suffer losses recover in time and actually return to their original level of happiness. If so, one implication is that damages based on hedonic losses may be systematically overstated.

4. PUNITIVE DAMAGES

In some tort cases, plaintiffs are awarded punitive damages or damages above those that would compensate them for the harm suffered. From the standpoint of minimizing accident costs and implementation of the Hand Formula, punitive damages appear to introduce the possibility that potential injurers will take inefficiently high levels of care. For example, suppose the burden of avoiding an accident is $100 and the expected harm (PL) is $90. In this instance, the efficient course of action would be to forego steps designed to avoid the accident.

On the other hand, if there is some likelihood that punitive damages will be awarded, the injurer must compare the avoidance costs with the total award including punitive damages. Suppose this is $150. Now it becomes rational for the injurer to spend up to $150 to avoid the accident. The problem, of course, is that the harm to be avoided at a cost of $100 is still only $90 and accident costs are not minimized.

It is important to note that the over-investment danger is not present if it already makes economic sense for the injurer to take precautionary action. Thus, if the burden of avoiding the accident is less than the expected harm, the injurer will take steps to avoid the harm. Adding more to the expected recovery would not change this outcome. Consequently, the effect of punitive damages will only be to encourage investment in avoidance efforts that are not justified by the harm to be avoided.

In this latter case, over-investment still may not occur. The basic model employed here includes the assumption that everyone harmed will bring an action and prevail against the injurer. If the injuries to the injured parties are relatively small compared to the costs to bring suit, the injured persons may just internalize the cost of the injuries by not bringing suit. This may be the case even though several people are similarly injured and, from an economic perspective, it would be efficient for the injurer to take precautionary action.

In these instances, the effect of punitive damages is to provide an incentive to plaintiffs to file an action. To the extent that the expected award, inclusive of the punitive damages, approaches the harm to all victims by the defendant's conduct, punitive damages may encourage more efficient behavior and lower primary accident costs. This is not, however, an outcome that can be depended upon. It is more likely a result of coincidence.

The United States Supreme Court has taken a decidedly non economic approach to punitive damages. The enforceability of punitive damages depends on the reprehensibility of the defendant's conduct, whether the award bears a reasonable relationship to the actual and potential harm caused by the defendant to the plaintiff, and the difference between the award and sanctions authorized or imposed in comparable cases. The key idea is "to the plaintiff." Consequently, in *Philip Morris USA v. Williams*, 549 U.S. 346 (2007) the Court ruled that a jury instruction under which a plaintiff was awarded $80 million in connection with harms from smoking and deception by a tobacco company had to be reconsidered. The reconsideration was required because the instruction allowed the jury to award damages based on the harm to parties other than the plaintiff. By taking damages to others off the table, the Court drove a wedge between the economist's notion of punitive damages and what courts may legally award.

The economic theory of punitive damages runs into additional problems. For example if punitive

damages were used to require firms to internalize
the full cost of its activities, what happens to subse-
quent law suits by additional victims? To the extent
they recover when punitive damages have already
been awarded, the level of internalization is inefficiently high. A second issue arises with respect to
the proper recipient of the punitive damages. Except to the extent necessary to motivate the plaintiff to bring an action, there is no economic reason
for the plaintiff to keep all of the punitive damages
awarded. Although economic analysis cannot provide an answer to the question of how the award
should be distributed, there may be good policy
reasons for the award to be distributed more broadly.

CHAPTER SEVEN

THE ECONOMICS OF SETTLEMENTS

As you may know, very few legal disputes go to trial. In fact, about 95% percent of cases settle. There are actually good economic reasons for why some cases settle and some do not.

A. WHY DO SOME CASES SETTLE?

A settlement is a contract and, like most contracts, they come into being when both parties feel they are better off by virtue of an exchange than they would be without the exchange. From the analysis of contract law in Chapter 5, you know the idea is that an exchange occurs when it results in a surplus. In a simple example, I may have a Ducati motorcycle that I value at $15,000. You think it is a particularly nice bike and would pay up to $20,000 for it. There is a $5,000 surplus and the decision on a price somewhere between $15,000 (the lowest I will take) and $20,000 (the most you will pay) has the impact of dividing that surplus.

In the case of a settlement, the plaintiff sells his right to sue to the defendant. Still, you may ask, where is the surplus? Generally, it comes from avoiding the costs of a trial and the expenses incurred leading up to the trial. Here is an example: Suppose you slip and fall on a wet floor in a grocery store. Your damages are $20,000. You are not sure you will win the case and calculate the probability at 60%. The trial itself will cost an estimated $5,000. The value of your case is $7,000. This is .60 times $20,000 or $12,000, your expected award, minus the $5,000 cost. In effect, a settlement offer in excess of $7,000 would be attractive to you. This is simpler than the reality, but the example is consistent with the theory.

Now switch to the other side of the case. As the grocery store owner, you think there is also a 60% chance that the plaintiff will prevail. The trial also will cost you $5,000. The expected loss to you is $17,000. This is .60 times $20,000, plus the $5,000. If you could avoid the suit for less than $17,000 you would be better off.

As plaintiff, you would be willing to sell your right to sue for anything over $7,000. As the grocery store owner, you would be willing to buy that right for anything below $17,000. There is a $10,000 range for bargaining just as there was a $5,000 range in the case of the motorcycle. The case is likely to settle because it enables both parties to avoid litigation costs. Another way of saying this is that under certain assumptions, because of litigation costs, the expected gain to a plaintiff of a lawsuit will usually be less than the expected loss to the defendant.

This is the simplest possible case and, as you would expect, there are a number of complications. The first is that the settlement process itself is likely to be costly. This is like a transaction cost of any contract. As you know from the chapter on the Coase Theorem, the higher the transaction costs, the less likely a deal will be struck. In effect, these costs offset the gains achieved by avoiding a trial. In addition, in most instances the parties will incur some costs before negotiations begin. The already-spent money cannot be saved and the range for settlement is narrower. In fact, by the eve of the trial it could be substantially narrower than when the lawsuit was initially filed. By that time huge costs associated with travel, discovery, photocopying and expert witnesses may already be incurred. They cannot be "saved" by settlement. Both of these types of costs narrow the settlement range. To be more exact, the savings by avoiding a trial or the surplus is equal to the *future* litigation costs avoided minus *future* settlement costs.

A second qualification of the model results from the reactions of the parties to risk. In the example, the least the plaintiff would take is $7,000. Is that really the case, though? The $7,000 value is an expected amount. The actual outcome will not be $7,000. It will be much higher—$15,000, or much lower—$5,000. In fact, there is a 60% chance of $15,000 and a 40% chance of $5,000. If the plaintiff is risk-averse, an offer of something less than $7,000 may very well be attractive to the plaintiff. Similarly, the grocery store is not going to lose

$17,000. The loss will either be $25,000 or $5,000. Given that its exposure is substantially more than $17,000, there is a strong likelihood, especially if it is a small privately-owned store, that it would be willing to pay a bit more than $17,000 in order to avoid a chance of losing $25,000. (Do you see how this could change if the plaintiff were a large national or regional chain?) The point is that if both parties are risk-averse, the range within which they can bargain may actually be larger than $7,000 to $17,000.

A third complicating factor comes into play if the parties lack confidence in their cases. So far the assumption has been that both parties think there is a 60% chance the plaintiff will prevail. Suppose the plaintiff is not positive one of her witnesses will be credible and thinks there is actually only a 50% chance of winning. In addition, the grocery store is not really sure that the floors were kept dry all the time and regards the chance of losing as 70%. Now the expected award for the plaintiff goes down to $5,000 and the expected loss to the defendant goes up to $19,000. The range between the parties has increased and there is more room within which to settle.

As you have seen already, the cost of litigating a case has an impact on the likelihood of settlement. High potential legal fees make settlement more likely. Low fees have the opposite effect. There are, of course, more complicated fee arrangements than the one discussed thus far. Go back to the original example again. The probability of a victory by the plaintiff is 60% and the damages are $20,000. Both parties agree on this. The expected award, therefore, is $12,000. The defendant's legal expenses (net of settlement costs) are fixed at $5,000, meaning that the defendant would pay up to $17,000 to settle the case. Now assume the plaintiff has a contingent fee agreement under which the legal fees are 33% of any award. The value of the case to the plaintiff is $.6(20,000) - .6(.33) (20,000)$ or $8,040. The expected attorney's fees are $3,960. The settlement range will be between $8,040 and $17,000. In this specific example, the settlement range is smaller because the expected litigation cost is lower. Put differently, the money saved by not litigating is lower and, thus, there is less incentive to settle. The range may be further reduced by the fact that there will be no legal fee at all unless the plaintiff prevails. In effect, the plaintiff is "playing with house money." As a general matter, people avoid out-of-pocket losses more than they avoid losing potential income. In the case of a contingent fee, the risk of an out-of-pocket loss is not present. If all other factors are constant, one would expect a contingent fee to result in fewer settlements.

This example involves the assumption that the alternative to a flat fee of $5,000 is contingent fee. The outcome is not always true. In reality, the impact of the contingent fee, as opposed to a flat rate or hourly fee, cannot be known without knowing the complexity of the case and the hours likely to be devoted to it. There is a way, however, to think about the issue. In the example, the expected contingent fee for the attorney is $3,960. You might ask what the attorney would find acceptable as a set fee in lieu of the contingent fee. Attorneys are like most others and are likely to accept a lower set fee over an expected fee of a certain amount. This goes back to the idea of risk aversion. After all, the attorney will not receive a contingent fee of $3,960. In fact, the actual fee will be $6,666 or less than zero when the costs incurred by the attorney in a losing effort are taken into account. Consistent with the risk aversion assumption, the attorney may well find a set fee of $3,500 acceptable. In fact, you would expect attorneys as a general matter to be willing to accept lower flat fee amounts over higher expected contingent fees. From this perspective, contingent fees appear to increase the likelihood of settlements over instances in which the attorney receives a risk adjusted flat fee. Still, the client makes the decision about the settlement and the contingent fee greatly decreases the likelihood of an out of pocket loss. The net outcome, again, is that one would expect fewer settlements.

Now suppose the loser pays the fees of both parties. Here again, assume the case involves $20,000 in alleged damages and a 60% probability that the grocery store will be found liable. For the plaintiff, the value is $.6(\$20,000) - .4(\$10,000)$ or $8,000. The value to the defendant of avoiding a trial is $.6(\$20,000) + .6(\$10,000)$ or $18,000. The settlement range is $10,000. The expected legal fee for the plaintiff is $4,000 and, for the defendant, $6,000.

You will note that the settlement range is $10,000, the same as it was when the parties paid their own fees. There is, however, a difference. First, the range is now more in favor of the plaintiff. This is because the 60% always favored the plaintiff but now the numbers to which that 60% is applied are bigger. Second, under the original example, both parties paid $5,000 in legal fees and there was no risk. Under the new example, the expected fee includes a possibility of paying nothing and a possibility of paying $10,000. If the parties are risk-averse, you would expect them to be more generous with their offers. The plaintiff may accept less than $8,000 and the grocery store is likely to be willing to pay more than $18,000. Consistent with common sense, a loser-pays-all rule is likely to encourage settlement.

The tendency to encourage settlement by increasing the risk of not settling is reflected in this Florida statute:

Offer of judgment and demand for judgment

(6) Upon motion made by the offeror within 30 days after the entry of judgment or after voluntary or involuntary dismissal, the court shall determine the following:

(a) If a defendant serves an offer which is not accepted by the plaintiff, and if the judgment obtained by the plaintiff is at least 25 percent less than the amount of the offer, the defendant shall be awarded reasonable costs, including investigative expenses, and attorney's fees, calculated in accordance with the guidelines promulgated by the Supreme Court, incurred from the date the offer was served, and the court shall set off such costs in attorney's fees against the award. When such costs and attorney's fees total more than the amount of the judgment, the court shall enter judgment for the defendant against the plaintiff for the amount of the costs and fees, less the amount of the award to the plaintiff.

(b) If a plaintiff serves an offer which is not accepted by the defendant, and if the judgment obtained by the plaintiff is at least 25 percent more than the amount of the offer, the plaintiff shall be awarded reasonable costs, including investigative expenses, and attorney's fees, calculated in accordance with the guidelines promulgated by the Supreme Court, incurred from the date the offer was served.

Another fairly obvious proposition is that settlement is more likely if the parties have different expectations as far as gains and losses, *and* the defendant's expected loss exceeds the plaintiff's expected gain. The possibility of different expected gains and losses takes on additional importance when you view the risks more broadly. Again, think in terms of the slippery grocery store floor. Suppose the current rule about store owner negligence is relatively favorable with respect to store owners. Thus, assume the chance of the plaintiff prevailing is only 40%. The expected gain (assuming fixed litigation costs of $5,000) to the plaintiff is $3,000 and the expected loss to the grocery store is $13,000. A settlement is likely on the basis of these figures alone. On the other hand, two factors may alter the analysis. If the grocery store is known to be willing to settle virtually any case when the issue is close, this may invite additional lawsuits. In other words, the expected cost of going to trial may be perceived to be small to potential plaintiffs and they will file suits more often and demand higher settlements. In effect, the cost of a settlement to the grocery store may be much higher overall than it would be in an isolated case.

Another influence has the opposite impact. As noted, the law is currently favorable to store owners. One of the risks of going to trial is that a court may change the rule and then be upheld on appeal. Instead of a 40% chance of winning, the probability may shift to 60%. With this example, the settlement range will not change but settlements would be higher. This change would be costly to the defendant and the possibility of a change may lead to a greater willingness to settle.

B.   WHY DON'T ALL CASES SETTLE?

Given that every case involves litigation costs, it would appear that there is always a "surplus" to be gained by agreeing to settle. And, in fact, settlement is the norm. Still, a number of factors work against settlement.

1. ASYMMETRICAL EXPECTATIONS

As you saw, asymmetrical expectations can be one of the most important factors encouraging settlement. In the context above, the asymmetry meant that defendants expected to lose more than plaintiffs gained. The opposite can also be true and the implications are different. For example, if a plaintiff's expected gain is $20,000 and the defendant's expected loss is $10,000, a settlement is not likely simply because neither party considers the settlement to be in its self-interest. This can occur if the parties have different estimates of the probability of success by the plaintiff, different views of the damages, or of the costs of the litigation itself.

When this asymmetry occurs it is, as you would expect, the result of disagreements about the facts or the law. Thus, in our grocery store case, the parties may have different interpretations of the liability standards in the jurisdiction as they pertain to store owners. This, however, is not the most likely source of asymmetry. Instead, in a case like the example here, the plaintiff may be absolutely sure she slipped on a wet spot on the floor. An employee of the store may, on the other hand, swear that he just mopped the floor, was present when the so-called slip occurred, and it appeared that the plaintiff tripped on her own shoe string. Both parties are 100% sure of their positions. Unless the attorneys can convince each party that the jury is as likely to believe one party as the other, the probability of settlement will decline.

Legal research can reduce disagreements about law and discovery can eliminate some disagreements about facts. This increases the chances of settlement. On the other hand, as these costs mount up, the benefits of settlement may decline. Consider how this might work in an antitrust case. Suppose a plaintiff claims that two suppliers have agreed on the price he is to be charged. The law on this is pretty easy: Under the antitrust laws it is unlawful to fix prices.

On the other hand, as a factual matter, did they actually fix prices? During the discovery the plaintiff will be permitted to inspect the communications between the two defendants. After considering all the writings and emails between the defendants, the plaintiff is unable to find a "smoking gun"—direct evidence of an agreement. In addition, the plaintiff takes the depositions of both the higher and lower level officials at both firms. All of them adamantly deny they agreed on a uniform price and explain their pricing decisions by increases in the costs of raw materials. At this point, the parties may still disagree but they will at least be closer in terms of how they believe a jury will interpret the evidence. This will bring them closer to settlement.

This does not mean that the parties have to come to exactly the same beliefs about the likely outcome of the case. The principal reason for settlement is still the existence of litigation costs. For example, suppose the plaintiff is 70% sure that the facts and law favor his side of the case on a $10,000 claim, and the cost of litigation for the plaintiff is estimated at $3,000. The defendant is equally sure of prevailing (70%) and faces a similar litigation cost. The value of the case to the plaintiff is $4,000 and the value of the expected loss to the defendant is $6,000. The outcome is that there is a $2,000 settlement range even though the parties have irreconcilable views of the merits of the claim. Furthermore, as explained above, risk aversion may expand this range even further.

2. BILATERAL MONOPOLY

A monopoly exists when there is one seller of a product or service for which there are no reasonable substitutes. Monopsony exists when there is but a single buyer. When a single seller faces a single buyer it is called bilateral monopoly. A settlement effort involves a bilateral monopoly. Put differently, the plaintiff is the only "seller" of a claim and the defendant is the only potential "buyer." When single sellers face off against single buyers they both may realize it is in their joint interest to reach an agreement. In the original example involving the shopper and the grocery store, both parties may realize that by settling they could avoid litigation expenses and be better off. The shopper was better off with anything in excess of $7,000 and the store would be better off by paying anything less than $17,000. The settlement range was $10,000. But suppose the parties dig in. The shopper demands an amount close to $17,000 and the store says it can go no higher than $10,000. Both parties have an incentive to bluff and claim that they could not settle for anything other than the amount that allows them to capture most of the benefit of the settlement. This is a type of transaction cost and it may prevent an agreement from occurring. In the case of a settlement, the trial date may be drawing closer. Moreover, the longer the haggling goes on, there may be less and less to be gained in terms of costs avoided.

There is another factor to consider. A negotiator may want to establish a reputation as a hard-nosed bargainer. It may make sense as an economic matter not to agree to a settlement even though it would make the negotiator better off in the short run if it pays dividends in the future.

3.   HUMAN FACTORS

This entire model of settlement is more or less based on the view of individuals as rational maximizers of self-interest with self-interest solely a function of monetary outcomes. In reality, a number of "human" factors come into play. For example, one reason for a settlement not to occur is that one or both parties simply make a mistake. The law or evidence may not be interpreted in the most reasonable manner. From this perspective, trials are actually mistakes. This is the essence of a theory proposed by George Priest and Benjamin Klein in their 1984 study of cases that did not settle.[1]

1.   George L. Priest & Benjamin Klein, *The Selection of Disputes for Litigation*, 13 J. of Leg. Stud. 1 (Jan. 1984).

Beyond the possibility of mistakes, it is not clear that human beings act in the manner that economic theory suggests. Different biases can result in asymmetries. One study suggests that two factors play a role in creating barriers to settlement. The study notes the possibility of a self-serving bias, especially when a litigant's self-image is on the line.[2] Consider an auto accident that has implications for the driving skills of each party, one of whom is elderly and very defensive about the possibility that his reaction time may be longer. An admission of that weakness by the elderly driver may involve a tremendous loss of face. The estimated outcome, case value, and settlement range all may be affected by self-serving biases. The same study notes that self-interest in the sense of maximizing utility and pecuniary outcomes may not be equivalents. People tend to place a "value" on being treated fairly. They may pass up offers that would increase their material well-being if the offer offends their sense of fairness.[3]

You have probably heard someone say "It's the principle of the thing." That too can explain why some cases do not settle. The possibilities range from relatively petty disputes about the location of a property line to far more important matters like child custody, freedom of expression, the right to have an abortion, the right to possess a firearm, and so on. Recently, for example, a case involving the

2. See George Loewenstien, Samuel Issacharoff, Colin Camerer and Linda Babcock, "Self–Serving Assessments of Fairness and Pretrial Bargaining," 22 *J. of Leg. Stud.* 135 (Jan. 1993).

3. You can read more on this in Chapter 3.

permissibility of including "under God" in the Pledge of Allegiance was heard by the United States Supreme Court. Settlement in these cases is unlikely for two reasons. First, they are often about "rights," and it is hard to identify a settlement range when the subjects of the disputes take on absolute values. Second, it is generally impossible to put values on the subjects of these disputes and then to compare them. In fact, they may be described as being of "infinite value." If so, even if these values could be monetized, the litigation costs saved by settling would have to be enormous for settlement to occur. The most important thing is that these suits are generally not about maximizing wealth.

4.   SOME EMPIRICAL EVIDENCE

As noted above, the Priest–Klein theory of settlement suggests that when parties do not settle, it is generally the result of irrationality or mistake. Mistake in this context does not necessarily mean that one party is careless or incompetent. Instead, the parties are simply unable to agree or at least get close enough to an agreement on the value of the case to allow for a settlement. When you think about it, these disagreements are most likely to occur when the question is a close one. For example, if you drive your car into another car stopped at a red light, there probably will not be any question about the applicable law, the facts, or the damages. Settlement is likely because there is little doubt about the outcome of a trial.

Suppose instead you nick the left rear of the car at a four-way stop at which you and the other driver had arrived at the same time. Here it is a close call and the parties may be unable to agree on the outcome of a trial or even the probability that it will go one way or the other. Thus, the Priest–Klein theory suggests that the most frequently litigated cases are ones that are close calls.

If the cases that go to trial are the close calls, you would expect that the outcomes would be about 50–50 in terms of favoring plaintiffs and defendants. This theory has been tested. One of the more interesting studies was conducted by Gross and Svyerud.[4] They found that the validity of the 50% theory varied by the type of litigation. The authors found that when plaintiffs must pay for the trial they have a higher win rate when they actually do take their cases to trial. This makes sense in the context of the model explained here. A litigant who must pay, win or lose, is going to lower his or her settlement demand and take great care in choosing which cases to try. These factors cut the other way when a contingent fee is involved. Another finding consistent with the theory is that when one party stands to lose more at trial than the other stands to gain, the number of trials decreases but the win rate for defendants increases. This can be explained by the fact that when defendants stand to lose more than plaintiffs will gain, the settlement zone will expand.

4. Samuel R. Gross & Kent D. Svyerud, "Getting to No: A Study of Settlement Negotiations and the Selection of Cases for Trial," 90 *Mich. L. Rev.* 319 (1991).

CHAPTER EIGHT

ECONOMIC ANALYSIS OF CRIMINAL LAW

A variety of issues can be raised when applying economic analysis to criminal law[1]—even more are raised if one extends the analysis to criminal procedure. In fact, a comprehensive application of economic analysis to criminal law issues would require consideration of substantive criminal law and criminal procedure together with mental health law and moral philosophy. The goal in this Chapter is much more modest. It addresses two basic questions. First, what are the economic bases for criminal law? Second, what factors are to be considered in determining the "right" level of punishment? It also includes a brief analysis of some criminal procedure issues.

More than any other area of law addressed in this book, the application of conventional economic analysis to criminal law will seem strained. First, and at a practical level, some of the conclusions that economic analysis presents with respect to why crimi-

1. For a look at the variety of topics see Richard Posner, *Economic Analysis of Law*, Chapter 7 (7th ed. 2007). Judge Posner addresses general criminal law matters as well as criminal intent, the war on drugs, organized crime, and various defenses.

nal law exists and why it is administered the way it is will simply not be consistent with common understandings of criminal law. For example, one is unlikely to treat seriously or even hear an argument that a shorter prison sentence for, let's say, car theft is warranted because current prison sentences create too much deterrence and inefficiently low levels of car theft. Yet this is the nature of the analysis when economics is applied to criminal law.

Second, criminal law seems influenced by moral considerations and the possibility that not all values in life can be reduced to the type of cost-benefit analysis favored by conventional economic analysis of law. Despite this, a great deal of the economic analysis of criminal law involves an assumption that those involved in criminal activities are not motivated by a sense of obligation to obey the law. Instead they are "rational maximizers of self-interest" and basically amoral. In fact, in the analysis of efficiency, general social welfare can be a function of a great many values that can change from era to era and which may seem irrational to some. Third, because what conduct is punishable is a political question to be answered by legislatures and there are theories suggesting that markets exist for legislation, it is useful to look at criminal law from the perspective of "public choice," a topic taken up in Chapter Fifteen.

A. WHY HAVE CRIMINAL LAW?

Chapter Six briefly addressed the issue of whether it makes economic sense to award punitive damages in the context of negligence. The answer there was that the use of punitive damages can mean that those who harm others may take inefficiently high levels of care to avoid accidents. Thus, when the goal is to minimize accident costs, the use of punitive damages is questionable. On the other hand, as noted in that Chapter, punitive damages may make sense when the harm to each person is so small as to mean that no one person will take legal action even though the total harm exceeds the cost of avoiding the harm.

Other than the possibility that no one person would be motivated to bring an action that would create an incentive for those causing harm to take preventative actions, what other bases exist for the use of penalties? At a fundamental level there are probably three. First, there are instances in which we would prefer exchanges to take place in the market. Criminal law can play a role in channeling them in that direction. Second, there are actions that we would like to avoid because we believe that the conduct, even if it is not against the will of the parties involved, may create external costs. Closely related to this is the possibility that the conduct will lead to external harms that offend our moral sensibilities. Finally, it is possible that criminal law, by stigmatizing some conduct, may actually have a preference-shaping capacity.

1. CREATING AN INCENTIVE FOR MARKET EXCHANGES

One of the economic functions of criminal law is to channel behavior that results in a transfer of property or rights into the market. In order to understand this connection it is useful to review the work of Calabresi and Melamed in connection with liability rules and property rules.[2] Calabresi and Melamed distinguish between liability rules and property rules as methods of protecting rights. Under a liability rule, individuals are permitted to make involuntary transfers from others but compensation at market value is required. This type of "protection" is appropriate when transaction costs are high and a voluntary exchange, even if the parties were, in theory, willing is very difficult or impossible. The danger of relying on liability rules is that the involuntary exchange may not actually be efficient. In other words compensation equal to the fair market value may not be equal to the value attributed by the losing party to what is taken.

Property rules, the authors suggest, make sense when transaction costs are low. In these instances, the transfer must be consensual. The idea is that when consensual exchanges are practical, the danger of an inefficient exchange can be reduced by requiring the parties to interact. An example may be useful. Suppose you have a mint condition 1966

2. Guido Calabresi & A. Douglas Melamed, "Property Rules, Liability Rules and Inalienability: One View of the Cathedral," 85 *Harv. L. Rev.* 1086 (1972).

Austin Mini with a market value of $5,000. Because of your attachment to the car you have turned down offers for it in excess of $5,000. In fact, you would not accept less than $7,000 for the car. Strict adherence to a liability rule would permit someone to take the car without your permission and compensate you at the market value. And that person may only attribute a value of $5,500 to the car. The liability rule would mean that an exchange could take place which would result in the car being owned by someone who actually values it less. The new allocation would be inefficient.

On the other hand, if car ownership were protected by a property rule, the car could not be transferred without your consent. In essence, the buyer would have to show you, by the amount offered, that he or she actually values the car more than you do. Criminal law is often seen as a means to assuring that the exchange is, in fact, efficient. Thus, the person who takes the car without permission runs the risk of being punished. In this context, it means the thief will be required to pay more than the market value of the item taken. In the criminal law and economics literature this is sometimes called a "kicker." The size of the kicker—the amount of punishment—is another question and is discussed in the second section of this Chapter. Suffice it to say at this point that a low level of punishment may not be enough to encourage the market exchange. For example, if there is a $10 fine for stealing a car, the thief is unlikely to find the market transaction preferable even if the likelihood of discovery is

100%.[3] Obviously, the penalty must be set high enough to make the market transaction preferable. Put differently, with an inadequate kicker, property rules can be made into liability rules.[4]

The notion of criminal sanctions as means of channeling transfers into markets is relatively simple to grasp when one considers protecting one's property. It may seem somewhat artificial, but one can stretch the analysis to bodily harm as well. For example, a person who harms another or commits rape could be viewed as a thief of a sort. The question then becomes whether he should be permitted to harm others as long as he pays the fair market value of the sex or harm. In other words, should a liability rule be applied? Here, though, objective market valuations are difficult to arrive at and seem even less reliable in terms of encouraging efficient transfers than in the case of property. The silliness of such notions is suggested by asking what would be the compensation in the case of rape. It could not be simply the price of sex in some area in which prostitution is illegal—like looking up the Blue Book value of a stolen car. For one thing, as Richard Posner points out, the rapist is not simply a thief of sex but may gain utility from the fact that it is coercive.[5] The same problems probably apply in other instances of those who get pleasure from

3. As explained later, the probability of detection is an important element in determining the proper level of punishment.

4. See Calabresi & Melamed, *supra* note 2, at 1125.

5. Richard Posner Economic Analysis of Law, *supra* note 1, at 216.

harming others.[6] A liability rule is obviously ill-suited.

The fact that transaction costs are low means that a property rule is more attractive in instances of rape or other assaults. This would seem to go a long way toward discouraging rape. First, the price is likely to be quite high. Second, if the rapist wants coercive sex, this is probably not available in the market at any price. The reason is that as soon as a price is agreed upon, the utility derived from the coercive nature of the act would disappear. Nevertheless, even though a property rule seems to achieve the desired outcomes in cases involving bodily harm, it is seems unlikely that the law is motivated by a desire to achieve an "efficient" level of rape or assault.

The property rule/liability rule distinction has logical appeal and can be reconciled with much of criminal law even if it is not the actual explanation for why the law is what it is. But there are many instances in which the coincidence of criminal law with the system of property and liability rules breaks down. First, there are instances in which transaction costs are low and property rules would seem to apply, but the law does not permit exchange to freely take place. This is especially true in the case of so-called victimless crimes. For example, there are laws prohibiting the sale of human organs and sex. Second, there are instances in which trans-

6. Unlike the case of rape in which the act is, by definition, nonconsensual, there are instances of people who do get pleasure from being harmed by others.

actions costs are high and a liability rule would seem to apply, but the law requires more than compensation of the victim. Thus, drunk drivers are not allowed merely to compensate those who they harm. Third, as illustrated above, only a very strained interpretation of economic interests can explain the existence of laws prohibiting rape and similar crimes. In all of these instances, broader moral concepts of right and wrong come into play. In effect, consent may have independent and high value so that it is the violation of one's autonomy that is protected rather than the fair market value of sex. Finally, some of the activities we label as criminal are not property rules at all but are rules of inalienability. In other words, they do not permit certain types of transactions. In these instances, the law itself can be seen as the transaction cost, and it is purposely high in order to eliminate such exchanges that might otherwise take place, not simply to make sure they are done efficiently. This category includes instances in which the criminal law is designed to prevent people from turning liability rules into property rules. As Jules Coleman notes, we might subject a polluter to tort liability but not permit the polluter to buy the right to pollute ahead of time.[7]

2. CRIMINAL LAW AND EXTERNALITIES

You would be hard pressed to reconcile all of

7. Jules L. Coleman, "Crime, Kickers, and Transactional Structures", *Nomos XVII: Criminal Justice* 313 (J. Panache & J. Chipman, eds. 1985).

criminal law with the simple notion of forcing exchanges to be consensual when transaction costs are low. For example, in many instances transaction costs are high, but the activity is a crime nonetheless. Generally, the law seems designed to prohibit activity that is likely to create externalities. Speeding, double-parking, and flag burning would seem to fit in this category. A special case of this is when the real or imagined externality flows from conduct that is consensual with respect to the primary participants. Crimes like consensual sodomy, prostitution, selling and buying of some drugs, and selling human organs and babies seem to fall in this category.

a. **Externalities Generally**

As the discussion in Chapter Six indicates, the central economic focus of tort law is on externalities. When a party does not take into consideration the harms to others of her activities, she is more likely to engage in activities that are inefficient. The tort system is designed to ensure that these external effects are internalized. In some instances, however, rather that channel harmful activities into market transactions through the use of a property rule or to rely exclusively on *ex post* compensation as a pricing mechanism, criminal sanctions are imposed. Thus, the speeding motorist cannot buy the right to speed from those who feel endangered by the speeding nor is it sufficient for the speeder simply to pay the damages of those who are actually injured by speeding. Similarly, the double-parker cannot negotiate in advance with those likely to be inconvenienced nor simply pay those whose trip across town was actually delayed by the congestion resulting from parking in the street.

The question from an economic point of view is why these types of activities having third party effects are treated any differently from garden variety torts. Specifically, why not rely on something as basic as the Hand formula to identify when speeding is negligent? When the probability of an accident occasioned by the speeding is multiplied by the loss and compared with the cost of prevention, the speeder will almost always be the negligent party. On the other hand, there may also be instances in which speeding would not be negligent, even though leading to an accident. For example, it might not be deemed negligent to speed across town to reach a hospital with an injured person. Basic tort law seems to have sufficient flexibility to respond to both these possibilities.

One way to understand these laws is to place them in the context of the Coase Theorem. As discussed in Chapter Three, a simple version of the Theorem is that, in a transaction-costs-free environment, rights will end up in the hands of those who value them the most. One corollary mentioned in Chapter Three and typically attributed to Judge Posner is that when transaction costs are high it makes economic sense for a court or a legislature to allocate the right initially to those who value it the most. In the case of speeding, consider two laws. One permits speeding and requires payment only of actual damages if the driver injures another and is successfully sued in a civil action. The counter-law is that speeding is penalized whether or not the speeder is involved in an accident. At one level this can be seen as a determination of whether drivers who speed from time to time value the right to do so more than other drivers, cyclists, and pedestrians value the extra security of less speeding. There is another way to frame the choice, however, which may be more important. The choice is whether people who choose to speed may harm others *without their consent*. Here the issue is whether people value being free of the threat of non-consensual harm to property or person more than they value a rule permitting non-consensual harm. If people generally place a high value on personal autonomy and the right to choose, a rule penalizing those who harm others without their consent can be squared with efficiency.

This explanation of some criminal laws is also consistent some other aspects of criminal law. While people may value a rule that protects them from involuntary transfers, they are not likely to oppose all such transfers. Thus, they may be willing to accept the risk of a non-consensual transfer if the motorist has a compelling reason to create that risk. The punishment for speeding is not, therefore, life in prison but is set at a level high enough to discourage those who might speed simply as a matter of convenience. Thus, the father speeding to the hospital with his injured son in the car would not be deterred. In effect, while the penalty is a cost of creating a risk of non-consensual transfer, it is not set so high as to deter all transfers.

In fact, variations in "price" make economic sense in a great many instances. For example, the speeding father may pay the basic fine for speeding. On the other hand, the penalty for drunk driving is much higher because there are few compelling reasons to drink and drive. In keeping with this theme, double-parking is at most an inconvenience for other motorists and the reason to inconvenience others need not be as compelling as the reason for speeding. The price is set low so as to discourage only the habitual double-parker. More generally what this suggests is that there are efficient levels of activities that technically are "against the law." It is fairly simple to understand this in the context of minor violations. But the rule also applies in all but the most serious crimes. Clearly, there are instances in which it is efficient to steal a car or even break into a house. The price of these crimes, however, is high because the harm is high as is the value the injured party is likely to attribute to being given an opportunity to choose to consent or decline.

b. Externalities and "Victimless Crimes"

The view that there are low transaction costs involved in the exchange of sex or drugs for money would seem to lead to the conclusion that criminal law should have nothing further to say about those who do make voluntary exchanges. There are, however, three economic rationales for prohibiting these sales. The first goes back to the basic teachings of contract law. The efficient exchange is that which takes place between people who are competent. In some instances of victimless crimes, there is a sense that both participants are not fully competent. For example, is it meaningful to say that the drug-addicted prostitute is really engaged in a voluntary exchange? Obviously, in a great many instances the decision about competence is a political one—what is viewed as competent seems to change with society's views of privacy and paternalism. Still, a voluntary exchange that takes place in the context of duress or a lack of clear understanding by one of the parties can be prohibited by reasoning that they do not produce allocatively efficient outcomes.

Probably more important than the efficiency implications of these exchanges are the distributive outcomes. Although economists are not comfortable, while acting within the constraints of the discipline, making decisions about the relative merits of various distributive outcomes, the information provided by economics is of value to those willing to consider distributive matters. Some of the so-called victimless crimes may be objected to on the basis of a perception that there is undue advantage-taking by one of the parties. This is, of course, bound up in the notion of competency as well, but the basic idea is one of prohibiting exchanges that are viewed as exploitative.[8]

8. Economists have a technical definition of exploitation. Here it is used in the more generic sense of taking advantage of someone to further one's own ends.

It is an unnecessary simplification to equate concerns about the possible prohibition of transactions that seem to systematically disadvantage one of the parties as exclusively reflecting distributive interests. In fact, the concern that one person or the collective feels about the way in which some bargains are struck may be also stated in terms of utility. For example, I may oppose baby-selling because I believe low-income mothers will be taken advantage of by well-to-do childless couples.[9] The existence of such bargains lowers my utility and perhaps that of others. From the standpoint of Pareto optimality, these exchanges are not efficient because some parties are worse off, even if the exchanging parties feel that they are better off. Even the more liberal Kaldor–Hicks standard would suggest that these exchanges are only efficient if the transacting parties could compensate those who are honestly offended by the outcome of the exchange. Two points are suggested by this analysis. The first is that the high tax rates associated with some exchanges that are not illegal may reflect a societal sense that the exchanges are somehow inappropriate and those who engage in those transactions should compensate the rest of us. Second, the complete prohibition of some of these exchanges may also be seen as indicating a government assessment that, whatever the gain to the parties from the exchange, it is unlikely to be sufficient to compensate those made uncomfortable by it.

9. *See In the Matter of Baby M, 537 A.2d 1227 (N.J. 1988).*

This efficiency-based analysis of distributive effects is one way of saying that victimless crimes are not always victimless. A more direct and conventional analysis is one that recognizes that some transactions do have the capacity to harm those who are not parties to the transaction. For example, prostitution may contribute to the spread of AIDs, meaning that third parties are required to expend energy and money to avoid contracting AIDs. Similarly, because drug transactions may involve large sums of money, those people who engage in the transactions may carry weapons. Concentrations of weapons create risks even for passers-by. These are relatively concrete externalities. In other instances they are harder to describe. For example, in the well-publicized *Baby M* case, in addition to the distributive issues discussed above, the decision also cites the "potential degradation of some women" resulting from enforcement of a surrogacy contract.[10]

As with the economic analysis of tort law, the issue becomes one of how to respond to these externalities. Like the channeling function of criminal law, the objective can be seen as encouraging efficient conduct. The standard liability rule/property rule analysis is, however, somewhat complex. In the case of the sale of drugs, babies, organs and sex, the agreement between the principle parties creates the harm. The property rule/liability rule model would then ask whether these consenting parties face high or low transaction costs. If transaction costs are

10.   Id. at 537 A.2d at 1250.

low, criminal sanctions would apply in order to require those engaged in the activity to get the consent of third-party victims. And, if the transaction costs are high, the activity would be permitted with compensation to come later. Obviously, in the case of drug and baby sellers and the like, a liability rule would seem to follow. In fact, the law imposes what looks like a property rule but which is in actuality a rule of inalienability.

Is there an economic basis for leaving high transaction cost exchanges in the realm of property rules? One possibility is that there is no meaningful likelihood that those harmed could be compensated by the consenting parties if a liability rule were used. For example, how does one compensate those who find market transactions for human organs morally repugnant? How does one locate and assess the damages to those offended? The law seems to signify any one of a number of possibilities here. One is that the costs of operating a system of compensation is much too high to justify what gains might be had from the "exchanges." Second, it is possible to reconcile the law with the view that the amount those willing to pay for the right to offend will almost never be more than the lowest victims are willing to take. Thus, what amounts to a per se rule against even attempting these transactions makes sense economically. Finally, to some extent the externality here is based on a view that certain things should not be bought and sold at all. The rule applied in these cases simply reflects the sense that if certain market transactions are offensive then so too are market transactions for the permission of those who are offended by the initial transaction.

3.   CRIMINAL LAW AND BEHAVIOR

As the above discussion suggests, it is possible to explain criminal law in terms that are obviously related to tort law. Much of the analysis focuses on the issue of externalities and forcing actors to internalize those externalities. Also at the heart of this analysis is the notion of an efficient level of crime which means that it includes the supposition that some criminal behavior is beneficial to society. At least one commentator writing from an economics perspective rejects these explanations for the existence of criminal law. Kenneth Dau–Schmidt rejects the view that society values criminal conduct. He argues that such a view is inconsistent with common sense and some aspects of our criminal law system.[11] For example, we increase punishment for repeat offenders yet the harm caused is the same for each offense.

If criminal law cannot be explained in terms of the traditional view that recognizes social benefits, it may be possible to explain it in terms of efforts to change preferences. That is, the goal is not to achieve some kind of balance in order to maximize social well-being. Instead criminal law may be viewed as an effort to change the things from which

11.   Kenneth G. Dau–Schmidt, "And Economic Analysis of the Criminal Law as a Preference–Shaping Policy," 1990 *Duke L. J.* 1.

people derive utility. It is important to note the type of behavioral change this suggests. In its simplest form, criminal law and the penalties that are involved raise the prices of some choices with the likely consequence that those choices will me made less often.[12] For example, in a world in which speeding is penalized, drivers are more likely to choose the substitute of leaving for their destinations earlier. And, if criminal prosecution is likely, those who would like the property of another and experience no moral qualms about stealing still may be more likely to buy the property. As economic theory would predict, when the price of one activity is raised, individuals tend to move to substitutes.

The preference-shaping view is quite different and can be understood by recalling what a demand curve represents. The curve shows the amounts that will be purchased at various prices. An assumption underlying all demand curves is that tastes and preferences are constant. For example, when prices increase and people demand less it is not because they find the item they are buying less satisfying. Their preference does not change. What has changed is relative price, and an increase in the

12. This is not to say that this is necessarily the case. Government action that creates a penalty or the appearance of a taboo actually may make the activity more glamorous and attractive to some. For example, penalties associated with flag burning may encourage flag burning because the penalties actually may make the meaning conveyed by the action of flag burning more powerful and the audience broader. Still, even though the level of impact is difficult to quantify, the direction of the impact is likely to be predictable.

price of one item is likely to mean that substitutes now are more attractive.

Within the context of demand curves, a change in taste or preference means a shift in the entire demand curve. An increase in demand in response to a change in tastes means that individuals are willing and able to purchase more of the item at each price. A fundamental economic teaching is that a change in the price of an item does not mean that tastes or preferences change. Whether that teaching is true in the context of criminal law is not clear. When an activity is criminalized it may affect the amount of the activity in two ways. First, the cost of the activity will go up and the amount "purchased" will decline. In Figure 1, if the sanction increased from S_1 to S_2, there would be a movement from point A to B on demand curve D_1. Suppose criminalization also causes the activity to become less attractive. This would be represented by a shift in the demand curve from D_1 to D_2. More importantly, consider the impact on quantity of the activity. As Figure 1 indicates, the level of the activity before it is criminalized is Q_1. After sanctions are imposed the quantity is Q_2 if there is no change in preferences. If the sanctions also affect preferences, the quantity is Q_3. The point is that the stigmas associated with criminal conduct, including revocation of voting rights and efforts to rehabilitate and condition violators, may be more consistent with demand shifting than they are with efforts to move people to different points on existing demand curves.

Figure 1

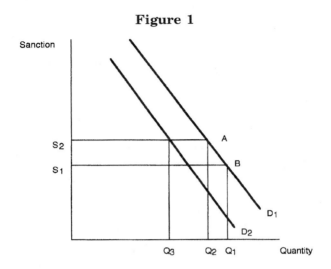

B. ADMINISTERING CRIMINAL SANCTIONS

If one adopts the preference-shaping role of criminal law, the amount invested in that effort could be determined by comparing the costs of various forms of preference-shaping measures with the benefits derived from changing what amounts to personalities. This approach gives rise to a great many philosophical questions that are difficult to answer. The more conventional approach to criminal law— the one that recognizes that some criminal behavior is part of overall social welfare—typically involves efforts to determine the optimal sanction. In other words, what price should society "charge" those who engage in prohibited activity in order to ensure that the benefits exceed the costs? The analysis has an allocative efficiency and a productive efficiency component. Thus, one objective is to find the right price to encourage the allocatively efficient level of criminal conduct. A related objective is to create a system that charges that price at the lowest cost to society.

1.   THE OPTIMAL LEVEL OF CRIMINAL CONDUCT

The first issue of encouraging the optimal level of criminal conduct can be depicted graphically. The underlying assumption of the presentation is that the actor is not influenced by the fact that the activity is labeled illegal. Put differently, the violator feels no moral obligations to obey the law simply because it is the law. In Figure 2, the Y axis measures benefits and the X axis measures the level of an activity. The downward sloping line, MB, represents the extra benefit of an additional unit of the activity in question. Suppose the curve relates to speeding. What it suggests is that there are a few instances in which the benefits of exceeding the speed limit are quite high. This might be consistent with the notion that there truly are emergencies in which speed can make a difference between relatively large or small gains. It also suggests that as more and more speeding takes place, the benefit decreases. In effect, people may be speeding simply to avoid being late for a movie or for class.

Figure 2

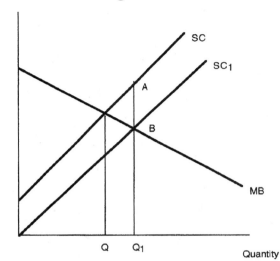

The other line on the graph represents marginal social cost. This is the cost to society of speeding. When the frequency of speeding is low the cost is low. As speeding becomes commonplace, the harm increases. The harm can be visualized as the probability the harm will occur times the severity of the harm. At low levels of speeding, the probability is low. It increases as more and more people drive in a riskier fashion. Returning to a familiar theme, the objective would be to permit speeding as long as the benefit of another incident of speeding exceeds the cost of that additional incident. This can be seen as an issue of involuntary transfers. MB represents what is taken by the speeder. SC is the value of what is taken. Based on the analysis presented above, the social cost function would include not just the harm times the probability of harm but would also include any aversion people feel about involuntary takings. As long as the marginal benefit exceeds the marginal social cost, net social welfare is increased by speeding.

As is typical in this analysis, the critical question is whether the speeder will react to the appropriate signal. For example, in the graph, the optimal level of speeding is Q. On the other hand, if speeders do not react to this actual social cost, they may act as though the social cost function were SC_1. The amount of speeding will be Q_1 which is inefficiently high. As Figure 2 indicates, the marginal benefit from speeding at Q_1 is below the social cost. There are a number of reasons the speeder may react to an inaccurate sense of social cost. First, although all speeders contribute to the risk of harm, only some are detected. Thus, the speeder does not react to the cost of speeding but to the cost multiplied by some probability that he or she will actually have to make a payment. Second, speeders may not factor in the aversion others have to involuntary transfers.

The role of the criminal law in this context is to add sufficiently to the perceived cost of speeding. A fine and a possible loss of one's driver's license are the typical measures employed here. Graphically, the result is a shift upward of the social cost curve from SC_1 to SC by an amount equal to the vertical distance between the curves or AB. In theory, the level of speeding would then be reduced to the socially optimal level of Q.

There is a high degree of artificiality in the model. On the other hand, if one accepts the basic rationale, the model is rather flexible. For example, rather than speeding, one could substitute one of the so-called victimless crimes. Suppose that crime is buying and selling marijuana. Again, if marijuana has therapeutic values, the benefits from a market in marijuana may be quite high for some. As one moves to more and more transactions the marginal benefit is likely to decline to the point that its use is entirely recreational. This is not to say that there are not positive benefits but that the level of benefit declines. On the social cost side, a few marijuana sales for medical purposes are unlikely to give rise to a great deal of social cost. On the other hand, if wide spread marijuana use is associated with poor driving, drug addiction, and expensive publicly-supported drug rehabilitation efforts, the marginal social cost curve will generally be upward-sloping as in Figure 2. In addition, since economic analysis validates all forms of disutility, the social cost curve would also factor in any moral objections to drug use. This latter point is important because in the case of some victimless crimes it is possible that the only social cost is the moral repugnancy experienced by those who object because the activity just seems to be "wrong."

While it can accommodate a fair amount of what is observable, the model cannot account for all criminal law. In the case of a great many offenses, it is hard to see any level as being efficient. For example, it is difficult to think in terms of an efficient level of baby selling, rape, or arson. In the case of baby and organ selling, it is hard to distinguish one sale from another. Either they are all objectionable or they all aren't. One might respond by saying that all baby and organ selling is equally costly. The marginal social cost in Figure 2 would be a horizontal line. And one could also argue the marginal benefits from buying a baby or a kidney do actually decline like the marginal benefits curve in Figure 2. Some people desperately want to be parents while others might just think it would be a neat idea. The conclusion one would draw from the model is that criminal law should accommodate those with particularly strong preferences.

This might be a palatable explanation in the context of baby and organ selling, but it seems far less acceptable in the context of rape and arson. While it is hard to imagine a situation in which any level other than zero would be efficient in the case of rape or arson, the economic model allows for that possibility. The model would seem to suggest the possibility that a person who gets tremendous utility from the act of rape may conceivably engage in efficient rape, and the pyromaniac may engage in efficient arson. One answer is that the punishment for rape and arson are high because it is so unlikely that the efficient levels are anything but zero. The problem with this argument is that it leaves open the possibility of the efficient rape and arson, and the individuals who the possibility is "open" for are the same people whose preferences are the most socially unacceptable. In other words, the model suggests that as a matter of public policy we want to permit some rape and arson if undertaken by the sufficiently depraved.

Obviously, this undercuts the model in those cases in which efficient criminal activity is likely only to occur when abnormal preferences are at work. It also raises more general doubt about the accuracy of the model. If the model fails to square with basic and intuitive notions of fairness in the context of crimes for which there appear to be no value, the question becomes whether it is any more accurate with respect to the policy—even intuitive—behind other aspects of criminal law. More specifically, is it really likely that laws about baby, organ, and marijuana selling are designed to permit certain levels of those activities because they create a net benefit for society?

2.   DETERRENCE OPTIONS

As noted above, the idea of creating disincentives for criminal conduct involves not just determining the level of punishment but how to most efficiently create the required disincentive. To understand the issue, go back to Figure 2. In that figure the optimal punishment was equal to the distance AB. But what is this punishment? It could be, as that illustration suggests, a fine. Or it could be imprisonment, caning, or pillorying. The critical matter is that it be seen as a cost of engaging in the activity.

In addition, the usual analysis stresses that the cost is an expected cost. Assuming that the violator is risk-neutral this means, for example, that a one percent chance of a $100 fine packs the same wallop as a twenty percent chance of a $5 fine. Thus the expected sanction can take the form of a high probability of a relatively low level of punishment or a very low probability of severe punishment. In effect the package of punishment (POP) is a combination of probabilities and various sorts of sanctions. The key in terms of economic analysis is to find the lowest-cost way of creating the POP.

The first impression one is likely to have is that the lowest-cost method of creating the proper incentive is to apply severe punishment in a low probability of instances. The reasoning is that the low probability is associated with lower costs of detection and lower budgets for law enforcement agencies. In addition, the POP should be in terms of fines or physical punishment because these forms of punishment are less costly than extended imprisonment.

Although this may be a valid starting point, several complexities arise. For one thing physical punishment is not accepted in the United States. This would seem to leave fines because the costs of administration would be lower than imprisonment. The problem is that not everyone is able to pay a fine. Thus, imprisonment must be considered. At first impression the norm would be fines and imprisonment would be reserved for those unable to pay. Now, though, the problem is one of equalizing the punitive impact of monetary sanctions with imprisonment. In addition, even the same level of fine will result in different levels of utility to those convicted.

The prospect for solving the problem of how to administer the proper level of punishing is made more complex by reactions to risk. Specifically, if those who commit crimes are risk-averse then the same level of expected punishment in an absolute sense may not translate into identical POPs with respect to behavioral reactions. For example, in absolute terms a certain one year prison sentence for selling marijuana is the same as a five percent chance of a twenty year sentence. On the other hand, if risk itself is a source of disutility, then the POP which includes the 5 percent likelihood of detection and a twenty year sentence will be perceived and responded to as if it is a higher cost than the certain one year sentence. What this means in terms of the optimal level of punishment is that you may over-deter law-breaking if the disutility of the risk is not factored in.[13] Thus, a certain one year sentence may have the same impact as an expected 10 month sentence.

Another complicating factor to be considered is that almost any POP is likely to involve price discrimination. In effect, different people will experience a different cost. This is exacerbated if the POP is composed of expected sanctions—a fixed fine or prison term multiplied by the probability of

13. A. Mitchell Polinsky, *An Introduction to Law and Economics* 82 (2d ed. 1989).

conviction. In these instances part of the disutility will be a function of risk, but this cost will vary from person to person depending on levels of risk averseness. In addition, if money is subject to diminishing marginal utility, relatively wealthy individuals may view the POP as being less expensive than poor people. Finally, some people may be more sensitive to the stigmatizing effect of a criminal sanction than others, and the level of stigma may vary depending on whether the POP is composed of fines or imprisonment. The more general point is that all of these factors make it impossible to charge each person the same price. People who are risk-averse and have strong reputational interests may be less inclined to commit a crime. On the other hand, changing and lowering the POP in recognition of this may mean that less risk-averse people and people with little to preserve in the form of reputation may undertake criminal activity when it is not efficient for them to do so.

Disutility from punishment may also have an indirect character. The stigmatizing effect of a conviction is obvious. Less frequently noted in the formulation of the POP is the fact that those convicted of felonies may lose voting rights and the right to participate in certain professions. Consideration of these and other negative consequences may seem like fine tuning an already shaky model. These seem unlikely to be the sorts of things even the rational, cost-benefit sensitive criminal might consider. This, however, may be a function of imperfect information, and a comprehensive POP would seem to include greater information for the individual contemplating an illegal act.

When one adopts a broader perspective with respect to the purposes of punishment an additional problem arises. The textbook analysis of criminal law usually lists deterrence as but one of a variety of purposes of punishment. Additional purposes are rehabilitation and retribution. Although in recent years the association of criminal punishment with rehabilitation has weakened, the issue of the efficient level of punishment seems to miss the point that punishment or some other response from law enforcement agencies may have a therapeutic effect. This "therapeutic effect" could take the form of reshaping preferences or more ordinary forms of behavior modification. For example, the modern trend toward requiring law-breakers to engage in community service may make them more empathic and less likely to break the law again. Whatever beneficial effects might be associated with personal reactions to punishment, they seem less likely to occur when the sanction is a fine only.

Finally a factor that is left out of most economic considerations of criminal law is the value of retribution. In economic terms, retribution can be said to be a source of utility to law-abiders. That is, the sense that people are punished simply because they deserve to be punished when they have committed a wrong is, to some, a value inherent in a system of criminal sanctions. Obviously this is a very different matter than punishing in order to deter or to make sure potential violators fully account for the social costs in their decision-making. In the usual economic model the sanction only produces disutility for those who violate the law. A comprehensive economic model of criminal law would recognize the utility-producing capacity of punishment as well. Such a consideration will influence the POP and support some types of punishment that are not necessarily the least expensive to administer.

C. CRIMINAL PROCEDURE

It may seem odd to think about applying the cost-benefit analysis of economics to safeguards for criminal defendants. You may regard these rights as "absolutes" that cannot be weighed against other interests. What this suggests is that the decision about whether or not to apply economic analysis is itself a philosophical one. In addition, the weighing, if it did take place, would be tricky owing to the nature of our system. To understand why, you must realize that in our criminal justice system there are two types of mistakes that can occur: an innocent party may be convicted, or a guilty party may be acquitted. On balance, it seems pretty clear that the system is set up to reflect the view that the second error is preferred to the first. Thus, an evaluation of procedure is not one that begins by assuming we are equally interested in minimizing all mistakes.

In fact, economic considerations enter the picture at a number of levels. For example, Professor William Stuntz makes a convincing argument that privacy rights and protection from surveillance under the Fourth Amendment vary from group to group depending on their relative economic conditions.[14] For example, poorer people are more likely than the affluent to use public transportation, live in smaller houses closer to public areas, and transact business in the open. In other words, like it or not, privacy and the avoidance of snooping can be bought on the open market.

Beyond this broad perspective, there are economic aspects of more specific criminal procedure issues. Some of these possibilities are obvious, as in the case of cruel and unusual punishment. If you view criminal law as about creating incentives for the efficient level of crime, the idea of cruel and unusual punishment can be easily connected. Forms of torture that might be inexpensively administered are unavailable. In addition, very high levels of imprisonment with very low likelihoods of punishment may also be prohibited. For example, twenty years of jail for a first time jaywalker—even if very unlikely to be administered—may be the lowest cost method of achieving efficient levels of jaywalking and may also be ruled cruel and unusual

One of the more interesting issues arises with the exclusionary rule. As you know, the rule prohibits the use of evidence obtained by an unreasonable search or seizure in a criminal trial. The benefits of the rule are that it provides freedom for all people from government intrusion, selective enforcement, and arbitrary uses of power. On the other hand, one

14. See William J. Stuntz, "The Distribution of Fourth Amendment Privacy," 67 *George Wash. L. Rev.* 1265 (1999).

of the costs of the rule is that guilty defendants may not be convicted if the crucial evidence either cannot be obtained or is obtained improperly.

An improper search can be viewed as a violation of a property rule. Typically the violation of a property rule means the party at fault is forced to pay damages or even penalized. In other words, the party who has acted improperly must internalize the costs of that conduct. The exclusionary rule may deter unlawful searches and seizures, but it does not, at least directly, involve internalization by those who have violated someone else's rights. In fact, it can be argued that the illegal search produces an externality in the form of an acquitted guilty party who is ultimately shouldered by society generally. In some sense, citizens may react to that cost by calling for the employment of people who are more careful about the Fourth Amendment, but it seems illogical to expect people to react to more crime by calling for fewer searches.

Richard Posner has made a case for replacing the exclusionary rule with more conventional tort remedies.[15] The idea is that the Fourth Amendment does not offer protection to criminals from prosecution. Instead, it provides a right for all people to avoid unreasonable searches. The damages from an illegal search may be fairly slight. Perhaps a door or door lock is broken and the victims distressed. As long as victims are adequately compensated for their loss by those guilty of the violation—excluding the loss of

15. Richard A. Posner, "Rethinking the Fourth Amendment," 1981 *Supreme Court Review* 49 (1981).

liberty if a victim is sent to jail—the economically proper level of internalization occurs. This leads to the question of what the compensation would be. If it is fair market value, the tort solution makes the Fourth Amendment into a liability rule. That might seem fine, but think about whether you would agree to a search and seizure at any time by public officials as long as they paid for whatever was broken. Issues obviously arise with respect to the price to be set for illegal searches. On the other hand, a property rule requires permission or punishment of those who attempt to change the property rule into a liability rule.

Although the Fourth Amendment and the exclusionary rule are amenable to economic analysis, albeit difficult economic analysis, other procedural issues are even more difficult to fit into an economic framework. In these difficult cases, it is possible to see the debate as existing at two levels. One level is whether a cost-benefit or economic analysis should take place at all. The other is what the relevant factors are if such an analysis is undertaken. Take, for instance, *Maryland v. Craig*, 497 U.S. 836 (1990), a case in which the Supreme Court considered the right of criminal defendants to confront witnesses as required by the Sixth Amendment when the witness is a child. The majority opinion amounts to an analysis of the costs and benefits of confrontation in the context of a right that the dissent views as absolute.

Whatever the implicit economic analyses of procedural issues, they can hardly be said to apply consistently. In the case of testimony by a minor, a weighing process is used that may reduce defendants' rights and, arguably, increase the likelihood of a mistaken conviction. The testimony is likely evidence that the Court evidently views as so critical that it should not be excluded. On the other hand, rock-solid evidence of guilt that is gathered illegally is completely barred. If the implied economic analysis of *Craig* were applied to search and seizure cases, the outcome could very well be a different rule than that which exists.

CHAPTER NINE

THE ECONOMICS OF ANTITRUST

Economic analysis has long been an important element of antitrust law. Even very early antitrust opinions used economic analysis to determine market share and the impact on competition of agreements among competitors. In addition, the calculation of damages is often based on economic projections.

Economic analysis became even more central to antitrust in the 1970's when the philosophy of the Supreme Court with respect to the antitrust laws took a decided turn. Prior to that time, purely economic concerns were often balanced against other social goals. In the 1970's, however, the Court adopted the view that the antitrust laws were designed solely to further economic objectives. These economic ends are efficiency and competition; they do not directly involve distributive issues.

Entire texts have been devoted to industrial organization and to the economic analysis specifically applied to antitrust law. The pages that follow, by necessity, have a narrower focus. The basic price theory that explains the advantage of competitive conditions over the absence of competition is presented first. The determinants of "market power" are explained next. The presence or absence of market power has become the cornerstone of modern antitrust analysis.

A. THE COMPETITIVE EXTREMES OF PERFECT COMPETITION AND MONOPOLY

The standard economic analysis applied to antitrust law involves a comparison of prices and output in an industry that is highly or perfectly competitive with prices and output in the same industry operating under monopoly conditions. In order to make this comparison, it is necessary to review some of the basic economic theory introduced in Chapter Two.

1. DEMAND AND SUPPLY

Perfect competition means that the industry is characterized by many small firms selling a homogeneous product, that there is easy entry into and exit from the industry, and that there is complete and inexpensive information for sellers and buyers. Basically, this means that all the firms are "price-takers." In other words, firms are powerless to raise prices above their costs without quickly losing all sales to competing firms. It is important to remember that "costs" in this context includes a "normal profit." A normal profit is the minimum necessary to keep investors from withdrawing their capital from the industry.

In perfect competition, the price in the market is set by the interaction of demand and supply. Demand for an individual buyer is a schedule of prices and the quantities that buyer would be willing and able to buy in that market at each price. Demand is usually illustrated graphically as a demand curve which plots the possible prices and quantities. For example, the demand of a single law student for ball point pens might look like Figure 1. At a price of $1, the student would be willing and able to purchase 10 pens. At a price of $2, the quantity would be 8 pens and so on.

Figure 1

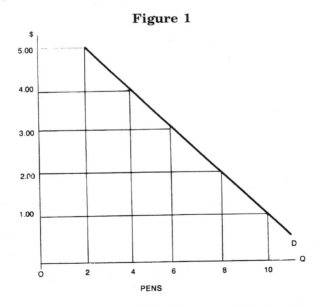

Total demand would be determined by "horizontally summing" the demand curves for all the possi-

ble buyers in the market. Suppose the market consisted of all 1,000 citizens of Lawtown. To derive
the horizontal summation, one would take a price
and add the total quantity that would be purchased
at that price by all buyers. The same process would
be repeated for each price. The result might look
like Figure 2. Now, for the market, the quantity
demanded at $1 would be 10,000. The quantity
demanded at $2 is 8,000 and so on.

Figure 2

Of course, to determine the price in the market, it
is necessary to have a supply curve. As indicated in
Chapter Two, an individual firm's supply is a series
of prices and the quantities that would be offered
for sale at each price. Figure 3 shows the prices that

might exist in a market and the quantities of ball point pens that would be offered for sale by a single supplier at each price.

Figure 3

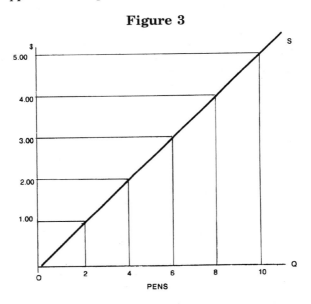

It is important for the analysis that follows to note that the individual firm's supply curve is the same as its marginal cost curve. Marginal cost is the additional cost of producing one more unit of output, and the curve simply shows the marginal cost at several levels of output. Thus, in order to derive the supply curve, one might ask the supplier how much it would offer to sell at a specified price. The supplier would presumably offer units for sale as long as the additional cost of producing each unit is less than or perhaps just equal to the price offered.

In other words, as long as the marginal cost of producing the unit was not in excess of the price offered, that unit would be offered for sale.

As with demand, the supply for the entire market can be determined by horizontally summing the supply curves of all the individual producers. Figure 4 illustrates the supply for the industry. The graph represents something of a simplification, as it is unlikely that supply would extend all the way down to a price of zero. In other words, the quantity supplied would probably reach zero (intersect with the y axis) at a price above zero.

Figure 4

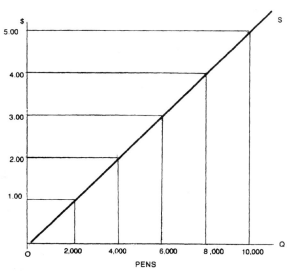

2. MARKET EQUILIBRIUM, PRODUCER AND CONSUMER SURPLUS

Figure 5 combines the industry demand curve from Figure 2 with the industry supply curve from Figure 4. In the graph, the curves intersect at a price of $3 and a quantity of 6,000. This is the equilibrium price and quantity. When price exceeds $3 it will tend to fall, and when it is below $3 it will tend to increase. The reasons are fairly obvious. Take, for example, a price of $4. At that price the quantity demanded is 4,000 and the quantity supplied is 8,000. There is a surplus of ball point pens in the market, and the tendency will be for sellers to lower their prices.

Figure 5

At a price of $2, on the other hand, the quantity demanded is 8,000 and the quantity supplied is only 4,000. Here buyers will begin to bid against each other for the pens, and the effect will be for prices to increase. Only at a price of $3, at which the quantity demanded and the quantity supplied are both 6,000, will there not be a tendency for prices to increase or decrease.

Figure 5 is also useful to illustrate what is meant by the important concepts of "consumer surplus" and "producer surplus." In the market for ball point pens, the price was $3, but in actuality, some people were willing to pay more than $3 for the pens. For example, the demand curve tells us that even at a price of $5, 2,000 pens would have been demanded. In effect, some people have paid only $3 for something they would have paid up to $5 to have. When a person is able to obtain something for less than the most they would have paid for it, they have received consumer surplus. If 10 people received $2 worth of consumer surplus, the total consumer surplus would be $20.

Similarly, in the Figure, even though the price is $3, there are some units that would be offered for sale at prices less than $3. For example, as the graph shows, even at a price of $1, 2,000 units would be offered for sale. When a producer receives more for a unit of output than the least it would take, it receives producer surplus.

Figure 6 illustrates total consumer surplus and producer surplus. The equilibrium price is P. The total consumer surplus is the area of the triangle PAC. In the graph, the total amount of producer surplus is equal to the area of the triangle P0C.

Figure 6

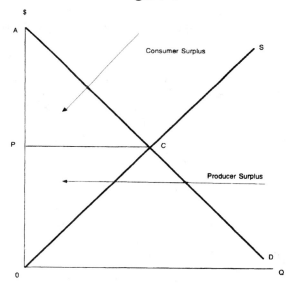

One can combine the surplus received by consumers with the surplus received by producers to determine the total surplus created by exchanges that take place in this market. This would be the area 0AC. As the graph shows, the process of determining the price also determines how the surplus created by the exchange is to be divided between consumers and producers.

3. THE INDIVIDUAL FIRM UNDER PERFECT COMPETITION: THE MARGINAL COST = MARGINAL REVENUE RULE

By combining demands of individual consumers and supplies of individual producers, the discussion so far has focused on the competitive industry as a whole. In order to fully understand the critical differences between competitive markets and monopoly markets, it is important to examine the decision-making of the individual firm.

Under conditions of perfect competition, the individual firm cannot control price. It responds passively to the price that is set in the market and sells as much as it would like in that market. Thus, if we assume that the competitively determined price in the ball point pen market is $3, the individual firm faces a demand curve that looks like curve d in Figure 7. The curve is really a horizontal line at the competitively determined price. This is because the firm will sell no units of output if it attempts to raise price to higher than competitive levels. It is not relevant to think of a price below $3 since the firm can sell all it wants at that price and would not, therefore, sell any for less.

Figure 7

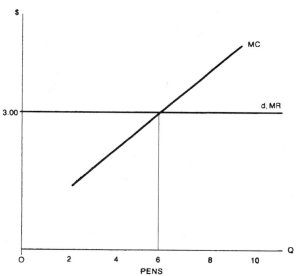

The demand curve also plots what is known as marginal revenue (MR). Marginal revenue is the additional revenue obtained from selling one more unit of output. For a firm operating under perfectly competitive conditions, the marginal revenue curve and the demand curve are the same. The significance of this will become evident shortly when conditions of monopoly are examined.

Figure 7 also illustrates the firm's supply curve. As explained above, the supply curve is the same as the firm's marginal cost curve. Just as in the industry as a whole, the firm's output will be determined by the intersection of the demand it faces and the supply curve. In the graph, this intersection takes place at 6 units.

For analytical purposes, it is more important to focus on the marginal revenue and marginal cost curves. The quantity sold by the firm is determined by the intersection of these curves. This makes sense when one considers the information provided by the marginal revenue and marginal cost curves: marginal revenue is the extra revenue from selling one more unit of output, and marginal cost is the additional cost of producing the unit. The rational producer will produce and sell any unit for which the additional revenue generated by its sale exceeds or is equal[1] to the additional cost of production. On the graph, if one starts at the origin and moves outward, it is evident that up until unit 6 marginal revenue exceeds marginal cost. At unit 6, they are just equal, and the firm would not produce additional units. The idea that a firm will produce until marginal revenue and marginal cost are equal is fundamental to price theory.

4.   COST CURVES

In order to further understand the general economic preference for competitive conditions over monopoly conditions, it is necessary to become familiar with an assortment of production costs in addition to marginal cost. Typically, production costs are classified as fixed or variable. Fixed costs

1.   Actually, the firm may be indifferent to producing the unit at which marginal revenue and marginal cost are equal.

do not vary as production increases. An example might be the rent paid for a factory. Variable costs increase as production increases. An example would be the raw materials used in producing a good. Total cost is fixed cost plus variable cost.

In most economics books, these costs are expressed as averages per unit of output. For example, if fixed costs were $200 and 4 units were produced, the average fixed cost would be $50 per unit. Average fixed cost will steadily decline as the level of output increases. This is because the same fixed cost is being divided by higher and higher levels of output. In Figure 8, the curve labelled AFC illustrates average fixed costs.

Figure 8

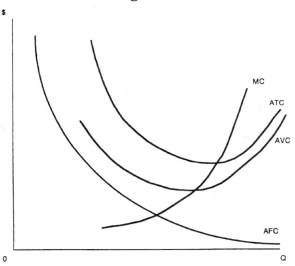

Variable cost is also typically divided by the level of output to get average variable cost. Here, though, higher and higher levels of output are divided into higher and higher levels of variable costs. As it turns out, average variable cost is likely to take on a U shape as illustrated by curve AVC in Figure 8. As production increases, the firm is likely to become more efficient. That is, its output will increase more rapidly than the increase in inputs used. This will cause average variable cost to fall. After some point, however, efficiency will no longer increase and, on the average, units will become more costly to produce.

ATC in the Figure illustrates average total cost. It is calculated by dividing total cost by the level of output. Or it can be seen as the sum of average fixed cost and average variable cost. Since it is the total of average fixed cost and average variable cost, it lies above average variable cost. The influence of average variable cost is reflected in its U shape. The average total cost curve draws closer to the average variable cost curve as output increases. This is because the difference between the curves is average fixed cost which steadily declines as output increases.

Figure 8 also illustrates the firm's marginal cost (MC) curve. It is drawn to intersect both average total cost and average variable cost at their lowest points. It is easy to understand why as long as one keeps in mind the information contained in the two types of curves. Marginal cost is the extra cost of producing a unit of output. As long as it is less than the average cost of the units being produced, it will have the effect of lowering the average. For example, if the average variable cost of 10 units is $10 and then an eleventh unit is added that has a marginal cost of $8, the average variable cost will decrease to approximately $9.80. On the other hand, if the marginal cost is above the average cost curve, it will tend to pull up average cost.

It may be useful to view the relationship of the curves in a slightly more technical way. When average variable cost or average total cost "bottom out," or reach their minimums, they are neither increasing or decreasing. For a very short span, they are flat. At this point, and only at this point, marginal cost exerts no upward or downward influence on these curves. The only way for marginal cost to exert no influence is for it to be equal to the average at that point. And, as the graph illustrates, marginal cost intersects the curves only at the point where they are neither rising nor falling.

5. EQUILIBRIUM AND PERFECT COMPETITION

Figure 9 includes all the cost curves from Figure 8 except average fixed cost which has limited usefulness. To those curves has been added the demand curve faced by the firm under competitive conditions. In the graph, the horizontal demand curve (d), which represents the market-determined price, has been drawn so that it intersects with the average total cost curve at that curve's lowest point. The firm will produce Q_c units. It is drawn this way because there is a tendency for this to be the long-term relationship between price and average total cost under competitive conditions. More directly, firms in perfectly competitive markets tend to charge prices that are equal to minimum average total cost.

Figure 9

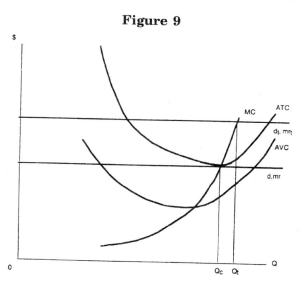

In order to understand why, focus again on Figure 9. In addition to demand curve d, another higher demand curve has been drawn at d_t. The firm might find that it is faced with this higher demand if there is an increase in industry demand that drives prices up. At this price, the firm would expand output to Q_t and, since price would be in excess of average total cost, it would be earning an economic profit.

In a perfectly competitive market, this can only be temporary. By definition, there is easy entry into the industry, and information is readily available. Thus, the presence of economic profits will quickly lure new firms into the market. The effect will be to increase supply and cause price to decrease back to levels that are equal to average total cost. Thus, under perfectly competitive conditions, consumers will tend to be charged a price equal to average total cost and average total cost will tend to be at its minimum.

An additional and important characteristic of perfect competition is that the industry price and output will be consistent with "allocative efficiency."[2] An allocatively efficient outcome is one in which resources are drawn into the production of a good or services in quantities that are justified by the value attributed by buyers to those goods or services. In order to understand why allocative efficiency is achieved, it must be recalled that the price and quantity in the competitive market are determined by the intersection of market demand and supply. Demand indicates the value attributed to units of output by potential buyers. The supply curve indicates the cost, in terms of resources used, of making the good available. Thus, as long as the value attributed to a particular unit of output, as indicated by the demand curve, exceeds the extra cost of producing the unit, as indicated by the supply curve, it is allocatively efficient to produce that unit. As Figure 5 illustrates, the competitive market encourages production of all the units that are valued more than their marginal cost of production. Production beyond that point, at least in theory, does not occur.

6. MONOPOLY

2. For a more detailed discussion see Chapter Two.

It is easiest to understand the objections to monopoly by comparing price and output under monopoly conditions with price and output under conditions of perfect competition. In order to do so, assume that through some unlikely merger, the ball point pen market that we started with is now served by a single firm. This means two critical things. First, the industry demand curve is now *the* demand curve facing the monopolist. Second, instead of reacting passively to the market-determined price, the monopolist will actually set the price. In fact, it is no longer meaningful to speak in terms of an industry supply curve showing prices and the quantities that would be offered for sale at each price. Instead, there will simply be one price—the price that maximizes the monopolist's profits.

In determining this price, the monopolist will follow the basic rule of finding the level of output where marginal revenue is equal to marginal cost. Things are different for the monopolist, however, in that the demand curve it faces is downward-sloping. This means that it must lower price in order to sell additional units. Moreover, it will have to lower the price for all units. Thus, in order to determine the marginal revenue from selling an additional unit of output, the firm must subtract the decrease in price for the other units from the price received for selling the additional units.

For example, suppose the firm is selling 5 units at a price of $10 per unit. If it wishes to sell 6 units, it may have to lower price to $9 per unit. Its marginal revenue from selling the sixth unit will be $4. This is a price of $9, which it gets for the sixth unit, reduced by a $1 per unit price reduction on the five units it was selling at $10. As a consequence, the marginal revenue curve for the monopolist is not the same as the demand curve but lies below the demand curve. This relationship is depicted in Figure 10.

Figure 10

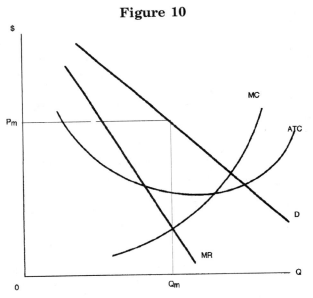

Figure 10 also includes the monopolist's marginal cost curve. In order to simplify the comparison with perfect competition, it is assumed that the marginal cost curve is the summation of all the marginal cost curves of the firms that previously existed in the industry.

To determine the profit-maximizing level of output, the monopolist goes through the same basic analysis as the firm in the competitive market. It will want to produce and sell as long as the additional revenue generated by selling an additional unit (MR) exceeds the extra cost of producing an additional unit (MC). In Figure 10, marginal revenue exceeds marginal cost for all units produced until the firm reaches unit Q_m. Thus, the monopolist will produce Q_m units of output.

The monopolist must also determine the profit-maximizing price. Obviously, the monopolist will charge the highest price that is consistent with selling Q_m units of output. One can find this by simply using the demand curve. Not only does it indicate the amounts that will be sold at each price, it also indicates the maximum price that could be charged and still sell any specified quantity. In Figure 10, the highest price that is consistent with selling Q_m units is P_m.

7. PERFECT COMPETITION AND MONOPOLY COMPARED

With this background, one can understand the general preference for competitive markets over those that are imperfect or have monopolistic tendencies. Figure 11 is useful in this comparison. The intersection of demand (D) and supply (S) in the graph determines the price (P_c) and output (Q_c) under competitive conditions. The intersection of the marginal revenue curve (MR) and the marginal cost curve (MC) determines the monopoly level of production (Q_m). The monopoly price is P_m. Thus, one of the obvious distinctions between the competitive model and the monopoly model is that price will tend to be higher and output lower under monopoly conditions than under competitive conditions.

Figure 11

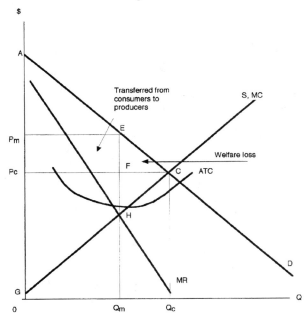

Another important distinction lies in the impact on consumer and producer surplus. Under competitive conditions, the consumer surplus is equal to the area of triangle P_cAC. Under monopoly conditions, consumer surplus is equal to the area P_mAE. Consumer surplus is, therefore, smaller under monopoly conditions.

The critical question is: what has happened to the portion of consumer surplus that is no longer enjoyed by consumers? First, a portion of it is captured by the monopolist in the form of producer surplus. In other words, under competitive conditions, the producer surplus was equal to area P_cCG. Under monopoly, this has been expanded to P_m GHE. Part of this new expanded producer surplus, area P_mP_cEF, was originally part of consumer surplus and now has been transferred to producers. Another portion of what was consumer surplus, area EFC, is not captured by the monopolist. This is part of what is called the "welfare loss" or "deadweight loss."[3]

In other words, part of what was consumer surplus under competitive conditions remains consumer surplus under monopoly conditions. A portion has been captured by the monopolist. This represents, in effect, a redistribution from consumers to the producer. Whether it is "right" or "wrong" or *ought* to happen is not a question that economics as a field of study is equipped to answer. A final portion of consumer surplus is lost and not captured by the monopolist. There is little controversy that this is a real loss in welfare. It was a measure of well-being or utility that has vanished.

   3.   Do you also see that part of producer's surplus has also disappeared?

Closely tied to this welfare loss is the impact monopoly has on allocative efficiency. It will be recalled that allocative efficiency is achieved when production is carried out to the point where demand and supply intersect. Under conditions of monopoly, production stops short of this level. The economic importance of this can be seen by focusing on the units between Q_m and Q_c. These are units that will be produced under competitive conditions and are not produced under monopoly conditions. Yet, for all of these units, the value attributed to them by consumers exceeds the value of the resources that would be used in their production. Under monopolistic conditions, the allocatively efficient level of output is not achieved.

Another cost of monopoly in the lure it represents to those who would like to achieve monopoly status and maintain it. In theory, the increased financial gains associated with the possibility of capturing a portion of consumer surplus can be regarded as a return to the investments devoted to gaining a competitive edge. This activity is referred to as "rent seeking." The problem is that it is directed dividing up wealth but not increasing it. Perhaps it is designed simply to hurt other competitors without making consumers any better off. If so, this expenditure is a waste as far as furthering consumer interests.

8.   SOME LIMITS ON THE COMPARISON

The models presented here and the discussion of the advantages of competition over monopoly in terms of price, quantity, and allocative efficiency represent a kind of first-level analysis. When one pushes the analysis a bit further the overall picture of monopoly versus competition becomes cloudier. One such complication arises from the fact that perfect competition requires a large number of firms. On the other hand, each firm may be too small to operate very efficiently. Figure 12 illustrates the problem. The average total cost curve is drawn so that the most efficient level of output is 10,000 units. The average cost of production would then be $1. This level of output may only be possible if one large firm buys an expensive but very efficient piece of machinery.

Figure 12

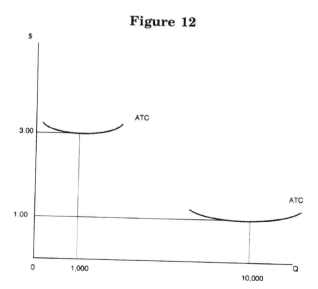

The graph also indicates that if 10 firms existed, each of which produced 1,000 units, the average total cost would be $3. Thus, while a market with 10 producers may be very attractive from the point of view of competitive pressure, the simple fact is that no matter how hard they compete, the price will remain close to $3. The problem is that the one large firm is able to take advantage of efficiency in production—productive efficiencies—that the smaller firms cannot. While the large firm, if left unregulated, may charge a higher price than the 10 competing firms, it is actually using resources in a more efficient manner.

This is not to say that the tension between competition and productive efficiency exists in every instance. In many cases, it may be that relatively small firms are able to take advantage of all the efficiencies in production. In other words, in some industries, the "minimum optimal size" for firms may be small enough that many firms can occupy the same industry, vigorously compete, and produce efficiently.

Another complicating factor for the simple model of antitrust is the "theory of second best." The problem can be envisioned by reexamining the notion of "allocative efficiency." A key requirement in achieving allocative efficiency is that marginal cost reflect the value of the resources used to produce the output and that the price paid be equal to marginal cost. As already demonstrated, this is the case in equilibrium under conditions of perfect competition. If, however, a firm is buying resources that are not supplied by perfectly competitive firms, the "signal" that drives output to the allocatively efficient level will be distorted. The point is that perfect competition as a means of achieving allocative efficiency really only works when all other related firms are also perfectly competitive. If they are not, one might more closely approach allocative efficiency in an economy of firms that are equally imperfectly competitive. This would be the "second best" solution. The theory of second best has not really influenced antitrust policy, but it suggests that policy implications of simply comparing monopoly to perfect competition can be misleading.

B. MARKET POWER AND MARKET DEFINITION

1. MARKET POWER

The second critical economic element of modern antitrust analysis is the determination of market power. It is important because the vast amount of antitrust litigation under the sherman and Clayton Acts requires plaintiffs to demonstrate that the defendant possessed market power.

Market power can be simply defined as the ability to raise prices above competitive levels and profitably keep them there.[4] In effect, any firm, including one that is in a very competitive industry, can raise

4. It is common to think of sellers as having market power. In fact, buyers too have power to deviate from competitive prices. This is called monopsony power. See generally. Roger D. Blair and Jeffrey Harrison, Monopsony in Law and Economics (2010).

prices. The issue is whether it can keep them there or whether buyers will turn relatively quickly to other products or whether suppliers will enter the market and begin selling the product in question. In either case, the price increase will not be sustainable.

Market power was traditionally assessed by determining the firm's market share. Market share is the firm's sales in the market divided by total sales in the market. Although market share is still the mainstay of market power analysis for antitrust purposes, it has given way to somewhat more sophisticated analyses that focus more on the actual factors that determine whether prices can be profitably raised above competitive levels.

2.   THE LERNER INDEX

The Lerner Index is a tool for measuring market power that captures more of the substance of market power than simple reliance on market share.[5] It is expressed as follows:

$$L = (P–C)/P$$

In the equation, L is the index, P is the firm's profit-maximizing price, and C is the firm's marginal cost at the profit-maximizing level of output. If the firm were operating under highly competitive conditions, P would approach C and the index would be very low. When the firm has market power, P can exceed C and the ratio will be higher.

5.   Abba Lerner, "The Concept of Monopoly and the Measurement of Monopoly Power," 1 *Rev. Econ. Stud.* 157 (1934).

Another way of expressing market power is to focus on the elasticity of the demand faced by the firm. Elasticity of demand is a measure of how responsive buyers are to changes in price. It is determined by comparing a certain percentage change in price to the resulting percentage change in quantity demanded. If the percentage change in quantity demanded is less than the percentage change in price, demand is regarded as "inelastic." A firm has greater market power—it is more likely to be able to raise prices above its marginal costs—the more inelastic the demand it faces. In fact, the Lerner Index is also equal to the reciprocal of the elasticity of the demand faced by the firm or $1/Ed$, where Ed is the elasticity of demand. Obviously, the lower the elasticity, the higher the index.

3. THE DETERMINANTS OF MARKET POWER

The Lerner Index can be reformulated to illustrate that the elasticity of demand faced by the firm and market power are determined by three factors.[6] The first factor is the elasticity of demand for the industry of which the firm is a part. The reasons are fairly straight forward. If the industry produces a good for which there are available substitutes, it is less likely that an individual firm in that industry will have market power.

A second critical factor is the elasticity of supply. Elasticity of supply, as the term implies, is a meas-

6. See Richard Posner & William Landes, "Market Power in Antitrust Cases," 94 *Harv. L. Rev.* 937 (1981).

ure of responsiveness to price changes by actual or potential producers of the good. In other words, it is a measure of how quickly producers can respond to price increases for a product by increasing the amount of it they make available. An increase in supply may come from firms already in the industry that have excess capacity. It also may come in the form of firms that are able to switch their productive capacity from one product to the one that now has the higher price. It might even come from firms entering production from scratch. If firms are very responsive in terms of increasing output—supply elasticity is high—it will be very difficult for an individual firm to increase price and keep it high.

Finally, market share also plays a role in determining market power and, if all other things are equal, firms with high market shares will tend to have higher market power. For example, a firm with a 90% market share may find that it can increase prices and actually lose substantial numbers of customers without suffering a large decrease in its overall share of the market. On the other hand, a firm in the same market with only a 10% share will not be able to sustain as much in the way of losses in volume of sales.

4. MARKET DEFINITION AND CROSS–ELASTICITY

Much of the foregoing discussion suggests a neat mathematical solution to the problem of market power. This is not, however, a real possibility. The problem is that the calculation requires a determination of the firm's market; for example, which products can be regarded as a part of the firm's market? Similarly, in order to determine the elasticity of demand for the industry, one would have to determine which firms are part of that industry.

Unfortunately, markets can rarely be defined with precision. Thus, market definition and the determination of market power remain activities that are "art" as much as "science." A useful, albeit imperfect, tool is the cross-elasticity of demand. Cross-elasticity is a measure of the responsiveness of the sale of one product to price changes of another. When an increase in the price of one product leads to increases in the sales of another, the products are substitutes. The greater this reaction, the more substitutable the products. There is no bright line test for when cross-elasticity is high enough for the products to be regarded as occupying the same market.

Furthermore, there are a number of pitfalls associated with a simplistic reliance on cross-elasticity. First, cross-elasticity may change and become higher as the period of time allowed for the reaction is increased. For example, if the price of coal as a home heating fuel goes up, people may not respond immediately by switching to natural gas because they are committed to furnaces that use only coal. When these furnaces wear out, though, they may switch to gas-burning furnaces and the cross-elasticity between gas and coal will appear higher.

Another problem is that the base upon which the calculations are made may cause a distortion. A firm that raises prices may find that it loses all of its customers. If, however, it loses them to a very large firm with a much higher volume of sales, the percentage increase in sales for that firm may be low, implying that the cross-elasticity is very low.

A final problem results from the fact that cross-elasticity may vary with the price at which it is measured. For example, a firm that is charging a relatively low price when compared to sellers of competing products may find that it can increase its prices without losing sales to those competitors. On the other hand, if it is charging a high price, it may be just at the point where consumers would abandon the product if prices were increased any further. Measuring cross-elasticity at the higher price will indicate a higher cross-elasticity than measuring it at the lower price.

5.   GEOGRAPHIC MARKETS

Antitrust market analysis focuses not only on products that are reasonably interchangeable but on the geographic boundaries of the market. The geographic market contains all those producers who, in the eyes of buyers, compete with the firm in question. In a sense, product market analysis concentrates on the products that are interchangeable and geographic market analysis concentrates on actual suppliers who are reasonably interchangeable. To fully account for all those firms that may limit the ability of the seller to raise price, both dimensions of the market must be considered.

The geographic market question can be approached with the same methodology as product market definition. The question is how responsive buyers will be to price increases in terms of buying from remote sellers. If they quickly move to remote sellers when local prices go up, the distant sellers are part of the market. If not, they are not part of the market. Again, there is no bright line test for including a firm in the geographic market. It is a matter of judgment and ultimately leads to the use of expert opinion at trial.

The primary determinant of the ease with which buyers will turn to distant sellers is transportation costs. Obviously, the more expensive it is to ship goods from distant locations, the less willing buyers will be to rely on those sellers. This can be refined a bit in the sense that the importance of transportation costs can probably best be judged in light of the cost of the product. Thus, one would expect the concrete block industry to be local because the cost of shipment as a percentage of the cost of the product is relatively high. The market for diamonds, on the other hand, may be international in scope.

6. SUPPLY ELASTICITY

As the expanded discussion of the Lerner Index indicated, one of the factors that affects the elasticity of demand faced by a firm is the quickness with which other firms can respond to price increases by making output available to customers. If there are no such firms, then no matter how willing buyers may be to switch to alternative suppliers, it will not make a difference in terms of limiting the ability of a firm to raise price. As already noted, the increase in supply can come from three sources: existing producers of the product who have excess capacity, firms that can switch existing capacity from the production of another good to the production of the good in question, and firms that enter the industry *de novo*.

One can best visualize the problem by thinking in terms of determining the firm's market share. If the market is defined to include only the production that exists in the market at the time of the evaluation, it may overstate the importance of the firm. In other words, the denominator in the market share calculation will be artificially low. This would be especially true if there were firms in the industry that could switch into the production of the good in question with very little effort. Once again there are no bright line tests for deciding when a firm should be included in a market even though it may not currently be producing the product in question.

The main determinant of supply elasticity is how fast production costs increase as output increases. The connection is obvious. If price goes up, firms will increase output as long as they can produce additional output at a cost that is less than the new price. If production costs rise very slowly as production increases, then suppliers are likely to play more of a role in limiting another firm's efforts to exercise market power.

In summary, market power varies inversely with industry elasticity of demand and elasticity of supply. It varies directly with market share.

7. A CLASSIC AND A CONTEMPORARY EXAMPLE

The complexities of market analysis can best be illustrated by reference to two important cases: one an antitrust classic and one a more recent headline grabber.

a. United States v. Aluminum Company of America (Alcoa)

Judge Learned Hand's market analysis in the 1945 Alcoa case is probably the most closely studied market analysis. Judge Hand reasoned that Alcoa was a monopoly by virtue of its possession of 90% of the market for virgin aluminum ingot. The 10% that was not sold by Alcoa consisted of imports. In effect, Judge Hand made decisions about what was to be included in the numerator and the denominator of the market share fraction. In doing so, Judge Hand did not have the benefit of the technical language found in today's judicial market analyses, but his reasoning, though possibly flawed, considered a number of the factors discussed above.

In coming to the decision about Alcoa's market share, Judge Hand took a series of steps. First, he excluded secondary or recycled aluminum from the market or the denominator of the market share fraction. He reasoned that secondary aluminum was not reasonably interchangeable because for some users it was not acceptable. In today's terminology, the cross-elasticity was too low. In addition, he was concerned that Alcoa had control over the production of aluminum that would be recycled. In effect, this type of competition was, in part, under the control of Alcoa. To include it in the market would, in his view, be misleading as to the potential for secondary aluminum to act as a limiting factor on Alcoa's control of price. Most scholars now feel that complete exclusion of secondary aluminum resulted in too narrow a market and an inflated market share for Alcoa.

In a second step, Judge Hand included in the denominator only foreign-produced aluminum that was already sold in the United States. The other possibility would have been to include all foreign-produced ingot. The issue was one of elasticity of supply. In other words, how sensitive would foreign producers be to price increases in the United States? It was probably incorrect for Judge Hand to include only the ingot currently imported, since additional imports would likely have occurred if Alcoa's prices increased. In fact, Judge Hand seemed to recognize this in some of his reasoning. As with secondary aluminum, most scholars now feel that the impact was to artificially narrow the market and inflate Alcoa's market share.

A third step taken by Judge Hand dealt with ingot that was fabricated by Alcoa. In effect, this was virgin ingot that Alcoa processed itself rather than selling to others. The question was whether ingot Alcoa processed should be included in the numerator. If it were included, Alcoa's market share would be higher, and if excluded, it would be lower. Hand elected to include the processed ingot. His reasoning was that the decision of whether to process or sell was one that had an impact on prices. To exclude fabricated ingot from the numerator would lower Alcoa's share and understate its power over price.

b. *United States v. Microsoft*

In the heralded 2001 Microsoft case, the Court of Appeals for the District of Columbia assessed Microsoft's market power in the market for operating systems. As in *Alcoa*, much of the controversy concerned what would be included in the relevant market or in the denominator of the market share fraction. Microsoft sought to include in the market the Apple operating system as well as operating systems for non-PC devices, including middleware. The court rejected all of these as failing the reasonably interchangeable test.

More interesting are two additional and less conventional arguments made by Microsoft. The first one was that a high market share overstated Microsoft's control over price because of the ease of entering the market. The court rejected this argument, reasoning that as long as most software was written for the Microsoft operating system, there was little likelihood of serious competition through new entry.

Microsoft also argued that whatever dominance it possessed was the result of the popularity of its system. This line of argument ties into the concept of network effects. Network effects occur when the desirability of a product increases as the manufacturer has greater market share. In the context of computers, the argument would be that the greater Microsoft's market share the better its product because it means a greater number of computer users have compatible systems. In effect, monopoly becomes consistent rather than inconsistent with consumer welfare. The court did not find the network effects argument compelling, but this particular type of reasoning may eventually lead to changes in conventional market analysis.

CHAPTER TEN

THE ECONOMICS OF GOVERNMENT REGULATION

With the exception of Chapter Nine, much of the material in the preceding chapters deals with the ways in which private law influences resource allocation or income and wealth distribution. There is, of course, a huge body of public law that is also specifically designed to achieve desirable allocative or distributive outcomes. In law school, this material is covered in courses ranging from regulated industries to securities regulation and environmental law. This Chapter, by necessity, adopts a more basic perspective than any of those courses. The focus is on the economic bases for regulatory intervention.[1] The critical question in the cases of all these rationales is whether the regulation produces a result that is more desirable than that which would be produced in an unregulated market. This Chapter also considers more recent attempts to connect regulation directly to increases in happiness.

1. The structure of this Chapter is based on Jeffrey Harrison, Tom Morgan & Paul Verkuil, *Regulation and Deregulation* (2003).

A. THE NATURAL MONOPOLY RATIONALE

1. THE THEORY OF NATURAL MONOPOLY

The bedrock justification for government regulation is the existence of natural monopoly.[2] A natural monopoly is said to exist when a market can be served most efficiently by a single firm. Table 1 illustrates how the costs of a natural monopoly may vary as output increases. The column for fixed costs shows total fixed costs of $10,000 for all levels of output. On the other hand, variable cost (VC) steadily increases with output. Thus, total cost (TC) also increases as output increases. The key column to examine, however, is the average total cost column (ATC). For every level of output on the chart, average total cost decreases. For example, at an output of 10 units, the average total cost has decreased to $1,000.64.

Table 1

Output	Fixed Cost	Variable Cost	TC	ATC
1	$10,000	$1.00	$10,001	$10,001.00
2	10,000	1.90	10,001.90	5,000.95
3	10,000	2.70	10,002.70	3,333.90
4	10,000	3.40	10,003.40	2,500.85
5	10,000	4.00	10,004	2,000.80
6	10,000	4.50	10,004.50	1,667.40
7	10,000	4.90	10,004.90	1,429.27
8	10,000	5.30	10,005.30	1,250.66

2. See Kenneth E. Train, *Optimal Regulation: The Economic Theory of Natural Monopoly* (1991).

Output	Fixed Cost	Variable Cost	TC	ATC
9	10,000	5.80	10,005.80	1,111.75
10	10,000	6.40	10,006.40	1,000.64

This steady decline in average total cost will occur when the firm's costs of production include a relatively large component of fixed costs. Fixed costs are those that do not change as the level of production increases. The typical example of a firm with large fixed costs is a utility. Since fixed costs are relatively large when compared to variable costs (those that do increase with the level of production) and do not increase as output increases, the average cost of production will fall even though some of the other costs of production are increasing.

Figure 1 illustrates the natural monopoly phenomenon graphically. The average total cost for the firm is depicted by ATC in the graph. The curve is drawn so as to steadily decline over most of the production levels graphed along the X axis. Curve D represents demand in the industry. As the graph shows, the average cost of production is falling throughout all levels of demand. In effect, from the point of view of production costs, the most efficient way to organize this industry is to have the total demand "served" by a single firm. The structure is called a natural monopoly, because if the market were unregulated it would evolve to the point at which only one firm survived.

Figure 1

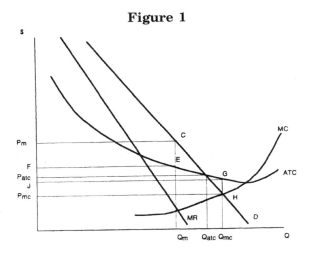

For example, suppose two producers of electricity were attempting to serve the same market. Given that they both would have high fixed costs, they would each need to serve most of the market in order to avoid losses. The ensuing competition could take the form of fierce price competition with each firm pricing below average total cost. Eventually, one firm would abandon the market, leaving it to the other firm.

The relationship of costs and demand resulting in natural monopoly conditions creates a dilemma. If the firms are left unregulated, prices will fall until one of them leaves the market. At that point, the remaining firm is a monopolist and will have the capacity to raise price. Following basic pricing principles discussed in Chapters Two and Nine, the firm would produce out to the point at which marginal cost (MC in Figure 1) and marginal revenue (MR) are equal and charge the price that is consistent with selling that level of output. In Figure 1, this results in the quantity Q_m and a price equal to P_m. The monopolist will earn a profit equal to the area of rectangle FP_mCE. Given the high costs of entering the industry, the likelihood is that the firm can keep its prices at supracompetitive levels.

A reaction to the threat of monopoly pricing is to regulate prices. If prices are regulated, the question then becomes: what is the appropriate rate? This question has both a general and a specific version. The specific questions are discussed below. At a more general level, there are two leading standards for the regulated price. The first is to choose the price that achieves allocative efficiency—marginal cost. For example, in Figure 1, if the allocatively efficient rate is chosen, the price would be set at P_{mc}. As was discussed in Chapter Two, this is because marginal cost reflects the cost to society of producing an additional unit of output, and the demand curve shows the value attributed to those units of output by buyers. From the point of view of overall welfare, it makes sense to produce as long as the demand curve is above the marginal cost curve.

The problem with this, as the graph illustrates, is that the price of P_{mc} is below the average total cost of production for the firm. In fact, the total loss to the firm is equal to the loss per unit times the number of units sold or the area of rectangle $JGHP_{mc}$ in the Figure. Thus, the firm cannot survive in the long run without some kind of outside source of funding, possibly a government subsidy.

Because of this, there is invariably pressure to allow the firm to recover its full costs of production including a normal profit. On the graph, this would mean charging a price equal to average total cost or P_{atc}.

2. AGENCY REGULATION

a. Revenue Requirement

Often the response to natural monopolies is to regulate prices through the use of a regulatory body. This actually involves two steps. One is the determination of the total revenue the firm will be permitted to raise through its pricing structure. As noted above, the typical approach is to permit the firm to collect revenue equal to its costs including a normal profit. The amount of revenue can be expressed as a formula:

$$R = C + Ir$$

where R is the total revenue, C is the operating expense or the costs of goods and services consumed during the relevant time period, I is the rate base or the assets that are not consumed during the relevant time period, and r is the rate of return.

In a rate hearing, each of the above components will be at issue, ranging from whether the executives of the utility are paid too much to calculating the utility's cost of capital. The issue is usually not whether the utility may incur a certain expense, but whether that expense may be fairly passed on to ratepayers. For example, a utility may choose to pay its president a salary of $200,000. A regulatory commission may determine that a fair salary is $150,000 and only permit that amount of the president's salary to be included in the charges that are passed on to customers. It has, in effect, "disallowed" part of the expense in determining the utility's revenue requirement.

If the regulatory mechanism is ideally working, the total revenue collected by the utility will be equal to its total reasonable costs including an acceptable level of profit. In other words, the total revenue would approximate the revenue collected if the firm were operating under competitive conditions. The problems of approaching this goal are well documented and fairly obvious. One key question is how to properly provide incentives for the firm to operate as efficiently as possible. If the firm is assured of recovering its cost and is restricted in terms of the profit it can make, many of the normal incentives found in an unregulated market are lost. To some extent, this problem is offset by the possibility that time will pass between rate hearings, during which time costs increase yet the firm must abide by the agency's decision about allowable costs. This "regulatory lag" can force management to be concerned about costs, but whatever impact it may have will only coincidentally match the pressure in an unregulated market.

Two problems associated with attempting to regulate the firm's rates and revenues in order to simulate an unregulated outcome are especially noteworthy. The first is the circularity in any effort to encourage efficient operation. For example, suppose the utility chose to pay its president an extravagant salary and to make large contributions to a local charity. At a rate hearing, the administrative body may determine not to allow the utility to pass these charges on to ratepayers. Since the expenses are already incurred by the utility, the net effect will be no different than had an unregulated firm been unable to charge a price at least equal to its costs—profit will decrease. Low or uncertain profits make it more difficult for the firm to attract new investors. The effect of this will be to make the cost of capital in the formula increase. Thus, disallowing a particular expense may not mean that ratepayers do not eventually pay for that expense in some other form.

Another widely discussed consequence of rate regulation is called the Averch–Johnson effect. Typically, the regulated firm is permitted to earn a "fair" rate of return on its invested assets. The money used for acquisition of these assets is the capital contributed by investors. If the fair rate of return is higher than the firm's actual cost of capital, the firm will have an incentive to invest in capital and substitute it when possible for other inputs like labor. The basic Averch–Johnson effect is that the regulated firm will be encouraged to use a different and less efficient mix of inputs than an unregulated firm.

b. Rate Regulation

The formula presented above only indicates the amount of revenue the firm is permitted to collect.

Another step in the process involves the determination of actual rates to be charged. There are two basic methodologies. One is to attempt to match users up with the actual cost of serving them. This "cost of service" approach can be based on the average cost of service or on the marginal cost of service. A second approach is sometimes referred to as being based on the "value of service." Typically, "value of service" pricing means that prices for different customer groups will vary inversely with the elasticity of the demand for that group. All of these approaches have complexities and shortcomings, some of which are discussed here. In addition, the two basic philosophies can be combined.

The problems with adopting one pricing strategy or another stem primarily from the tension between the need to raise revenue equal to the total cost of operating the firm and the desire to send the right pricing signal to consumers as a means of achieving allocative efficiency. Thus, as noted above, a price equal to marginal cost may mean that a firm is unable to meet all of its expenses. A response may be to try to allocate to each user the "full cost" of production. In other words, all of the fixed costs of the firm would be allocated so that each unit is priced in a way that the consumer pays some portion of the total costs of production. Of course, this means losing the advantages of marginal cost pricing in that the pricing signal sent to consumers will no longer encourage the socially optimal level of consumption.

A related possibility is called two-part or multi-part pricing. In this case the consumer is charged some price for simply being able to consume at all and then a price per unit actually purchased. The fixed part of the charge could be designed to insure that the firm recovers the fixed costs of production. It might be allocated to customers on the basis of how much they demand at the highest period of demand. The per unit charge could then be set to reflect marginal cost. This approach to rate-setting is something of a hybrid in that the objective is to enable the firm to collect its revenue requirement while providing consumers information about marginal cost.

In the form described here, the two-part price is also a type of peak load pricing. Peak load pricing involves charging different prices depending on the time of consumption. To the extent a consumer's demand coincides with the time of overall peak demand on the system, one could say that she is responsible for the costs associated with the firm's acquisition of the fixed plant necessary to serve all customers at the peak period of demand. In a sense, she is charged in a way that matches her responsibility for marginal investment costs.

"Value of service" pricing involves a different perspective than "cost of service" pricing. Instead of attempting to match consumers up with the costs they cause the producer to incur, the focus is on the elasticity of demand of the consumers. Those consumers with relatively inelastic demand are charged a higher price than those with relatively elastic demands. This is not to say that the consumers with inelastic demands actually "value" the service any more than others; other factors may influence their responsiveness. For example, the shipper of a relatively valuable commodity may be willing to pay a higher freight rate than the shipper of a less expensive commodity because the cost of shipping is an insignificant element of the total cost of the commodity.

One advantage of the value of service approach over the cost of service approach is that it provides a way for the seller to charge a rate in excess of average total cost to some consumers—those with relatively inelastic demands—in order to offset charging a price which is below average total cost to other consumers—those with relatively elastic demands. Under an approach called "Ramsey pricing,"[3] the goal is to charge different prices depending upon elasticity of demand in order to just meet the total cost of production.

Figures 2 and 3 illustrate this possibility. In Figure 2, the demand curve for one group of consumers is drawn to be relatively flat, indicating that demand is relatively elastic. The firm's average total cost and marginal cost curves are also on the graph. The price (P_1) is set at the intersection of the demand curve and the marginal cost curve. This group of consumers is making no contribution toward the firm's fixed costs, and the "loss" associated with serving this group of consumers alone is equal to the area of rectangle P_1ABC.

3.   See Kenneth E. Train, *supra* note 2, at 117–125.

Figure 2

Figure 3

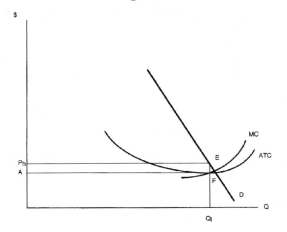

In Figure 3, the demand curve of a second class of consumers is relatively steep in order to illustrate a relatively inelastic demand. In this case, the price charged is equal to P_h, which is in excess of average total cost. The area of rectangle P_hEFA is the total "profit" recovered from this group of consumers. As long as the area of P_lABC in Figure 2 is equal to the area of P_hEFA in Figure 3, the firm is able to cover its total costs of production.

c.   Cross–Subsidization

The possibility of charging different prices to different groups of customers brings up the issue of cross-subsidization or, as Richard Posner calls it, "taxation by regulation."[4] As a general matter, the subsidization occurs when one group is charged above-cost rates so that another group can be charged below-cost rates. There is an obvious relationship to value of service pricing since the subsidizing group will typically have the relatively inelastic demand for the service.

Even at this simple level, two things should be clarified. First, it is not just relative rates that determine whether one group is subsidizing another. Thus, one group, to which it is very expensive to provide service, may be charged a higher price than a group that is less expensive to serve. The group paying the higher rate could still be the subsidized group if the rate charged is lower than cost.

4. Richard Posner, "Taxation by Regulation," 2 *Bell J.* 22 (1971).

A second point is that it is sometimes difficult to determine which group is being subsidized and which group is subsidizing. For example, suppose group one pays a rate below average cost but above marginal cost and group two pays a rate in excess of average cost. In a sense, group two appears to be subsidizing group one. On the other hand, if it were not for the contribution that group one is making towards fixed costs by paying a rate that is in excess of marginal cost, the rates paid by group two would have to be raised even further. Indeed, if group one had a very elastic demand for the good or service because there were many good substitutes available and would stop purchasing altogether if rates were any higher, one might conclude that its members were actually subsidizing the members of the higher-paying group.

A better example of cross-subsidization is when one customer or a group of customers is not paying a charge equal to marginal cost. The classic example is a remote purchaser of electricity or telephone service who pays the same rate as customers living in concentrated areas. Unless the remote purchaser has paid the full cost of constructing the necessary cables or lines to the remote location, that cost must be accounted for elsewhere in the system, most likely in the rates of others. Another prominent example is the effort to provide electricity to the needy through what are called "life-line" rates. Again, unless the life-line rate is equal to or above marginal cost, the "loss" must be made up in the form of higher rates elsewhere in the system.

True cross-subsidization, where the customer pays a rate that is lower than marginal cost, is hard to defend on traditional economic grounds. The most obvious problem is that below marginal cost rates send the "wrong" signal to consumers in the subsidized group and encourage an allocatively inefficient level of consumption. This is because marginal cost reflects the actual cost to society of producing the output. Consumers who purchase at a price that is less than marginal cost cannot be said to "value" the output at a high enough level to justify its production over the production of other goods or services for which those inputs might be used.

Although narrow conventional economic reasoning does not support true subsidization, there may still be economic or perfectly sound moral reasons for subsidizing the consumption of a product. For example, there may be sufficient positive externalities associated with the use of electricity by the needy for warmth that the demand they express in the market actually understates the "value" associated with their consumption of electricity. Similarly, the fact that traditional economics defines demand as a willingness and ability to pay may give one pause about allocating necessary goods and services to only those who "demand" them.

Another problem has less to do with allocative efficiency than with the taxation character of cross-subsidization. It is hard to distinguish cross-subsidization in the regulatory context from any other policy-based decision to subsidize one group at the expense of another. Thus, subsidizing the purchase of electricity is really no different from issuing food stamps or providing subsidies to tobacco farmers. Any system of widespread subsidization should at least strive for some semblance of coherence and consistency. Whether participation by a regulated firm and its regulating agency detracts from or assists in achieving this coherence is highly questionable.

3. CONTESTABLE MARKETS

Another approach to natural monopolies is one that does not so readily give up on the use of the market as an allocative mechanism. The basic idea here is that the condition of natural monopoly does not mean that prices must be regulated in order to avoid monopoly pricing. Instead, the focus is on *which* firm will be the single supplier. This can be determined by competition.[5] The competition is not, however, for individual customers; it is for the market itself.

One version of this approach is to make the determination of which firm will operate in the market by auctioning the right to operate. For example, a local government might auction off the right to be the exclusive supplier to the firm that bids for that right by offering the lowest pricing schedule and the highest quality of service. The local government might own the fixed resources

5. Harold Demsetz, "Why Regulate Utilities," 11 *J. L. & Econ.* 55 (1968).

required to operate in the market and, in effect, auction off the right to use these resources to a single firm.

This alternative is not without complications.[6] For example, the auctioning agency would presumably have a contract with the winning bidder for a substantial duration. Most likely, the contract will provide for price adjustments. The process of deciding when an adjustment is called for can begin to resemble a more typical rate-making process.

Another theory is that under certain conditions, it will be impossible for a monopolist to charge prices at which it earns above a normal profit. The key here is that entry into and exit from the industry by a newcomer must not be more expensive than for an incumbent. Under these conditions, if an incumbent monopolist attempted to charge a price that resulted in a profit that was higher than the minimum necessary, another monopolist could enter and charge a lower price and completely take away the incumbent's market. Presumably, this constant threat would be sufficient to force the incumbent monopolist to hold prices down. It is not clear just how often monopoly producers are as fungible as this theory requires.

B. EXCESSIVE COMPETITION

At times, regulations have been enacted in response to what is termed excessive or "destructive" competition. These regulations typically take the

6. See Kenneth Train, supra note 2, at 297–315.

form of restrictions on entry into the market or on minimum prices that can be charged. In general, the destructive competition rationale has been invoked in four different types of cases. The first is related to the value of the service pricing approach discussed above and to a policy of cross-subsidization. In these instances the "losses" incurred by serving one group are made by the extra revenue generated from serving another group—typically the group with a relatively inelastic demand. It would be profitable if a new firm could enter the market and serve only the group with the inelastic demand. The name that has been attached to this practice is "cream-skimming." As the label implies, the cream-skimming firm enters the market and takes only the very "best" customers, leaving those who are willing and able to pay a price below average total cost to the remaining firm. The obvious response to cream-skimming is to protect the incumbent firm from new entry.

A second reason for regulating entry or setting minimum prices arises when cream-skimming is an issue but involves a more direct response to the types of costs a firm has. It must be recalled that fixed costs are those that do not vary with the level of output. The firm must pay even if it produces nothing. If the firm has a high level of fixed costs, it is especially vulnerable to competition. Increases in competition, including competition for the most desirable customers, may mean that the firm cannot charge a price equal to average total cost. Moreover, since most of its costs are fixed, it cannot escape these losses by simply closing.

This predicament can be visualized by referring back to Figure 1. The firm will sell output as long as its price is no less than marginal cost. This is because that price at least covers the costs that are incurred by deciding to produce and allows for some contribution towards fixed costs. A price below average total cost cannot, however, go on indefinitely. Eventually, a firm that cannot cover all of its costs, including fixed costs, will go out of business. Thus, in order to avoid the risk of chronic losses and the possibility of a general hesitancy to enter the market in the first place, cream-skimming may be prevented by regulating new entry and setting minimum rates.

A third basic category of "destructive" competition is of a totally different character than the high fixed costs case. Sometimes rates and entry have been regulated simply because the firms in the market are inherently unstable. In other words, entry and exit from the market are relatively easy, price-cutting is the predominant method of competing, and there can be widespread business failures. Of course, this is not a pleasant prospect for the actual participants in the market, and there is likely to be political pressure brought to bear in order to protect them from the rigors of the market. This appears to have been the impetus behind the Motor Carriers Act of 1935, which provided this type of protection to the trucking industry. That protection was motivated more by Depression-era concerns about the general welfare of the individual trucker than by concern that the industry would either cease to exist or become highly concentrated.

A final justification for reducing competitive pressure in an industry is based on the possibility that intense competition results in a decrease in the quality of service. Sometimes the argument, when made in the context of something like the airline industry, preys on the fears of customers and relates specifically to safety. Although the quality of service argument has some appeal, there are a series of responses, based on conventional economic thinking, that tend to undermine it as a basis for regulating competition. The first starts from the assumption that every profit-maximizing firm is constantly on the lookout for ways to increase profit, including ways that involve reducing costs of production and possibly quality. Unless this quest for higher profits is somehow different or more relentless during periods of intense competition, it is not clear that quality will be any different than under normal market conditions.

In addition, the argument that quality will suffer seems based on the belief that consumers either do not value higher quality or are unable to assess differences in quality. If the former is the case, the reduction in quality is actually desirable. The second possibility has a little more appeal, although it once again suggests that firms have not taken full advantage of profitable strategies until faced with competitive pressure. But suppose that market imperfections relating to information costs really do render the consumers unable to effectively express preferences for higher quality and that it is only during periods of intense competition that quality suffers. Even here it is not clear that the most effective method of assuring higher quality is to decrease competitive pressure; directly regulating minimum quality standards may make more sense.

C. THE ALLOCATION OF INHERENTLY SCARCE RESOURCES

A rationale that is sometimes offered for regulation is the allocation of inherently scarce resources. This general justification probably stands for two more basic concerns. Broadcast frequency regulation illustrates these two concerns. The justification for the regulation of broadcast frequencies was that unrestricted and unregulated use would mean that competing broadcasters would interfere with each other and thereby severely limit the usefulness of the broadcast spectrum. This particular problem could have been solved simply by creating a system of exclusive broadcast rights, a step which would have been sufficient to overcome the "tragedy of the broadcast commons." This is probably the strongest basis for regulation since a system of property rights and means of enforcing those rights is basic to an efficiently operating system.

The second concern is about how the limited resources are to be allocated. Thus, in the case of broadcasting, auctioning the broadcast/property rights would have been one possible solution. The market would determine eventual ownership. Alternatively, the rights could be, and were, assigned on the basis of factors other than the willingness and ability to pay. In all likelihood, the "allocation of scarce resources" rationale reflects concerns about distribution as much as it does concerns about setting up a system of property rights.

This is not meant to imply that economic factors are only at work when rights are sold on the open market. In fact, there are often sound economic reasons for deviating from market solutions. In the case of broadcasting, there is an economic justification based on the presence of positive externalities. In other words, the benefits of having a broad range of views heard over the broadcast spectrum may accrue to people other than those vying for broadcast rights. This is one of the economic gains from favoring racial diversity in the allocation of broadcast rights.

In recent years, the allocation of scarce resources problem has been played out in the context of the geosynchronous zone. The geosynchronous zone is 22,300 miles out in space. Satellites placed there travel at roughly the same speed as the rotation of the earth and are, therefore, "stationary" with respect to the earth's surface. The zone is the primary location for communications satellites. The geosynchronous zone is inherently limited in that only so much of it exists. In addition, much of the zone is over oceans and, therefore, less valuable than other spaces. Finally, satellites in the zone are capable of crowding one another.

These problems are like those encountered in early broadcast regulation. One option is a massive "land rush," with the first parties successfully launching satellites, in effect, laying claim to the space occupied. This is comparable to a market solution in that the parties or countries that are willing and able to pay the most and take the risk are like the high bidders in an auction. The problem that has been recognized and treated, if not absolutely solved, by international treaty, is that many Third World countries are not as able to join in the "auction" as are more affluent countries. Here again, the decision has been made to deviate from a simplistic market solution.

A question that arises in virtually all decisions to allocate rights in a way different from the market allocation is whether the recipients of the rights can then resell the rights to the highest bidders. If they can, the eventual outcome in terms of ownership is unlikely to be much different from that resulting from an auction. And whatever positive externalities were behind the initial assignment will be lost. Of course, there are important distributive consequences in that the original recipient of the right will experience an increase in wealth.

D. REACTIONS TO TRANSACTION COSTS AND EXTERNALITIES

A great deal of the regulation encountered on a day by day basis concerns government efforts to respond to transaction costs and externalities. Transaction costs, as discussed in Chapter Three, are the costs of actually making an exchange happen. Transaction costs are not the actual consideration flowing from one party to another, but the costs associated with such things as locating each other, gathering information, negotiating, and drafting the terms of the exchange. High transaction costs may cause otherwise beneficial exchanges not to take place. Sometimes regulations are designed to make transactions smoother or less costly to those involved.

In general, there are three broad areas of responses to transaction costs. The first amounts to setting standards that "rationalize" an industry. The most basic of these rules relates to the assignment and definition of property rights or entitlements. The second general response is to require that information is made available. Third, a great deal of regulation is a direct response to externalities. In each instance, it is important to ask whether the market, left alone, could work around the transaction costs problem and reach an efficient outcome.

This is not to suggest that these responses are found in neat self-contained regulatory compartments. Take, for example, the regulation of drugs. Some drugs are sold without a prescription, some are sold only with a prescription, and some cannot be legally sold at all. From one perspective this classification system creates the standards for drug manufacturers to use in the development of new drugs. They amount to rules or rationalizing devices that indicate what it takes to acquire different levels of marketing rights. The different classifications are valuable sources of information for manufactures, as well as consumers. In addition, consumers benefit from the requirement that certain warnings and information be provided. Finally, a policy designed to keep some drugs off the market entirely can be explained by possible negative externalities.

1. RATIONALIZING AN INDUSTRY

One can garner an understanding of the importance of government regulation as a means of setting up the basic format of a market or an industry by recalling the initial justification for broadcast regulation discussed above. Without an initial assignment of broadcast rights, it is unlikely that anyone could claim the exclusivity that would then permit them to exchange or even use a broadcast frequency successfully. Although there may be a theoretical possibility that all people interested in broadcasting could somehow buy out the claims of other potential broadcasters and set up a system of privately determined property rights, such an effort would be incredibly costly and is subject to major problems of extortion, hold-outs, and enforcement. The industry is made rational or predictable by government intervention which defines the rights involved.

The same sort of thing happens when the government defines what it means to own a patent, copyright, or trademark. Similarly, decisions concerning water rights or whether one has a right to collect damages from a polluting factory establish entitlements that the parties can then exchange. Without this initial entitlement, however, it would be difficult for meaningful exchange to take place.

The rationalizing function can also be seen at work in the context of professional licensing. Imagine, for example, a situation in which an individual needs medical care but lives in a state in which there are no formal licensing procedures. Perhaps anyone could hang out a sign advertising that he or she is offering medical care and use the "M.D." label. In this instance, "M.D." would be a fairly valueless piece of information for the consumer. By permitting only those with a certain level of training or expertise to use the label "M.D." and offer medical care, the government promotes standardization in labeling and makes comparisons more feasible.

2. INCREASING THE AVAILABILITY OF INFORMATION

In the example described above, the regulated use of the label "M.D." rationalized the industry by encouraging standardization. The standardization also carries with it the information that all those calling themselves medical doctors are of a certain quality. Without this standardization and the information about minimum quality standards implicit in the permitted use of the label, consumers concerned about the quality of the training and expertise of potential medical care providers would face incredibly high information costs. These high costs may mean that, in some instances, the consumer makes no choice at all and does not participate in the market. In other instances, the consumer runs the risk of making a poor choice.

The requirement that sellers provide certain types of information—whether it is the nutritional content of foods, the health hazards associated with smoking or drinking, the gas mileage of a new car, or the "plain language" disclosure of credit terms— is no more than a requirement that sellers produce and provide a "product" in the form of information to consumers. The requirement that this service be provided is almost uniformly a reaction to the belief that information would be expensive for the individual consumer to discover and that it enables consumers to make better choices.

As an economic matter, it is important that this requirement have either a desired distributive or allocative consequence. The possible distributive objectives associated with requiring that information be provided are fairly obvious. To the extent the information makes consumers better able to compare producers, market power may be lowered and sellers forced to price more competitively. For example, by reading the label on a can of tuna, a consumer may find that the generic or house brand has the same nutritional qualities as the higher-priced, nationally-advertised brand. When prices are more competitive than they otherwise would be, the distributive impact is in favor of consumers. This is why sellers resist making information available even if it is relatively inexpensive to produce.

This is not to say that the distributive consequences of information requirements exist apart from allocative consequences. In fact, as discussed in Chapter Nine, the elimination of market power has very important allocative effects as well as distributive effects. The fact that the labeling of the cans of tuna means that the market is more competitive also means that prices will be lower, output higher, and the outcome more allocatively efficient. The same reasoning is behind the requirement that the terms of loans be explained fully and in some detail; borrowers are better able to shop for better deals and lenders less able to conceal the fact that money is essentially fungible.

Still, from the standpoint of traditional notions of efficiency, a different focus is useful. The requirement that information be made available really is a requirement that sellers produce and sell information to consumers as a condition of selling the product. In addition, no one should suffer from the illusion that the cost of supplying information will not be treated as a cost of production. Since consumers end up making what amounts to a forced purchase, it is important that the "exchange" be one that might take place if the market for information were perfectly fluid.

This leads to the question of why the information is not viewed as being produced in sufficient quantities without regulation. After all, unlike the distributive justification, the allocative justification lies in the belief that the information is more valuable to buyers than it is to potential sellers. Provision of the information and the resulting adjustments in demand will not happen, however, if there are transaction costs that impede the smooth working of the information market.

An obvious type of transaction cost that impedes the free flow of information is that potential consumers of the information to not know it exists or are unable assess its value. In these instances, the actual demand for the information will understate its value. A good example might be the warnings about the health or safety hazards of various products ranging from cigarettes to athletic equipment. In order to demand the information in efficient quantities, consumers would first have to be "educated" about the existence of the information and its relevance. Having been enlightened about the existence of hypothetically useful information, demand for the information would appear. Of course, this intermediate step would alone require the production of information that consumers may mistakenly undervalue, possibly by discounting the eventual benefits of having access to the information.

But even if they were entirely enlightened about the existence of such information, there may be free-rider problems. For example, if one person bought the information, there is little guarantee that the information could be kept secret. Thus, each potential consumer may simply wait in hopes that the demand of others will result in the production of the information.

The free-riding problem also plays out on the supply side of the market in a different context. Suppose the problem is not one of danger, but of the important properties of a product. Suppose further that, in order to understand these properties, consumers require some basic education. This was the case with respect to R-values on insulation materials.[7] While R-value was a useful way to compare materials, its use required that some basic information be provided. The problem is that any supplier of the information would be unable to capture all the benefits of providing the information; consumers might well use the information and then buy from other producers. The problem is similar to that which would be faced by a composer of music in the absence of copyright protection. The outcome is that it may not be rational for any individual producer to supply information which

7. See Trade Regulation Rules: Labeling and Advertising of Home Insulation, F.T.C., 1979, 44 Fed. Reg. 50218.

actually is of sufficient value to consumers to warrant its production. Required production by all is one solution to this problem.

3. REACTIONS TO EXTERNALITIES

As discussed in Chapter Three, externalities can be either positive or negative. Positive externalities exist when the producer is unable to "internalize" all the benefits of what has been produced. The classic example is that of an inventor who has no control over the use of his invention after it is put into use. Goods or services that are likely to result in positive externalities tend to be produced in inefficiently small quantities because much of the motivation to produce is siphoned off by those who enjoy the benefits without paying. Some possible reactions are to require users to pay for their use through a regime of copyright or patent law or to subsidize the production of the good. As just illustrated in the context of information, another reaction is to require some producers to provide the under-produced good as a condition of operating at all.

Most government regulation, as opposed to subsidization, concerns negative externalites. These are costs of production or consumption that are not borne by the producer or user. The polluting factory and the person smoking a cigarette in a crowded room are good examples. It should be noted that defining something as an externality raises one of the issues addressed here: the factory that emits smoke is only creating an "externality" if the people surrounding the factory have a right to clean air.

A decision that an activity produces an externality sets up a framework in which the "offending" party can buy the right to continue his activity. It also creates a situation in which the injured parties can vindicate their property rights by seeking compensation or injunctive relief. In these situations, which are discussed in Chapters Three and Four, the private party is permitted to sell her right or entitlement.

In this section, the focus is on action that not only assigns the right, but preemptively protects the right by banning activity that may interfere with it. In effect, the right cannot be sold—voluntarily or involuntarily—by the owner. A good example of this is the requirement that certain safety features be incorporated into new cars. The buyer has, in a sense, the right to buy a car that complies with certain safety standards. On the other hand, she is not permitted to sell that right back to the manufacturer and buy a less safe car at a lower price. Other examples include workplace safety, meat inspection, and prescription drug effectiveness.

Before examining some specifics it is useful to note that in these situations two less restrictive regulatory possibilities are passed up. The first, as already noted, is to permit the buyer to sell her "right" to the safe car or safe workplace. The second is to provide information about the product or service to the consumer and allow the consumer to adjust demand accordingly.

The important question is why go further than defining the rights, making information available, and allowing the parties to express their preferences in the market? Perhaps some people would prefer automobiles without air bags and seat belts at lower prices than they must pay for automobiles equipped with these features. Perhaps some people are also willing to take their chances with drugs that have not been proven to be "safe and effective." From the standpoint of economics, regulations that go further than these alternatives make sense only if they result in a better allocative or distributive outcome.

One strong possibility is that owners are prevented from selling rights that they may tend to undervalue. This may be the justification for safety standards in the workplace and in the manufacture of automobiles as well as in the case of the application of building codes. For example, suppose workers were assigned the right to safe working conditions and these rights could be sold; employers could offer higher wages for working in hazardous conditions. It is possible that these "rights" are actually more valuable than the potential sellers realize, so much so that it would be allocatively inefficient for the rights to be sold. You might argue that workers with accurate information will not tend to undervalue these rights. Technically this may be correct, but efforts to inform workers so thoroughly that they will make the right valuation may be more expensive than simply preventing the sale of these rights in the first place.

In other instances, like automobile safety features, there may be important benefits to third parties associated with the regulation. For example, potential victims of accidents may benefit from better braking systems and better visibility. The features may be undervalued by buyers because the benefits of the features do not accrue to buyers alone. At the same time, huge transaction costs preclude translating these third party benefits into market demand.

While potential mistakes in valuation explain some regulations, distributive goals are also relevant. General requirements about minimum product quality or workplace safety standards can be seen as ways of favoring purchasers or workers with respect to the terms of the exchange. In other words, they are presumably made better off at the expense of the other party. Just how effectively distributive goals can be achieved through regulations forcing one party to internalize a cost is open to question.

For example, in Figure 4, the Y axis is the cost of labor and the X axis is units of labor. D_1 is the demand for labor before a factory is required to install an air filter and other safety devices. It is important to remember that the demand curve shows the most the firm is willing to pay for each quantity of labor. S is the supply of labor. The cost of labor and the wage paid is equal to W_1. The

installation of the equipment is viewed by the owners of the factory as another cost of using labor and
in that regard this cost is indistinguishable from the
payment of wages. The fact that some labor cost is
now used to improve working conditions does not
alter the amount the firm is willing to pay for each
quantity of labor.

Figure 4

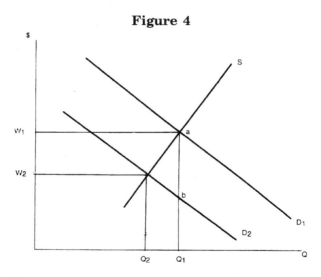

There is a difference between the amount the
firm is willing to pay for each quantity of labor and
what it is willing to pay in the form of wages. This
means there is a new demand curve that shows the
maximum wage the firm is willing to offer for each
quantity of labor. This is D_2 in the graph. The
vertical distance between D_1 and D_2 (ab in the
graph) is the cost of the safety measures.

The new wage is determined by the intersection of D_2 and S and indicates that wages will fall from the initial level to W_2. In addition, the quantity of labor employed has dropped from Q_1 to Q_2. Thus, although the workers still employed may enjoy a safer workplace, it has come at a price to them in terms of wages and employment opportunities. Clearly, the distributive impact is not as simple as adding better working conditions to the value of existing wages.

This does not mean that this effort to achieve distributive ends through the control of externalities must fail. First, although wages fall, they do not fall by as much as the total cost of the safety measures. One can see this by comparing the difference between W_1 and W_2—the wage decrease—with the vertical distance between D_1 and D_2—the cost of the safety measures. The amount of the cost of the safety measures that will be passed on to workers in the form of lower wages will vary depending on the relative elasticities of demand and supply.

Second, the simplistic model used here and favored by conventional economists does not allow for the fact that workers may become more productive with safer working conditions. Consequently, demand may not change at all. Third, demand and supply models like that in Figure 4 are not representative of labor markets in which employers have monopsony power (power on the buying side of the market). In these markets, the forced increase in compensation may not lead to lower wages or lower levels of employment.[8] Third, safety regulations like those discussed here may be beneficial to both parties. For example, workers may prefer better working conditions over higher wages, and employers may prefer to offer better working conditions and lower wages, but transaction costs have prevented the exchange. Still, there is the strong possibility that desired distributive outcomes will be difficult to achieve.

The final reason for prohibiting some activities because of external effects deserves more than the passing mention it gets here. It is illustrated by regulations that prohibit activity that endangers a species of animal or its habitat. In effect, these regulations grant a "right" to exist to the species or at least to those who favor preservation. The negative externality is the elimination of the animal. If left to the market and the judicial system, the problem becomes one of measuring the damages associated with the destruction of the species. In fact, some would argue that the "damages" are immeasurable.[9] Clearly, the preferences of those currently wanting to preserve the species and those who will live in the future and might wish that the species had been preserved will be drastically understated in the market due to transaction costs. But much of this may miss the point. Here the step of preemptively protecting the right seems to flow

8. Jeffrey L. Harrison, "The New Terminable-at-Will Employment Contract: An Interest and Cost Incidence Analysis," 69 *Iowa L. Rev.* 327, 340–42 (1984).

9. See *Tennessee Valley Authority v. Hill*, 437 U.S. 153 (1978).

not so much from the sense that, if left to the market, it will not be protected at economically efficient levels. Instead, the right to be protected transcends traditional economic measures.

E. SOCIAL JUSTICE REGULATIONS

Many regulations seem impossible to square with conventional notions of efficiency. Instead, these regulations exist as a result of a sense of injustice and an effort to correct that injustice. This does not mean that economic analysis is irrelevant, for a number of reasons. First, much of the search for justice really means "economic justice" or the feeling that individuals are economically better off. This usually means there is a redistributive objective. Second, there is a cost associated with most efforts to adjust market outcomes to achieve just outcomes. Third, a decision must be made about who will pay the cost of increased social justice. Finally, the objectives of justice and efficiency are not necessarily inconsistent. For example, think about even the most expensive plan of redistribution you can imagine. As long as those who benefit directly from the plan and others who favor it could compensate those who are made worse off, the plan is Kaldor–Hicks efficient.

A great many social justice regulations fit into one of two categories. The first category includes those instances in which equally productive people are discriminated against. This is likely to be the case when gender or racial discrimination is involved. Here, if employers simply keep their eye on the bottom line of profitability, the discrimination should eventually disappear. For example, if employers discriminate against women who are just as productive as men by not hiring them, there will be an excess of women in the labor market. The excess will drive the wages of women down and the wages of men up. Employers hiring women would eventually experience lower costs of production and be able to increase profits and sales. Those firms continuing to discriminate would either fold or catch on in order to survive. In effect, the employer who discriminates on the basis of race or gender has an expensive habit that is inconsistent with maximizing profits.

If the market will cure gender and racial job discrimination, why is any regulation necessary? The principle reason is that markets work slowly and may bog down. For example, suppose labor costs are a small part of the costs of production. In those instances, employers who discriminate may not get the message for some time. Or, if an employer has market power, he may not feel great pressure to overcome his workforce preferences. In addition, a history of discrimination may affect the training (human capital) certain groups acquire as well as their aspirations. By not acquiring the same training as men due to the perception that men's jobs are closed to them, the productivity of women may remain lower, but not for reasons that have to do with gender per se. The point is that regulations can require employers to act as though markets are working effectively, and the eventual outcome may be greater equality and efficiency.

Perhaps more interesting are regulations that require employers to ignore what the market would dictate. A good example is the Americans with Disabilities Act. The Act is quite complex but basically prohibits discrimination based on disability as long as the disabled person can, either with or without a reasonable accommodation, perform the essential functions of the job. The concept of "reasonable" under the Act does *not* mean "cost-justified." In other words, an employer cannot avoid the responsibility by showing that the accommodation is more expensive than the productivity gains. In economic terms, employers are required to hire and subsidize workers who, from one perspective, actually make the firm less profitable than it would otherwise be. Of course, the presence of those with disabilities may increase the morale of the workforce or have some other beneficial effect that turns out to be profitable. This is not, however, the goal. A cap on the subsidization is provided by the stipulation that employers need not undergo "undue hardship."

There are obviously great benefits associated with hiring the disabled. Aside from the impact it may have on self-esteem, the likelihood is that dependence on the government will be reduced if more disabled individuals are employed. There are, in fact, two possibilities. One is that the regulation is Kaldor–Hicks efficient. Benefits accruing to the disabled and their relatives, co-workers, and society in general as a result of a sense of living in a more just world may exceed the costs to employers. On the other hand, it may not be Kaldor–Hicks efficient but perhaps justified on more philosophical grounds. Even if this is the case, the costs are probably relevant if for no other reason than to determine whether the same benefits might be achieved at a lower cost or whether greater justice could be achieved at the same cost.

Economics also enters the picture when determining how to finance efforts to achieve social justice. Under the ADA, the costs of accommodation will be shared by the firm's customers and shareholders. Whether the cost should be shared more generally by all taxpayers who favor the subsidy is another possibility, and it may actually lower the costs—as far as utility goes—if these costs are more broadly distributed.

F. REGULATION AND HAPPINESS

For about twenty years economists, sociologists, and psychologists have focused on the factors that explain actual happiness. This has lead, in turn, to a consideration of how regulatory efforts might be designed to emphasize happiness as opposed to economic efficiency.[10] This is an important, albeit new, area of study because increasingly it appears that wealth and happiness do not necessarily run hand in hand. In fact, you probably know very wealthy and successful people who are not happy and other

10. See e.g. Cass Sunstein & Richard Thaler, Nudge (2008); Derek Bok, The Politics of Happiness (2010).

less wealthy and successful people who seem quite satisfied. One way to think about this is that preferences people are willing and able to express in markets may not ultimately maximize happiness Similarly, regulatory efforts that focus on conventional economic analysis may not advance happiness.

As noted in Chapter 1, the introduction of happiness into the analysis of what government should do is a complicated matter. For example, should the goal be to maximize measures of objective well-being or subjective ones. The problem is that some things that make people feel happy or better off are actually harmful in a more objective sense. There is also the issue of balancing current and future happiness. Or, is the relevant happiness how one feels when undergoing an experience or how one feels about it later. In short, the goal of maximizing happiness is a laudable one but difficult.

Still one can fairly easily imagine places where happiness could enter into the analysis. For example, the fact that some people may not be able to afford the basics of life can be interpreted as an indication that it is inefficient not to provide these things to the needy. If one switches from desires as expressed in the market to increased happiness, the rationale for providing these basics become clear. In particular, "life line" rates can be viewed as inefficient if the price charged is below marginal cost. On the other hand, when actual happiness or satisfaction is accounted for, life line rates are far easier to justify.

As another example, consider airline deregulation. Presumable deregulation was undertaken to increase welfare. On the other hand, think about air travel today. Are you enjoying it? Even the chief architect of airline deregulation observed a few years after the fact, "Most of us probably did not foresee the deterioration in the average quality of the flying experience, and in particular the congestion and delays that have plagued air travelers in recent years.[11] The point is that much of regulation and deregulation seems disconnected from how people actually feel.

Obviously, the slippage between choices people make and government regulation and how happy people actually end up being can be traced to the inability to assess how individuals will feel in the future. If this is the case one could argue for greater regulation that encourages the provision of information. In effect, advertising might include not just the benefits of a particular experience but routine ratings by those who have undergone the experience. Interesting this is currently the case with respect to many on-line services ranging from Trip Advisor to Amazon. First person reports assist current decision-makers to make wiser choices.

Some aspects of happiness probably lie outside anything most governments can influence. For example, it appears that people are happier when they feel they are treated fairly, when they feel that have

11. Alfred Kahn, The Surprises of Airline Deregulation, 78 Papers and Proceedings of the One–Hundredth annual Meeting of the American Economic Association 316, 320 (May, 1988).

some direct input into government, have significant social contact, and engage in acts of kindness themselves. The potential for government regulation to be increasingly focused on actual well-being as opposed to the well-being associated with standard cost-benefit analysis is something which will be much more accurately assessed over the coming decades.

CHAPTER ELEVEN

INTELLECTUAL PROPERTY

Interest in intellectual property law has exploded in recent years, and it is an area that is readily amenable to economic analysis. Interestingly, the area has not been the subject of as much scrutiny from an economic perspective as others discussed in this book. This may be because copyright and patent law, in particular, are very complex and may be viewed as the domain of creative and eccentric people. Since the law and economics of intellectual property can be linked to antitrust law and economics, we are likely to see more analysis of this field. This chapter is limited to patent, copyright, and trademark law. Much of the analysis can be carried over to the law of trade secrets as well as state common law intellectual property doctrines.

Before starting, a cautionary note is in order. After reading about the costs of monopolies in Chapter Nine, you may wonder why the government would set up systems to protect intellectual property and seem to grant the owners monopoly power. If that was your line of thinking, you have fallen into a common misperception. Patent, copyright, and trademark law do not in and of themselves result in market power. They do, as you know, afford owners a right of exclusive use, but that does not mean that owners will reap monopoly power unless the underlying property has consumer appeal. To understand this, think of the last illustration that you saw on a restaurant napkin. In all likelihood it was copyrighted, but there are probably thousands of illustrations that would serve the same purpose. The point is that patent, copyright, and trademark define property rights and limit access to private property. In many cases they are necessary but not sufficient to create monopoly power.

A. THE ECONOMIC RATIONALE

There are a variety of theories or rationales for the development of a system of intellectual property. The economic approach, however, principally centers around the idea of providing incentives. This is captured by the Supreme Court in *Mazer v. Stein*, a landmark copyright decision: "The economic philosophy behind ... patents and copyrights is the conviction that encouragement of individual effort by personal gain is the best way to advance public welfare through the talents of authors and inventors...." (347 U.S. at 219 (1954)).

In many respects, this is no different from the economic logic for defining any kind of property right. For example, suppose you "own" a plot of excellent land that is great for grazing cattle, but you cannot erect a fence. Not only that, you cannot enjoin others from entering or even expect to collect damages if their cattle come onto your land to sample the fare there. You are likely to find that your land is not worth very much, and you would be foolish to invest in finding and cultivating the best quality grazing area. Just shift the idea to a useful device, a well-done photograph, or the name of a product you are attempting to promote. Now suppose anyone who would like to can take your device, figure out how it works, and manufacture his or her own. Or, having taken your photograph, suppose anyone who wants to can reproduce it and call it his or her own. Finally, suppose you develop a chain of restaurants that bear the name "Joe's Chop House," and you strive for uniformity and quality, but anyone who cares to can call his or her restaurant "Joe's Chop House." In all these cases—patent, copyright, and trademark—you are a victim of free-riding. In other words, you may be unable to fully internalize the gains from your efforts. If you are unable to profit from your efforts, you are less likely invest in those efforts in the first place. This is why you often hear the argument that pharmaceutical manufacturers need patent protection in order to justify high research and development expenses.

This is the problem, but in order to justify a public system of intellectual property you must also consider whether a private system is practical or less expensive. For example, every person who comes into your art gallery could be required to sign a contract in which he or she promises not to make copies of what was displayed there. The transaction costs here would be high, and it does not take long to realize that the costs of operating a system that protects intellectual property are probably lower if it is publicly maintained.

This basic incentive rationale applies to patent, copyright, and trademark, but there are important differences. Both patent and copyright are designed to reward those who create something new. They are similar in this respect but different in another. For a device or process to be patentable, it must be novel, meaning the first. In copyright, the protection is for something that is original. This does not mean that it must be the first, but it must not be copied. For example, a person who writes a poem that is the same as one already copyrighted would not be guilty of an infringement if he or she had not actually copied the first version.

Trademark is a somewhat different matter and works on a broader scale. The goal is to reduce transaction costs by reducing confusion—specifically, the costs buyers face in identifying the source of products and the confusion if one seller attempts to "pass off" his product as that of another seller. For example, if you had a great meal at Joe's Chop Shop, which happens to serve the best soy chops around, you would probably like to repeat the experience. If everyone could use Joe's Chop Shop as the name of his or her restaurant, the problem for you would be obvious. Of course, the original Joe's could begin calling itself "The Original Joe's Chop Shop" but you can see that this would ultimately not do much good.

Despite these differences, the same issues affect all intellectual property. The questions are: how broad is the protection and how long should it be? Going back to the example of the cattle ranch, the issue can be visualized as one of determining the boundaries around one's property. In the context of intellectual property, one can see the process as putting a fence around an idea. There can be narrow protection, in which only exact copies might be viewed as infringing, or broad protection, in which the inventor or author is protected from those who do not make exact copies. In addition, protection can be defined in terms of duration. In patent and copyright the duration is in years while a trademark is lost when it is abandoned. Longer protection is obviously comparable to owning more property.

Although the notion of property ownership generally can be seen as an economic device for reducing uncertainty, allowing exchange, and creating incentives, the rationale for most property ownership doctrines also lie in history and tradition. From an economic standpoint, however, a system of intellectual property exists and is designed to increase social welfare. In essence, people are permitted to create and claim certain property rights as long as the net effect is socially beneficial.

Social welfare, in the instance of intellectual property, involves a tradeoff. The tradeoff is between the benefits derived from creative efforts and the costs resulting from exclusivity and the operation of a system of intellectual property protection.[1] Some of the costs of exclusivity are related to possible market power. For example, a powerful new drug may be very expensive due to the inventor's monopoly. Other exclusivity costs are related to challenges to other creative people whose costs of creativity go up because they cannot make use of ideas claimed first by others. Finally, there is a cost of administering the intellectual property system. This cost of administration includes a great deal of activity that has little to do with innovation but with dividing up of the profits from innovation.[2]

From the standpoint of economic theory, and perhaps only from that standpoint, the breadth of protection is determined by balancing costs of protection against the social benefits.[3] In fact, a number of the doctrines that define the breadth of protection can be reconciled with an effort to strike an efficient balance.

B. LIMITING PROTECTION

A challenge that arises in patent, copyright, and trademark is defining just what is protected. Although governed by different doctrines, the basic

1. See generally, William M. Landes & Richard A. Posner "An Economic Analysis of Copyright Law," XVIII *J. Leg. Stud.* 325 (1989).

2. See Jeffrey L. Harrison, "Rationalizing the Allocative/Distributive Relationship in Copyright," 32 *Hofstra L. Rev.* 853 (2004).

3. See Jeffrey L. Harrison, "A Positive Externalities Approach to Copyright Law: Theory and Application," 13 J. *Intell. Prop. L.* 1 (2005).

idea is not to extend protection so far that it grants more exclusivity than is necessary. In copyright this is captured by the notion that one can copyright an original expression of an idea but not the idea itself. For example, suppose you had the idea to paint a picture of a dog running through a field of wheat. Your concept would not be protected, but your execution of the idea on canvas would be, subject to exceptions too numerous to discuss here. Similarly, one may not copyright facts no matter how much work was involved in discovering them.

The economic rationale for this distinction—between ideas and facts as opposed to expression—is fairly obvious. First, to allow you to have exclusive rights to the painting of dogs running through fields is likely to be much broader protection than necessary to bring forth your painting. In effect, the protection would be inefficiently broad. Second, assessing whether there has been infringement of an idea as opposed to an expression is likely to be a complicated and expensive task. For example, suppose someone paints a dog running through a corn field with a fence around it and a car and Lou Reed, both sitting on cinder blocks, in the middle. Would that be an infringement? The point is that it is a simpler—but by no means simple—matter to examine your actual expression and determine whether it has been copied than it is to define your idea and then assess whether it has been copied. If ideas were protected, the costs of exclusivity and administration would almost certainly outweigh the benefits. In the existing system, costs of administration are further reduced by the requirement that the expression must be "fixed" in order to be copyrightable.

A similar theme is found in patent law with the requirement that patents are available only in the case of "any new and useful process, machine, manufacture or composition of matter." As in copyright, an idea or concept is not patentable. In addition, unlike copyright, patent law includes a utility requirement. One may take an idea and from there create something that is novel and useful, but the protection extends only to that which is created and does not relate back to the idea itself. From an economic standpoint this limits the amount of exclusivity granted and lowers costs of administration.

In trademark, a similar objective is approached by allowing the owner of the mark to identify a specific source but not to extend to a broader or more generic claim. The critical concern is that the mark distinguish one seller from another. For example, "Bill's Best Hamburgers," distinguishes one provider. On the other hand, granting trademark protection to "Hamburgers" has an effect similar to the impact of allowing an idea to be copyrighted or patented: it would allow the user an unnecessary measure of monopoly power and raise the costs to competitors who also sell hamburgers. This is not to say that trademarks may not be descriptive, but they must also have what is called a secondary meaning that distinguishes a specific supplier.

C. STRIKING THE BALANCE

The doctrines discussed above are, from an economic perceptive, the measures through which holders of intellectual property are prevented from preempting entire areas. Aside from these broad limitations, there are numerous other rules, requirements, and exceptions that play a role in the balancing process. This is not to suggest that all of these measures can be explained by reference to efficiency. In fact, one reading of the Copyright Act of 1976 reveals that far more than efficiency, the underlying motivations are about distributive outcomes. Still, it makes sense to examine how economic analysis can be applied to some of the more important doctrines.

1. THE DOCTRINE OF EQUIVALENTS

As you would expect, it is relatively easy to establish a patent infringement when the infringer has exactly duplicated the patented device or process. More difficult is the softer analysis that must take place when there is not literal duplication but a great deal of similarity. This is where the doctrine of equivalents comes into play. The issue arises in the context of an infringement action when the alleged infringement is not exactly the same as the patented process. In effect, the question is just how close one may come to the original before it is viewed as an infringement. Ultimately, the decision determines how far a patent holder's property right extends.

The larger economic importance of this decision should not be understated.[4] You can understand this if you take the perspective of the party who comes into a field of research after the original patent is granted and thinks about the way research investment might be most efficiently directed. Broad protection of the original patent will discourage investment that runs the risk of being too close to the original. This may seem like a good idea. It will force competitors to concentrate efforts on inventions that are true breakthroughs. In addition, the patent holder will have an incentive to make improvements to the original work without the risk of losing the gains to a second comer who makes slight changes. On the other hand, perhaps there are small and important improvements that could be made and which have not been undertaken by the patentee. If so, broad protection may allow the original work to stagnate.

Narrow protection, on the other hand, encourages investment in research that may be very similar to that which led to the patented work. This may mean that research investment is channeled away from "breakthroughs" that will seem relatively risky. Some small improvements may only be product differentiation improvements with little social value. On the other hand, if the incumbent is enjoying monopoly position, narrow protection is advantageous to consumers because it lowers entry barriers and may mean lower prices.

4. See Hilton Davis Chemical Co. v. Warner–Jenkinson Co., Inc., 62 F.3d 1512 (Fed.Cir.1995).

2. FAIR USE

Within copyright law, probably no doctrine has been scrutinized more closely than fair use. Unlike the doctrine of equivalents, a fair use analysis takes place after it is determined that the copying would otherwise be an infringement. It is a defense. Like the doctrine of equivalents, the process is one of defining the limits of one's property rights.

A fair use analysis involves weighing four factors. First is the "purpose and character of the use." A relevant distinction here is whether the use is educational or commercial. An additional inquiry is whether the use is transformative. In general terms, if someone is permitted to copy the work of someone else it is more likely to be a fair use if something new is created. The second factor is the nature of the original work. Creative works, as opposed to those based primarily on fact, are likely to be afforded greater protection, and a fair use defense will be more difficult to mount. A third factor is the amount of the original work that is used relative to the whole. Copying should be no greater than necessary to serve the new work's purpose. Moreover, as the amount of copying increases, the character of the new work should be of greater importance. The fourth factor is the impact on the value of the original work. The greater the impact, all other thing being equal, the less likely that the use is "fair."

The radical nature of fair use can be understood by comparing it to patent law, which has no similar doctrine. In effect, fair use says that you may, in some circumstances, copy the work of another and make adjustments to it in order to produce a new work. In patent law this would be like permitting an inventor to copy the work of another inventor and then employ a defense that the new product is socially useful and did no great harm to the original inventor. Or, in the conventional grazing example, it would be similar to but not quite the same as being required to allow others the use of your land as long as they have a socially beneficial use. The extreme nature of the exemption can also be understood by noting how much further it goes than a liability rule. That is, in the land example, a person could make an involuntary transfer (trespass) and pay the fair market value. In fair use the user does not pay fair market value. In effect, the copyright is limited in the first place.

There are a number of ways to square fair use with efficiency. In some instances, a user might be willing to pay and the copyright holder willing to accept a fee for the use, but transaction costs are so high that the exchange is impractical. Fair use here is Kaldor–Hicks efficient. The transaction cost possibility extends beyond just the obvious one-to-one relationship. For example, suppose consumers value the work of a book, film, or play reviewer and that an effective review requires copying some portion of the original. The value of the information and, thus, an informative review may exceed the value the copyright holder places on continued exclusivity. Here, free-riding and transaction costs may prevent the reviewer from generating enough revenue from his or her own work to pay the copyright holder's asking price. Here again, fair use may lead to a Kaldor–Hicks efficient outcome.

One implication of the transaction costs justification for a fair use defense would be that the defense would not be available when transaction costs are low. This is not, however, how cases have been decided. Repeatedly, defendants have successfully employed fair use as a defense even when transaction costs are low. Conversely, the fact that transactions costs are high does not work in the favor of the infringer. For example, a bar band in, say, Archer, Florida covering a Lucinda Williams song will not be able to assert as part of its fair use defense that the cost of contacting and negotiating with Williams far exceeded any benefits derived from performing the work.

Another possibility is that transaction costs are low but that copyright holders possess a level of monopoly power. The demand for a high licensing fee would exacerbate the transaction cost problem described above by further decreasing the likelihood that the second user will be able to pay the copyright holder's asking price. Also, the asking price may be inflated if the copyright holder anticipates the copying is part of direct criticism or parody. In fact, the elevated price may be of a predatory nature since it is driven by a desire to limit consumer information that might undermine the copyright holder's market power. In all these instances, fair use may allow the original work to be used in ways that are socially beneficial but which would not take place if a transaction were required.

In fact, many instances in which fair use is employed can be explained by a sense that the copying party will put the copyrighted work to a better use. When the "better use" is not reflected in economic terms, the fair use exception permits that use to take place nonetheless. This might be the case when the purposes are primarily educational.

What is most difficult to fit into an efficiency framework are instances in which transaction costs are low, the copier's use is for commercial purposes, and there is little or no critical element in the second work. In some of these instances the fair use defense is unavailable, but not always. A case to examine from this perspective is *Campbell v. Acuff–Rose Music, Inc.*, a 1994 Supreme Court decision, in which the rap group Two Live Crew recorded a parody of "Pretty Woman" after attempting to purchase the right to do so. That case can be explained by the monopoly/predatory price rationale discussed above, but it seems unlikely that the owner of Pretty Women was worried about the impact its use by a rap group would have on Pretty Women fans. Still, even when the three conditions—low transaction costs, commercial use, no critical element— exist, it still may make economic sense to permit fair use. First, the copyright holder cannot claim that the original creation was motivated by a use he or she had intended to exploit. Thus, fair use has no adverse incentive effect. In addition, from a Paretian perspective, the copyright owner suffers no harm while society and the copying party are made better off.

In instances like the one discussed above, it is tempting to argue that the fair use defense amounts to a redistribution from the owner of the original work to the infringer. This is probably incorrect. First, if the derivative work is one that would not have been anticipated by the owner, it is difficult to see wealth as having been taken from one party and distributed to the second one as opposed to new wealth simply being created by the second party. Second, the notion of a redistribution presupposes that the owner of the original work possessed something in the first place. As a technical matter, the copyright owner never possessed the right to block what is fair use. Thus, there is no redistribution. Granted, there is some circularity in this reasoning, but it is important to keep in mind that intellectual property is a legislative creation, and one cannot lose what the legislature did not grant in the first place.

D. DURATION

Part of the definition of one's intellectual property rights lies in the length of time for which those rights exist. From the standpoint of investment, the longer the term, the greater the likely return and the higher the amount of investment. Thus, as a matter of economic analysis, the balance struck is between the increased incentive effects and the additional costs of exclusivity and administration resulting from additional years. There is not a single term that maximizes efficiency across all areas of inventiveness and creativity. In addition, there is a tendency to overstate the impact of distant earnings on current investment. This is because earnings that accrue fifteen or twenty years hence must be discounted quite heavily to present value in order to be compared with current research dollars.

On the other hand, duration is still important to those considering creative effort investments and to those who hold existing patents and copyrights. In fact, for those holding existing patents and copyrights, a term extension, unless anticipated at the time the rights were purchased, can be viewed as a windfall. This does not make the additional income less attractive to those holding current rights, but it does weaken the incentive rationale for extending the term of existing intellectual property. This is a matter that will be discussed more fully below, but first it is important note that trademark terms work differently from copyright and patent terms and that the trademark approach may make more economic sense.

While patent and copyright terms are of fixed duration, the right to a trademark can last indefinitely depending on use by the owner. The indefinite duration seems harmless given the infinite number of potential trademarks. The right to the trade mark ends when the mark is abandoned either intentionally or by actions, or the lack thereof, that cause the mark to lose its distinctiveness. In effect, the loss of the right to the mark ties in with the rationale for trademark in the first place. When the mark loses its effectiveness as a way to lower search costs for consumers, the mark is abandoned.

As already noted, fixed terms are rather arbitrary. There seems to be constant political pressure to extend terms by those who stand to benefit. Recently the issue of term extension was addressed by the Supreme Court in *Eldred v. Ashcroft*, 537 U.S. 186 (2003). The Court examined the Copyright Term Extension Act of 1998 which had the effect of extending most copyright terms from the life of the author plus 50 years to the life of the author plus 70 years. The specific question was whether the extension could be retroactive. Part of the Court's analysis dealt with the economic incentive issues. The problem with a retroactive extension is that it cannot easily be said to be responsible for works already in existence. Thus, to the extent that the Constitutional provision authorizing patent and copyright law seems to call for a functional or utilitarian approach to term lengths, retroactive extension would appear to be off-limits.

Rather than deny the functional goals of term duration, the Court sought to reconcile approval of retroactive extension with providing incentives even in the case of works already in existence. The reasoning offered by the Court was that term extensions had always been retroactive. Thus, when the implicit bargain was struck between those investing in creative efforts and the public, it was understood that the inventors or authors would receive the benefit of the existing term and any extensions that might take place during that term. In effect, retroactive extension was part of a bargain that had already been struck, and Congress, by making the extension retroactive, was merely holding up its end of the bargain. In other words, the calculating author or inventor of 1940 or the parties acquiring the rights to protected works would figure into their future income stream any income likely to be earned during the current term plus some figure for additional years if and when Congress decided to extend the term.

E. REMEDIES

Like most rights, copyrighted and patented works as well as trademarks could be protected by liability rules, property rules, or rules of inalienability.[5] None of the rationales for inalienability, however, apply very easily to property that comes about as a form of investment, so that possibility is largely irrelevant.

As you recall, in a general sense, liability rules may work better from an economic standpoint when transactions costs are high relative to the gains from the exchange and property rules are preferred when transaction costs are low relative to the gains from the exchange. Although it is a broad generalization, intellectual property often is, when compared to typical high transaction cost contexts, a

5. A thorough analysis is found at Roger D. Blair & Thomas F. Cotter, "An Economic Analysis of Damages Rules in Intellectual Property Law," 39 *Wm. & Mary L. Rev.* 1585 (1998).

domain of relatively low transactions costs. Most owners of intellectual property rights are anxious to make their identities known and to inform potential infringers that the rights are already claimed.

Under a liability rule, an infringer would essentially be able to force a sale of a license. In theory, the infringer who was able to make a more profitable use of the work could use the work and pay damages to the owner at an amount less than that earned by the infringement. The analysis is similar to the efficient breach of contract. The same questions about the efficiency of a contract breach can be raised with respect to the efficient infringement. In effect, are the damages set high enough that the person whose property right has been violated is left in a position that is no worse? The problem is that damages equal to fair market value may not serve this function. In effect, there is no guarantee than an infringement will be Pareto Superior or Kaldor–Hicks efficient. Another element of liability rule protection ties to the issue of incentives. Incentives are likely to be higher if the owner is able to fully internalize the gains generated by the work. It is interesting to note that some copyrighted works are subject to compulsory licensing which is not unlike a liability rule and may involve the same inefficiencies. The possibility of an involuntary exchange and an award of damages can only reduce the incentives created by intellectual property law. A property rule, on the other hand, requires a voluntary exchange, and the outcome should be Pareto and Kaldor–Hicks efficient.

All three regimes of intellectual property examined here permit a plaintiff to obtain injunctive relief and, thus, have elements of a property rule. Beyond that, there is an important difference that bears on the analysis. An infringing party in the case of both copyright and trademark can be liable for damages and any gains resulting from the infringement. In effect, there is a possibility of disgorgement of the gains. For example, an infringing party that uses a copyrighted song in a Broadway show would be liable for the portion of the profits generated by the show that were attributed to the song that was used without permission. This allocation is not an easy process, but it is still a far cry from patent law, at least as the law is written. In patent law, the owner is entitled to damages that are no less than an established or reasonable royalty. At least expressly, disgorgement is not possible.

The different between copyright and trademark, on the one hand, and patent, on the other, is fairly extreme. Patent law remedies reflect a liability rule approach in that the infringer is liable for the fair market value. The possibility of "efficient infringement" is, therefore, a real one, except that some courts are quite generous with awards with the possibility that they approach disgorgement levels. In addition, the authority of the courts to award treble damages, to the extent the power is used, offsets the liability rule-like nature of patent remedies.

As a result of the disgorgement possibilities in the context of copyright and trademark, the remedies come closer to a property rule regime in their effect because they tend to channel secondary users into voluntary transactions. This is because if detection were 100%, the potential infringer would be faced with disgorging all the gains made possible by the infringement or entering into a transaction that would likely permit him or her to keep at least a portion of the gains. Obviously, detection is not 100% which indicates that some kind of punitive damages would be appropriate to raise the expected costs of infringement. Copyright law does provide enhanced damages when a plaintiff is awarded statutory as opposed to actual damages, but there is no express provision for punitive damages.

The overriding question is which is the more appropriate regime for intellectual property? In the context of providing maximum incentives for creativity, the key element is the ability of the creative or inventive person to capture all the rewards for his or her efforts. A system that allows for efficient infringement by allowing damages equal to the owner's losses falls short of this goal, and, perhaps more importantly, does not assure that use by the infringing party is the more efficient one. The efficiency of property or disgorgement rules are, however, affected by transaction costs and bilateral monopoly problems which may mean that efficient uses are not realized.

In the context of copyright, most of the remedies analysis must be viewed in the context of fair use which can be analogized to compulsory licensing at no price. There is no particular guarantee that the fair users are more efficient users. In fact, the use of another's work can be viewed as having a variety of prices ranging from zero, in the case of fair use, to disgorgement. In between are prices established by compulsory licenses. Any comprehensive view of efficiency would have to account for all these possibilities.

CHAPTER TWELVE

THE EVOLUTION OF LAW

As you know, law tends to evolve. It may be slow and haphazard, but it obviously changes from era to era. When statutory law changes, the process tends to be relatively clear. Common law is different. Unlike statutory law, a judge cannot decide one day that the law of torts or contracts needs to be changed and then write an opinion changing it. For one thing, because 95% of cases settle, judges do not see all the opportunities for change. Second, the cases and issues the judges do address are selected by private parties.

This all leads to a number of interesting questions that have intrigued scholars for the last forty years: Do the cases that parties choose to try and even press to appeal share common characteristics that are somehow different, at least in some respects, from the general run of cases? If so, do these cases follow a predictable path toward more efficient rules? Is there an economic explanation for the process itself?

A. THE EVOLUTIONARY PROCESS

A discussion of how law may evolve to be efficient

starts with the pioneering efforts of Paul Rubin[1]
and George Priest.[2] The theory is that the rules
that are most frequently challenged by private parties are inefficient rules. Consequently, the issues
that trial and appellate judges will be asked to
address are largely ones that deal with some form of
inefficiency. This leads to an evolutionary process
toward efficient rules. And, since inefficient rules
are more likely to be challenged, once a rule is
efficient, it is less likely to come back to a court for
review.

So, how does this work? A numerical example will
help you understand what is meant by an inefficient
rule. Suppose you own a restaurant and once in a
while someone slips on spilled water. The current
rule is that owners are liable for any injury resulting from falls inside restaurants. On average, you
have one slip every other month that costs about
$40,000 for a total annual average of $240,000. You
pay the damages because you have discovered that
it would cost you $300,000 a year to hire extra
personnel to keep an eye on the floors all the hours
you are open. On the other hand, slips could be
avoided if customers were a little more careful—by
walking a little slower. The total value of the lost
time (from moving slower) per year is $60,000. As
you know from the Chapter 6, or from common
sense, a rule that requires you to pay $240,000 a

1. Paul H. Rubin, "Why is the Common Law Efficient?" 6 *J.
Leg. Stud.* 51 (Jan. 1977).

2. George L. Priest, "The Common Law Process and the
Selection of Efficient Rules," 6 *J. Leg. Stud.* 65 (Jan. 1977).

year for damages that could be avoided for $60,000 is inefficient.

To understand why you—the restaurant owner—would be inclined to go to trial, suppose someone slips and falls on a very obvious wet spot on the floor and claims damages of $40,000. The trial would cost you $5,000. What happens if you go to trial? You will probably lose the case, but there is some slight chance that the court will change to a rule that says you are not liable for slips caused by obvious wet spots. Let's say that without that change there is a 25% chance you will win based on some factual dispute. Without regard for the benefits of a rule change, the value of the case[3] to you is a *loss* of $35,000 [(.75 x 40,000) + 5000] and you would be prepared to settle for anything less than that. On the other hand, there is a 25% chance that the court will alter the rule so that you will save $240,000 in just the first year. This changes things dramatically. Thus, even for one year, the expected outcome of trying the case is $25,000. [.25(240,-000) − .75($40,000) − $5000]. In effect, because you have a chance to get a very favorable change in the law, it is actually worth a positive $25,000 to you to try the case. This actually understates the value because you stand to avoid $240,000 every year.

Now switch your perspective and examine the issue from the point of view of the customers. Also assume they can be treated as one entity. If the case goes to trial, the expected value of the case, assum-

3. You may want to review Chapter 7 and the discussion settlement and the determination of the value of a case.

ing the cost to them is also $5000, is $25,000 [(.75) $40,000 − $5000]. But there is a big risk: There is a 25% chance that the court will change the rule so that customers will have to absorb the costs of the slips or walk more carefully. From their perspective, the overall expected outcome of a trial is $10,000. This is calculated as [.75 ($40,000) − .25($60,-000) − $5000].

In effect, the restaurant will happily go to trial and take the risk of a rule change. Any effort by the customers to settle the claim will meet a brick wall. Why is the case worth so much less to the plaintiff/customers? Principally it is because if the customers lose and the law does change, the impact on them is far less severe than the gain to the restaurant owner.

Now using these same numbers, assume the rule already is that the restaurant is not liable. Again assume the probability of a rule change is 25%. When the customer suffers a $40,000 fall, the expected value of the case is $20,000 [(.25($40,000) + .25($60,000) − $5000]. Any settlement offer above that amount will keep the case out of court. From the point of view of the restaurant, however, the outcome of a trial has an expected value of negative $75,000. [.25($40,000) + .25($240,000) + $5000)]. Avoiding a trial for anything less is a better position to be in. The plaintiffs will accept anything in excess of $20,000 to settle the case and the restaurant will be willing to pay up to $75,000. There will be a settlement and a court will not have an opportunity to change the rule.

The example seems to confirm the theory that inefficient rules are more likely to be presented to judges to rule on. Efficient rules, on the other hand, are likely to go unchallenged because they will settle if they are filed at all. A number of factors are at work here. The more inefficient the rule is, the more likely it is to be challenged. Another important factor is the probability that the rule will be changed. The example here—25%—is probably quite high. Think of how unlikely litigation would be if the probability were only 5%. One more factor is the cost of litigation. As you know from Chapter 7, high litigation costs mean a higher likelihood of settlement. In effect, litigation costs are like transaction costs and, if they are high, the "judicial transaction" will not occur.

The first step in the evolutionary theory is that inefficient rules find their way to the courts. Of course, some of the rules will stay the same. Others will change. It almost does not matter. Any rule that is changed from inefficient to efficient, whatever the rationale, becomes "sticky." Inefficient rules, on the other hand, are likely to be challenged repeatedly. Over time, efficient rules will prevail regardless of the economic sophistication of judges.

B.   A CLOSER LOOK AT THE EVOLUTIONARY THEORY

One issue that arises with the evolutionary theory is that it seems to involve an assumption that the parties are aware of and/or care about the consequences of a rule change. What happens if this is not the case—only one party or neither party has gone through the calculations presented here?[4] If only one party cares about the value of the rule, whether or not the current rule is efficient, that party will be motivated to bring it to the attention of a court even if the change it seeks is ultimately to an inefficient rule. For example, in the restaurant example, the restaurant "protected" the efficient rule by keeping it out of court because it understood the consequences of the rule change. If a case does not settle, the court may address and change an efficient rule to an inefficient rule. If neither party has a stake in the rule as opposed to the outcome in a particular case, the law is unlikely to change at all. The case will settle or not settle based on what the current rule is and not on the willingness of either party to advocate changing the rule.

Why would a party not be interested in a change from an inefficient to an efficient rule? One important reason is that the effort to change rules has a public good character. That is, the party who takes on the task of changing an inefficient rule may not be the only victim of that rule. More specifically, maybe the rule is only inefficient because thousands of people are negatively affected by only by a small amount each.

This possibility presents a serious challenge to the "evolution to efficient rules" theory. In order to understand why, think about what public goods are.

4. See Rubin, supra note 1, at 54–56.

They are goods or services that, when produced, the producer is unable to internalize all the benefits. This means that, even though the benefits may be great, producers will not be motivated to produce the goods because there is only a modest reward.

To understand the implications of this, go back to the "slip in the restaurant" example. Assume that you own a chain of 10 restaurants and the total of $240,000 is for all the restaurants in your chain. Each time someone slips and falls you pay damages. You are motivated to challenge the rule because you internalize the entire gain of $240,000. Now switch it around and all 10 restaurants together pay $240,000 in damages but you only own one of the restaurants. The benefit to the group of a rule change is the same. The benefit to each individual, including you, will decline substantially.[5] In effect, if you challenge the rule and win, all the restaurant owners are better off, but you are only better off by avoiding paying for a fairly rare slip and fall incident. And remember, there is only a 25% you will prevail if the case goes to trial. The other restaurant owners are free-riding on your effort. In fact, if you are unable to capture enough of the benefit, it may be rational for you avoid the trial altogether.

It is also possible to use the free-rider analysis to explain why some rules would switch from efficient to inefficient. In this regard, keep in mind that in the original example, the decision to litigate was based on a cost-benefit analysis—not on the deter-

5.   See Gordon Tullock, "Public Decisions as Public Goods," 99 *J. Political Economy* 913 (1971).

mination that one rule or the other was necessarily more efficient. Put differently, the decision is based on the so-called "bottom line," not a quest for efficiency. This being the case, it is entirely possible that an efficient rule—like the one saving $240,-000—could be in effect with the benefits spread thinly over a number of restaurants. And, as in our example, the cost to all customers of avoiding injury may only be $60,000. If the customers are viewed as a single entity, they would be motivated to challenge the efficient rule. If the restaurant owners act only individually, a "bottom line" analysis could mean a successful challenge to the efficient rule. In addition, if one party internalizes the benefits of an inefficient rule while those favored by an efficient rule are scattered, challenges to the efficient rule may result in settlement and the inefficient rule will persist.

Obviously, free-riding does not mean that all cases with efficiency implications are not heard. Several factors account for the fact that they make it to court anyway and, of course, once there the evolution to efficient rules may begin. For instance, although settlement is the norm, it does not always occur. In some cases a party plays "hardball" and resists settlement as a way of establishing a reputation for future settlement negotiations. In other situations, the bilateral monopoly comes into play. The parties bluff and posture and find they end up at trial when both would have been better off with a settlement. Once the issue is before the court, the rule may be changed to the efficient one. The problem for the evolutionary theory in these cases, though, is that both efficient and inefficient rules may be brought to the court's attention. This means the theory that courts will only change or be more likely to change inefficient rules because those are the ones they predominantly see no longer holds.

Class actions, which allow parties to combine relatively small claims, and punitive damages may offset the impact of free-riding. In these instances, cases make it to court because the gain to plaintiffs is made larger. Here again, both efficient rules and inefficient rules can make it to court and both types of rules may be switched. Whatever rule is established in the case of these magnified damages can be quite unstable. The problem is that magnification may be temporary and when it is less of a threat, a party may decide to challenge the rule.

C. EVALUATION AND EXAMPLES

The evolutionary theory of law is not that law will be efficient but that there are economic factors at work that tend to move law in the direction of efficiency. Testing the theory is very difficult. In his important book, The Economic Analysis of Law, Judge Richard Posner makes a fairly convincing case that most common law rules are actually efficient. Going back through this book and reviewing contract and tort rules, especially, you can see that he has a point. If he is correct, then, according to evolutionary theory, one would expect relatively little investment in attempts to change rules.

Though it is impossible to quantify this, it may very well be the case. But it could be the case for reasons other than the fact that efficient rules tend to be "sticky." The common law changes slowly and the norm would be few challenges and few changes under any circumstances. In addition, as the analysis above indicates, current rules tend to be sticky either because they are efficient or because those benefiting from inefficient rules are able to internalize the benefits of those rules. Little can be determined by observing that most common law rules seem stuck in place.

One can also approach the issue of validity of evolutionary theory by examining changes that have actually occurred. Here, too, it is difficult to find the kind of evidence that would satisfy a scientist. In contract law, the most radical change in the last 100 years or so is the adoption of promissory estoppel. Promises that were not supported by consideration were not enforceable. Now it is common for them to be enforced. In Chapter 5, you were introduced to several lines of reasoning that support the idea that the enforcement of gratuitous promises is efficient. This could support evolutionary theory, in part, if the new rule goes unchallenged for a substantial period of time.

It probably does not support the part of the theory that predicts that inefficient rules are the ones courts will be asked to rule on. In particular, promissory cases are nearly always brought by individuals who are unable to internalize the gain from a change in the rule. Thus the number of cases brought is hardly an indication either way with respect to the efficiency of the older rule. On the other hand, some of the early cases leading to promissory estoppel involve educational institutions that rely on many gratuitous promises and are able to internalize the economic advantages of a rule change as opposed to simply the benefits of a favorable outcome in a single case.[6] In short, these cases and parties seem to fit the evolutionary model. This lends support to the evolutionary theory but does not prove it. More specifically, the fact that a rule forcing people to keep promises is very valuable to a charitable or non-profit institution tells us nothing about how valuable a rule of non-enforcement might be to thousands of individuals and unorganized potential promise-breakers.

A big change in the law has taken place with respect to the habitability of property that has been rented or purchased. As you know, the traditional rule was "buyer beware." A tenant or renter who moved in and discovered a leaky roof or roaches had little recourse. At one time this may have been an efficient rule. People moved less frequently than they do today and they moved shorter distances and stayed longer. This meant they were more knowledgeable about the community and housing conditions. In effect, the information costs of avoiding unexpected problems were lower for tenants.

As people became more unsettled, moving more often and longer distances to new communities,

---

6. Allegheny College v. National Chautauqua County Bank of Jamestown, 159 N.E. 173 (N.Y.1927).

things changed. Now the cost of the information needed to avoid making a mistake can be quite high. On the other hand, the owner of the property may be in a far better position to understand the condition of the property and to address whatever problems there are at a lower cost. Consequently, many states now have an implied warranty of habitability. This means that the seller or lessor is held to certain standards. This is likely to be a more efficient rule. Moreover, it probably confirms the second part of the evolutionary theory in that it is unlikely to change. Still, whether the early challenges to the old rule resulted from some notion of inefficiency is more difficult to determine.

Along with promissory estoppel and implied warranties of habitability, product liability law has also changed and probably in the direction of greater efficiency. Clearly, a great deal of the harm resulting from the use of defectively designed or manufactured products can be avoided less expensively by the manufacturers themselves as opposed to purchasers. Again, though, it is hard to see this as an example of an evolutionary theory. Manufacturers, in particular, are likely to capture most of the benefits of an inefficient rule while consumers/plaintiffs are certain to run into free-riding problems. Thus, even if the rule has become efficient, it is not clear that it got that way through the process the evolutionary theory suggests.

If the theory does not work every time or even rarely, what would account for changes in the direction of efficient rules? One possibility is that judges simply choose efficient rules. To some extent, the rules that are efficient just have a common sense appeal. For example, the rule that someone is liable if he or she rams into the rear of the car in front of him or her is efficient and it is also common sense. No doubt judicial common sense could also explain the change in rules about products liability and habitability as well as many others.

Perhaps the most promising area in terms of verifying the evolutionary theory is antitrust. A possible explanation is that commercial entities are better able to internalize the benefits of rule changes. Antitrust is technically statutory law but, in practice, the law is very generally stated and its interpretation and evolution track what is found in common law. To understand how the theory may work, it is necessary to know that two sets of antitrust rules have developed. Some practices by firms are per se unlawful. They are illegal without a detailed analysis of their actual economic impact. Other practices are only determined to be unlawful after an actual comparison of the anticompetitive effects with possible procompetitive effects.

In 1967, the United States Supreme Court adopted a series of per se rules that most economists disfavored.[7] One rule prohibited manufacturers from selling to a retailer and then restricting the geographic area within which the retailer could resell. Firms had adopted this practice because it was felt that having two retailers of the same brand

7. United States v. Arnold, Schwinn & Co., 388 U.S. 365 (1967).

competing was actually harmful to the competitive fortunes of the firm itself. At one level—between the retailers or intrabrand competition—the restriction was clearly anticompetitive. On the other hand, so the theory goes, the practice prevented retailers of the same brands from free-riding on each other. Without the restriction one retailer might do a great deal of advertising then find that its competitor, selling the same brand, would make the sale at a lower cost. By eliminating this possibility, retailers would be more aggressive in their sales efforts with respect to competing brands. In effect, the per se rule was seen as protecting intrabrand competition while harming interbrand competition. You should also recall that the per se rule allows for no exceptions. This means even restraints that might increase competition and increase consumer welfare were unacceptable.

The Supreme Court changed the rule in 1977, after nearly unanimous criticism from economists and the business community. It switched the analysis to the rule of reason.[8] The Court recognized that the restraint could have both procompetitive effects and anticompetitive effects and opted to allow these effects to be balanced. It is generally accepted that the Court changed an inefficient rule to an efficient one. The question is whether the process of change is consistent with the evolutionary theory.

As with the common law, antitrust law requires litigation to change. In the case of restraints on

8. Continental T. V., Inc. v. GTE Sylvania, Inc., 433 U.S. 36 (1977).

reselling, it is clear that manufacturers—those challenging the original rule—were likely to internalize the benefits of a rule change. In fact, the firm that challenged the rule before the United States Supreme Court was one that had grown substantially by employing restrictions on competition among its retailers of the same brand. It was able to encourage retailer loyalty by protecting them from other retailers selling the same product. Retailers objecting to the rule change were likely to be much more limited in size and stood to lose less by virtue of the rule change than manufacturers stood to gain.

This scenario seems to track the evolutionary model fairly closely. First, the existing per se rule that always prohibited restraints on resale was almost certainly inefficient. The only way for it not to be inefficient would be for the restraint to almost always harm consumers. The problem was the rule precluded even determining when this was true. Second, a firm that was able to internalize the benefits of a rule change was motivated to litigate the matter. This evolutionary story falls short of the ideal only because there were potential free-riders on each side of the issue. Many manufacturers gained from the Court's reversal but did contribute to the cause, and many retailers who stood to lose by virtue of the rule change also were not engaged. Still, the example comes very close to conforming to the model.

Ultimately, law does evolve and many of the rules are consistent with efficiency and common sense. The outcome, may be the result of the evolutionary theory described here or it may be that some judges just prefer efficient rules. There are examples that support both possibilities. On the other hand, there are also rules that are technically inefficient but which seem to comply with common sense. This is because values like "fairness" or "justice" are important ones and have a common sense appeal. Not all of the rules chosen because of these values, however, can be squared with economic efficiency.

CHAPTER THIRTEEN

TAX POLICY AND TAXES ON INTERGENERATIONAL TRANSFERS

Although not a mainstream law and economic issue, one matter that consistently draws attention from those interested in tax and equity is intergenerational transfers. Typically this concerns transfers of wealth, but consider the following. Your friend's parents both have I.Q.'s of 160 and, as a result of their genetic mingling, your friend's I.Q. is also 160. She finds this book easy and goes through math courses the way some people go through comic books. She has high-paying job offers by the handful. In the meantime, you are smart enough, but good grades come with a great deal of effort. Did it ever occur to you that the government should levy a tax on your friend's intelligence? Every year, when filling out her tax forms, she might be asked to pay $100 for every I.Q. point over 120. No doubt the idea seems preposterous but ideas related to it have been discussed by some well-regarded economists.[1]

1. One of the first Nobel Prize winners in economics, Jan Tinbergen, proposed such a tax, which he called the "talent tax". One way to make this idea practical would be to define and tax "earning capacity" rather than earnings. See Plug, E.J.S, Van Praag, B.M.S and J. Hartog, "If we knew ability, how would we tax individuals?," *Journal of Public Economics*, May 1999, 183–

Suppose instead your friend seems no brighter than you and seems no more motivated to do well in school. Both of you work fairly hard, live in the dormitory, ride motor scooters to class, and are careful with your money. One day your friend learns that a long lost aunt has died and left her $50 million. She moves to a nice apartment, begins driving a Porsche to class, starts cha-cha lessons, and spends weekends at the beach after being transported there in her private airplane. It occurs to you that your friend did not work any harder than you and seems no more deserving of living the good life. In fact, now it appears your friend has little motivation to work hard in the future. In addition, you begin to realize that because of the randomness of who your parents are, not only is your friend better off, but someday your children will occupy a spot in society with your friend's children who presumably will also be rich or at least have a leg up on your children in pursuing their goals. If you are like many others, there is a good chance you might not find the idea of an inheritance tax all that preposterous.

Although this book does not include a comprehensive look at tax policy—a course in public finance or tax law would be the place to go for that—the disposition of assets at death is traditionally an issue in which lawyers are deeply involved.[2] The

211. See also Lawrence Zelenak, "Taxing Endowment," 55 *Duke L. J.* 1145 (2006)

2. Technically, inheritance taxes are assessed against those receiving a bequest, and estate taxes are assessed against the issue has a great deal to do with what it means to be "related" as well as property rights; it is ultimately a question of one's ability to control property after death. As this introduction suggests, the issue of inheritance raises issues that are both economic and emotional. It also tends to bring to light our ambivalence about inheritances of various kinds. For example, why tax inheritance but not above-average looks, intellect, or height—especially if it is enough height to slam-dunk a basketball? This ambivalence is borne out by some surprising statistics. For example, although inheritance taxes are paid by only 2–3% of the population, they are objected to by 70% of Americans.

The section that follows includes some introductory information that will provide a context for what is to come. After that, the economic characteristics of inheritance taxes will be explored. Then the standards for evaluating taxes are explained. Inheritance taxes are then examined in light of these standards. The final section returns to the issue of whether the inheritance tax is likely to solve any problems caused by intergenerational transfers of wealth.

A.   THE INHERITANCE TAX

estate of the deceased. Here, the term "inheritance" is used to denote any type of tax on wealth left at the time of death. Also, bequests are specific designations of who receives what in a will. When no one is named, the law steps in and assets are transferred to heirs—typically family members. In this Chapter, the language used is not intended to distinguish these methods of intergenerational transfers.

Inheritance taxes of one kind or another have been around since Egyptian times. In the United States, inheritance taxes started with the Stamp Act of 1797, which was actually a charge to probate—legally process—a will. In 1862, the tax was altered so that it varied not with the amount of money but with how closely related the relative receiving the bequest was to the decedent. Now the tax is calculated as a percentage of the amount passed to heirs.[3]

The general controversy about the inheritance tax is fueled by a number of arguments that are often more impressionistic and emotional than economic. On one side, arguments are made that everyone should have an even start in life and that an inheritance gives some people an advantage. In addition, individuals with large inheritances may be lazy and not contribute much to society. Furthermore, inheritances perpetuate the status quo in terms of economic power. On the other side, people who are free from having to make ends meet on a day-by-day basis have the potential to be imaginative or, at least, generous. And, once a person has earned money, it is his or her property to spend or give away even upon death. In fact, removing the incentive to make your heirs better off upon your death may mean that you are less motivated and less productive. To some extent, the controversy is of limited relevance since the tax contributes only a very small percentage toward the United State fed-

3. A fairly large amount is excluded from the federal inheritance tax.

eral budget. Obviously, this is just a sampling of the possible arguments and, although this list may seem a bit simplistic, some of these ideas are relevant in the context of a more careful economic assessment. The first step is to lay the groundwork for what one might look for in all taxes. That is, what are the common characteristics of ''good taxes?'' The next question is whether taxes on the wealth that people possess when they die have these characteristics.

B. THE GOOD TAX[4]

In order to begin an economic assessment, it is important to remember the ideal that government takes money from people—makes them worse off— only when the funds are then used to make the public even better off. Whether it is in terms of allocative efficiency or Kaldor–Hicks efficiency, the hoped-for transfer from private spending to public spending is one that increases welfare. This is more likely to be the case when the cost of raising any particular level of revenue is at the lowest cost. This means putting aside the question of how much benefit the public derives from a particular project and concentrating on the cost side of the equation. The goal from this perspective is to generate a particular level of revenue fairly and efficiently. Fairness is obviously hard to define, but one stan-

4. For more detail see Krisanne M. Schlechter, ''Repeal of the Federal Estate and G.A. Tax: When Will it Happen and How will it Affect our Progressive Tax System?'' 19 Va. Tax Rev. 781 (2000).

dard is that similarly situated people pay the same amounts.

Efficiency in this context is analogous to productive efficiency. The challenge is to generate tax revenues at the lowest cost per dollar of tax revenue generated. When considering the efficiency of the revenue-raising, there are a number of possible costs to be considered. First and most obvious is the disutility of those from whom funds are taken. In fact, those who support progressive taxes do so in part on the basis of the sense that money itself is subject to diminishing marginal utility. The idea is that those with a great deal of money feel the sting or disutility of being taxed less acutely than those with less. This obviously involves an implicit interpersonal comparison of utility and might justify taxing the rich quite heavily. In Figure 1 illustrates a diminishing marginal utility curve showing that "rich" individuals who own $100 have a marginal utility of 3 for their hundredth and last dollar, whereas "poor" individuals who own only $10 have a marginal utility of 40 for the tenth and last dollar. Each time a rich person is taxed $1, 3 utils are lost, whereas if a poor person is taxed the cost to society is 40 utils.

Another approach is to spread the tax over a great number of people. This too is based on the idea that money is subject to diminishing marginal utility. Again, look at Figure 1 and assume that society consist of 50 people. All individuals are the same and each individual has $100. Now suppose we need to raise $50 through taxes. If we tax everyone at a rate of $1, the total units of lost utility will be 150 (50 times the loss of 3 utils). As can be seen from Figure 1, the marginal utility of the ninety-ninth dollar is 3.2 utils. It is now decided that half the population has to pay $2 in taxes (total tax revenue is still $50) and the other half of the population has to pay nothing at all. What is the total utility loss of this unequally spread tax system? On their first tax dollar, the 25 taxpayers lose a total of 75 utils (25 times 3 utils) and on the second tax dollar they loose a total of 80 utils (25 times 3.2 utils). Total utility loss is now 155 (75 + 80). Hence, the more equally spread tax system among similar individuals implies lower social utility loss.

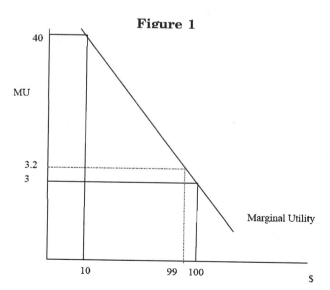

Figure 1

The second thing to consider in examining the soundness of a tax is the cost associated with administering the tax. Some of these costs are the result of efforts to avoid taxation. Avoidance in this context means efforts by taxpayers to continue the taxed activities but not pay the taxes on those activities. This in turn gives rise to the costs of government collection authorities and all the sums spent by private individuals on attorneys and efforts to avoid the tax. This is a true social cost because it only has distributive consequences (activities related to this type of tax avoidance do not produce anything useful for society).

There is yet another type of avoidance cost. Here, avoidance takes the form of substituting no-tax or low-tax activities for those that are taxed. Ideally, a tax would not do that; it would be "neutral" in the sense that it would not cause any substitution or shifts in productive choices. It is hard to devise a really neutral tax. Those types of property and income on which taxes disproportionately fall tend to be disfavored although the substitutes may not be as effective. For example, if home ownership were heavily taxed, more people would rent. If labor is heavily taxed, people might prefer to take more free time. Why take a second job if most of the income is taxed away?

Similarly, suppose a person with altruistic motives wants to provide for his children. He could choose to make lifetime gifts or leave wealth by way of inheritance and might prefer inheritance as a more effective way to achieve her ends. A tax on inheritance could result in a shift to lifetime gifts—the less preferred choice. Neutrality cannot be achieved perfectly, but one can devise a tax system whereby the substitution effects are as small as possible. In earlier days, governments often relied on a salt tax. One of the reasons for the salt tax was that, in those days, salt was an essential ingredient in food preparation and there were hardly any substitutes available. A good or a service that has few substitutes is usually characterized by a low elasticity of demand. Hence, if the price is increased (because a tax is added to it), the quantity demanded does not decrease very much and the tax revenue is higher than if the good or service were more elastic. We will come back to the relationship between tax and the inelasticity of demand later in this Chapter. It should be noted, however, that in some instances a tax is employed specifically for non-neutral purposes. For example, taxes on automobiles that get poor gas mileage are intended to encourage people to shift to more economical automobiles.

Finally, aside from what the revenue is used for, it is possible that some taxes may increase or decrease welfare in less direct ways. For example, if a person were envious of those who have inherited wealth, an inheritance tax would increase that person's sense of well-being. In addition, it has been argued that an inheritance tax is even beneficial to those upon whom it falls. The reasoning is that consumption is like spending the money of heirs and, thus, it creates social pressure on the wealth holder. The tax, so the argument goes, takes the pressure off the wealth holder, permitting her to do what she "really" would prefer to do.[5] Finally, since statistics show that most Americans oppose inheritance taxes, the existence of the tax, whether or not a person actually pays it, is likely to be a source of disutility.

In sum, aside from being fair, a "good" tax is one that generates revenue at a low cost. Expenses can come in a variety of forms, but the three principle ones are costs of administration and enforcement, the losses from market distortions (through shifts from preferred but taxed activities to less preferred, less taxed activities), and the disutility of those taxed. Naturally, all of this is made more complicated by the fact that there are different tax rates and different types of taxes that, in an ideal world, would be balanced to generate the ideal level of revenue at the lowest cost. In reality, the most efficient combination is impossible to determine because it would require interpersonal comparisons of utility.

C. HOW DO INHERITANCE TAXES MEASURE UP?

The question of how inheritance taxes fare when compared with the ideal is not an easy one to answer. As with many economic matters, it depends on the assumptions one makes about why people

5. Roland H. Koler II, "Inheritance Justified: A Comment," 16 *Journal of Law and Economics* 423 (1973).

hold wealth at their death and the reasons for limiting inheritance.

1.   COST OF ADMINISTRATION

The cost to administer a tax probably has less to do with the type of tax than it does with the specific wording of the tax law and the way it is interpreted by the courts. It is obvious that the cost of tax avoidance efforts is likely to be lower when the tax itself is low; one is unlikely to invest $15,000 to avoid a tax of $10,000. In addition, these costs will be lower when the laws are drafted so they are well understood. Complex and ambiguous tax laws, on the other hand, raise costs; a great deal of money may be spent attempting to decipher the rules or developing arguments for how they should be interpreted. To a great extent, this cost is directly related to the drafting of specific tax provisions and beyond the scope of this analysis of inheritance. Suffice it to say that there is a huge industry composed of thousands of attorneys who engage in a process called "estate planning" that is in large measure a euphemism for tax avoidance. By no measure can this be regarded as a relatively uncomplicated area of law.

2.   AVOIDABILITY

An inheritance tax does not seem to perform well when it comes to avoidability. Again, though, this depends on assumptions and certain empirical questions. The crucial question is why people desire to hold wealth at their death.[6] To be more specific: Is the sole reason for holding wealth at death to benefit heirs? Or is it possible that wealth is held as a matter of status or as a hedge against contingencies?[7]

A good starting point for understanding the importance of this question and its relevance to avoidability is to view wealth held at death as a good or service. From that perspective, one can formulate something analogous to a traditional demand curve with price being the tax on wealth held at the time of one's death. Figure 2 illustrates the relationship one would expect.

One of the curves, D, represents the assumption that the only reason for holding wealth is to benefit one's heirs. This is implicit in the fact that the curve intersects the Y axis at a tax rate of 100%. The logic is that if the only reason to hold wealth is to benefit one's heirs, then a 100% tax will completely remove the incentive to do so. Curve D_1, on the other hand, represents the possibility that there are other reasons for holding wealth beyond benefiting heirs. For example, people may hold savings

6. See William G. Gale & Maria G. Perozek, "Do Estate Taxes Reduce Savings?" in Rethinking Estate and Gift Taxation 216 (W. Gale, J. Hines, J. Slemrod, eds. 2001, Brooking Institution Press).

7. A well-known discussion of why one holds wealth and the implication of a 100% tax rate is found in Gordon Tullock, "Inheritance Justified," 14 *Journal of Law and Economics* 465 (1971); Thomas R. Ireland, Inheritance Justified: A Comment," 16 *Journal of Law and Economics* 421 (1973); Richard Posner, The Economic Analysis of Law 539–542 (2007).

in order to provide for their needs as they age. Typically, they do not know exactly when they will die. Thus, the best policy is to be conservative and not spend it all. This means there will be wealth held at death. Similarly, for some, the accumulation of wealth may be associated with status or just a hobby. Thus, even at a 100% tax rate on inheritance, some wealth would be retained and some taxes generated.

Curves D and D_1 also have different slopes. The relative slopes depend on the number of ways one can hold wealth for the particular purposes associated with each curve. Although it is counter-intuitive at first, D_1 is the more inelastic demand and indicates that some of the reasons for holding wealth are not ones likely to be affected by a tax on inheritance. Plus, for these people, there are not good substitutes for having personal control over one's wealth. On the other hand, D is relatively elastic. The principal goal of these people is to benefit heirs by making bequests and, thus, they will be responsive to the "price" of doing so. Plus, there may many ways of benefiting heirs other than leaving them assets upon death.

In the case of both demand curves, as tax rates go up, the levels of wealth held at death will decline as will the tax revenue generated.[8] And in both cases,

8. The means that although the curves differ in their relative elasticity, they are both elastic. See Wojciech Kopczuk & Joel Slemrod, "The Impact of the Estate Tax on Wealth Accumulation and Avoidance Behavior," in *Rethinking Estate and Gift Taxation* 299 (W. Gale, J. Hines, J. Slemrod, eds. 2001, Brooking Institution Press).

there is a downward slope, with more wealth being held at death at lower tax rates. There are, however, important differences between the curves. For example, suppose you view inheritance taxes as a fair way to raise revenue and favor a very high tax rate—even 100%. If the curve looks like D, the impact of a 100% tax rate will be that no tax revenues are generated. You will have eliminated inheritance and raised no tax. (And you probably have not stemmed the types of transfers from one generation to another that you opposed.) On the other hand, if the curve is D_1, some revenue will be generated because these people have needs that require them to hold wealth until they die.

Figure 2

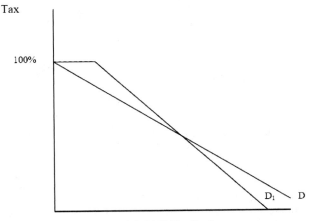

Tax

100%

D_1 D

Wealth Held at Death

In the case of each curve, at some point analogous to the point of unitary elasticity on a conventional demand curve, the amount of tax revenue generated would be maximized. The revenue-maximizing tax rate will be higher when the curve is relatively inelastic. Thus, the ideal tax rate will be higher on D_1—when there are fewer substitutes available to achieve one's goals—than on D where the number of substitutes are relatively plentiful. Consequently, one cannot determine the most effective tax rate without understanding the motivation of holding wealth—is it for the benefit of heirs or the wealth-holder?

It is not possible to specify the position or the slope of the actual curve, but in all likelihood the actual curve will lie closer to D_1 than to D. Almost certainly, some people will die with accumulated wealth even if the inheritance tax is 100%. This may be a result of bad planning or because wealth is held for reasons other than inheritance. Analysis of the substitutes for holding wealth at death also cuts in favor of D_1. The reason for this can be understood by thinking of the three principal purposes for holding wealth—security, status, and intergenerational transfers. A demand curve reflecting only the latter would be very elastic because there are a multitude of ways to provide for others upon one's death. A parent can pay for an expensive education, provide low or no-interest loans, or make outright gifts to his or her children. In some instances, these gifts themselves are subject to taxation, but with very little imagination these taxes can be minimized or avoided all together.

Likewise, maintaining wealth is only one way to achieve security. In particular, one can buy an annuity. An annuity is a type of insurance that pays a set amount during one's life and then stops upon death. Thus, if a person has $500,000 in savings and the inheritance tax is viewed as excessive, he or she might buy an annuity that pays $75,000 for the reminder of his or her life and then end. An annuity is not, however, as flexible as having one's savings on hand (or not perceived to be even if it is) and therefore may not be as readily used as a substitute. As for experiencing the status gained from simply having on hand a great deal of wealth, there may be no substitutes. In sum, when all three goals are considered together, the elasticity (with respect to the tax rate) is likely to be less than it would be if intergenerational transfers of wealth are the only goal.

The reasons for holding wealth and the availability of substitutes lead to a number of implications. First, the ideal or revenue-maximizing tax rate is probably higher than if the only purpose for holding wealth is to make intergenerational transfers. Second, it means that those who favor an inheritance tax must anticipate responding to and taxing a variety of methods individuals may use to achieve intergenerational transfers other than inheritance. This means taxing or prohibiting all forms of these transfers in order to channel those who want to benefit their heirs into the inheritance route. This too adds to the cost of administering an inheritance tax. Finally, there are implications for those who favor eliminating inheritance as a means of "evening the playing field" or addressing their envy. The fact that there are numerous methods of making intergenerational transfers means that an inheritance tax alone is an ineffective tool for this purpose.

Since the ideal tax rate hinges so much on the reason people hold wealth at their death, you would expect economists to come to some firm conclusion on the matter. In fact, a great deal of disagreement continues.[9] Some economists believe that the demand curve looks more like D_1. If this is correct it suggests that annuities are poor substitutes for holding wealth on hand in terms of providing security. It also means that maintaining money in the bank leads to the perception of success, power, and prestige. Increases in inheritance taxes will not affect these goals. Other economists believe that savings are linked to a desire to make bequests and thus the curve looks more like D. Under this view, a tax on inheritance would mean a drastic decline in bequests.[10] Some evidence even suggests that savings increases as the tax rate increases. This may seem counter-intuitive, but if savers have certain fixed goals (such as a certain after-tax amount of wealth that they want to leave their heirs), higher

9. See Mark L. Ascher, "Curtailing Inherited Wealth," 89 *Mich. L. Rev.* 69 (1990).

10. Id.

tax rates require more savings to achieve those goals.

3. NEUTRALITY

An assessment of the neutrality of an inheritance tax is different in some respects from an assessment of other types of taxes. As an example, a tax on yachts is destined to channel funds away from buying yachts. A tax on gasoline may reduce the level of driving. In the case of inheritance, the tax is on wealth left at death. The channeling effect here, as suggested above, would be in the direction of increased lifetime transfers, the purchase of annuities, and increased consumption. Like any tax, the impact is not entirely neutral, but the distorting impact of taxes on inheritance is likely to be minimal. Two of the reactions—annuities and lifetime gifts—are merely transfers from one possible saver to another. Insurance companies pool funds and invest them in a matter that is in a general sense similar to the individual saver. Similarly, lifetime gifts are made to people whose savings patterns may resemble those of their benefactors.

This leaves the unusual case of the saver who, as a result of an inheritance tax, decides not to save at all and not to transfer the wealth to surrogate savers but to spend every last cent. The spending itself is not likely to create any noticeable distortion unless people who save in order to make bequests have very narrow and similar preferences for what they spend their savings on when it is shifted to consumption. On the other hand, could a decrease in savings by all these people somehow reduce the money available to borrowers and lead to an increase in interest rates? This seems unlikely. Aside from the series of assumptions that would have to be true for this to happen, the fact is that people receiving income as a result of this new propensity to consume would probably have some motivation to save. This would offset, albeit partially, the savings that had been withdrawn.

D. INHERITANCE IN CONTEXT

The case for inheritance taxes is a hard one to make. As the above analysis suggests, the revenue-raising potential is limited by the fact that there are good substitutes for making intergenerational transfers. The consequence is that the impact of a heavy inheritance tax may be that very little tax is generated at all. In addition, any effort to close off all the ways that can be found to make intergenerational transfers is likely to be prohibitively expensive, impractical, or impossible. In a sense, this is unfortunate because an inheritance tax, as was explained above, would appear to have a relatively neutral effect.

Where does this leave those who feel that inheritance is unfair in a social sense? Here, the objection is that people become better off not because they are more productive or even better in a moral sense but because of the sheer randomness of parenthood. Obviously, this randomness cannot be overcome by taxing inheritance alone. The intergenerational transfers that give some people a head start can be genetic and environmental as well as financial. In addition, even the financial ones can take place well before the matter of inheritance becomes relevant. It is not clear that taxing inheritance would put more than a small dent in the lopsidedness that results from being born into an affluent family. What is needed is a much broader plan that taxes all inherited advantages. Many, if not most, people would find this objectionable, and it may be too expensive both financially and utility-wise to justify any offsetting gains. Another way would be to try to compensate the disadvantages of children from poor backgrounds with special preschool programs (e.g. with low student-teacher ratios) or with investments in schooling and training in general[11].

11.   For a general discussion of these type of policies and their effects, see James Heckman and Alan Krueger, Inequality in America; What Role for Human Capital Policies? MIT Press, 2003.

CHAPTER FOURTEEN

MARRIAGE AND DIVORCE

One of the more intriguing areas for applying economics to law is marriage and divorce. Contract law is especially relevant. It may not have occurred to you, but when you become engaged to be married, you essentially promise your partner that you will marry him or her in exchange for the same promise in return. A few decades ago, lawsuits based on breach of the contract to marry were not unusual. At the time of the marriage, it is customary to again exchange promises. To be sure, these promises can be a little vague—"love and obey in sickness and health till death do us part"—but they are promises nonetheless. In fact, although you do not hear about marriage involving a contract, even today courts and scholars analyze marriage as a form of contract. Moreover, the increased willingness of courts to enforce antenuptial agreements suggests that marriage is becoming increasingly contract-like. When one party or the other violates the marriage vows, it is analogous to a breach of contract. In effect, one party or the other does not deliver what was expected. Although the contract analogy holds up pretty well in some respects, the advent of "no-fault" divorce tends to reduce the similarity.[1]

This chapter focuses on the economics of marriage including why people marry. The analysis focuses on the economics of marriage as pioneered by Gary Becker.[2] It also considers the questions of how law has an impact on the marital relationship and its efficiency. As it turns out, the impact of law on the formation of a marriage and even on the way it is conducted is not as important as the matter addressed in final section: How does law influence whether and the conditions under which a marriage may be ended?

A. THE ECONOMICS OF MARRIAGE: GENERALLY

Although the general themes of marriage are similar to more traditional contracts, when you take a close look at the legal implications, the analogy is far from perfect. One important difference is that although parties may freely enter into marriage, they cannot exit as easily as the parties to a contract. In addition, traditional contract law generally assumes that parties bargain at "arm's length" in order to maximize their individual gains from the contract. When it comes to the marital contract,

1. Along with contract, marriage is analogous to a partnership. In effect, marriage involves a contract to enter into what amounts to a partnership.

2. See Gary S. Becker, "A Theory of Marriage: Part I," 81 *Journal of Political Economy* 813 (July, 1973); Gary S. Becker, "A Theory of the Allocation of Time," 75 *Economics Journal* 493 (1965).

interdependent utility functions come into play. That is, one person's happiness will be a positive function of the other party's happiness. This ultimately may not be inconsistent with the idea of maximizing individual utility, but it makes the legal analysis of offer, acceptance, consideration, and fairness more difficult. It also may result in outcomes that legal authorities will mistake as unfair when, in fact, they are the result of love and generosity. The motivation of someone working a minimum-wage job or earning a comfortable salary is very different from that of a stay-at-home mother working hard for even longer hours. In addition, it is clear that marriage involves a multitude of unwritten and tacit agreements and understandings that vary greatly from couple to couple. For these reasons and others related to protection of privacy, courts are far less likely to apply traditional contract standards to family issues.

Once the marriage contract is obviously at an end, however, courts cannot help but become involved. Here again, the legal analogy to contract law is a bit strained. For example, is there such a thing as an "efficient divorce" comparable to the efficient contract breach? How is one to determine who breached an unwritten contract with terms that are implicit and constantly evolving? In addition, if there is a breach, how is the expectancy of the non-breaching party to be valued? Is an antenuptial agreement comparable to liquidated damages? Despite the vagaries of these concepts, it is clear that law has its greatest impact on the marital relationship at the point that one or both parties want the relationship to end.

Before continuing, three points need to be made. First, it is useful to consider that the notion of "marriage" may have a variety of meanings. People can live together and share the costs and benefits of life without a formal agreement and with a right to terminate the relationship at any time. In other instances, they can exchange formal promises but have the right to terminate the relationship with no questions asked. In fact, today most divorce is "no-fault," meaning that it is not necessary to show that one person has breached the agreement. Finally, there is the possibility of an agreement in which both parties are committed unless one of them commits an act comparable to a contract breach. What these variations involve are different costs of dissolving the relationship. As you will see below, it is not always clear that it is efficient to have the lowest possible cost of dissolution.

Second, it is generally accepted that it is economically efficient to encourage marriage, including efforts to make marriages work. The source of the utility is two-fold. First, when individuals join, they tend to become more productive as a result of opportunities to specialize. Second, most people who marry intend to and do have children and children become, in effect, third party beneficiaries of the marriage. The time, money, and risks of child-rearing tend to be less onerous if shared. In sum, most of the economic analysis of marriage begins from the premise that marriage in one form or another offers efficiencies.

Finally, the economic approach to marriage may itself carry a bias. It starts from the basic assumption that individuals are rational maximizers of self-interest and are guided by these characteristics in making choices within the marriage. This approach has been questioned because it may explain too little. Another approach, called "provisioning," focuses on how decisions are made, who gets what, and the impact of legal and social factors on marital behavior.[3] The tension between the approaches is important. It is possible that the economics of marriage is forced into the utility-maximizing model because that is essentially what economists do. The argument is that the dominant approach to the economics of marriage is a bit like the tail wagging the dog. Rather than extending the analysis to answer critical questions, the subject (marriage) is analyzed to fit the methodology (maximization theory). Maximization often is the result of specialization. Thus, there may be a bias in the approach toward seeing men and women in traditional roles at the expense of considering gains in utility that are more difficult to specify. This, of course, opens the larger question of applying the "rational self-interest maximizing model" to other issues, like the decision to have children or how to vote on issues of broad social importance.

3. Julie A. Nelson, "I, Thou and Them: Capabilities, Altruism and Norms in the Economics of Marriage." *84 Am. Econ. Rev.* 126 (May, 1994).

B. WHY MARRY?

Or why enter into any contract? In the context of a conventional contract, we think in terms of increasing the utility of both parties and allocating risks. The increase is a result of the "benefit of the bargain." For example, if I own a car that I place a $1000 value on and you value it at $2000, our exchange creates a surplus that could not exist without our "partnership" in the form of a contract and, ultimately, the exchange. The benefit of the bargain is $1000 as the car moves from somebody who values it at $1000 to somebody who values it by twice that much. Part of the process of making the exchange is determining how the benefit of the bargain will be divided. If the price is $1100, I gain a relatively small share of the benefit and you get a relatively large share. Of course, the opposite is true if the price is close to $1900.

The suggestion above is that all contracts have a partnership-like element. In fact, the opposite is true as well—partnerships come about as a result of contracts. The economic approach is one that stresses the partnership-like nature of marriage. To understand why, you may want to think about why business partnerships are formed. Usually the partners have somewhat complementary skills and together can produce more output and profit than the sum of their individual profits. There can be a variety of reasons for this. A partnership allows for specialization. It also permits a greater variety of outputs that possibly satisfy a greater variety of customer needs. On a practical level, renting one place of business may be less expensive than renting two. This is also the case for two electric bills, two telephone bills, and so on. The source of these economies of scale is two-fold. First, the actual amounts owed for service provided by others is likely to be less than the total for two separately. Second, the transaction costs of acquiring necessary inputs are drastically reduced.

Marriages are not about making profits per se, but they are about efforts to maximize net utility or the difference between utility and disutility. Some of this utility can be traced to the same types of factors that make conventional partnerships attractive. For example, when you marry, you are likely to pay rent on one apartment instead of two and share a telephone as well as heat and air conditioning and the light from a single lamp. These economies make income available to purchase utility-increasing goods and services. In addition to utility derived from ordinary goods and services purchased in the market, there is utility from sources of satisfaction associated with the relationship itself. Waking up next to a person you love may result in feelings of warmth, security, and well-being.

As with a conventional partnership, a marriage also allows for specialization. For example, a single person may work outside the home, do the cooking and cleaning, pay the bills, and feed the pets. A married couple can divide these tasks and presumably each partner can become more adept at his or her specializations. This type of specialization may be especially desirable when young children are involved. Although there is a great deal to be said for both parents being equally involved in the child-rearing, one is likely to be better at it as a general matter based on his or her own physical characteristics, skills, and interests prior to the marriage.[4]

The contributions of inputs of the parties to this utility-producing effort may come in the form of work done outside the home from which monetary income is derived or from work inside the home. For example, one partner may earn the income necessary to purchase food while the other may prepare the food, do the laundry, or simply discuss an interesting book. In short, both partners provide inputs and enjoy the outputs of the relationship. Unlike a conventional partnership, the exact division of the utility provided by joint effort is obviously very hard to predict. This is especially true since most marriages involve partners with interdependent utility functions. On the other hand, like conventional contracts and partnerships, a great deal of attention is likely to be paid to distributive matters before the marriage. For example, qualities such as "demanding," "high-maintenance," or "poor health," all other factors remaining equal, are likely

4. Curiously, the returns to scale and specialization arguments for marriage stop at two-person marriages. Clearly, the returns to scale continue for more than two persons, and specialization gains still increase with more than two persons. If fact, communities may be more efficient than couples. Yet they are not very common. Maybe free-rider problems kick in when the number of persons involved gets higher. And the interdependent utilities might become too intricate with more than two persons.

to make a person less attractive as a partner. In effect, people who marry are likely to think they know a fair amount about how the marriage will "work for them" before entering into the formal relationship.

C. LAW AND THE MARRIAGE MARKET

Assuming rationality in the selection of a mate, it makes sense to think in terms of a market for mates or a "marriage market." In fact, magazine and television advertisements promote businesses that lower transaction costs in the marriage market. The process is one of finding the partner that will assist in the process of maximizing utility. The possibilities are vast and law properly stays out of what are highly individualized taste-driven decisions. For example, if you are a recent graduate of a prestigious MBA program, your search might rule out a poorly educated person. All other factors being equal, your utility would probably be increased by being able to converse intelligently with someone who understands your working life. In fact, insights from that person might assist you in your job. Compatibility, however, does not mean sameness. For example, a hard-driving executive may find the company of a soothing artistic type preferable to another executive type. The complementary partner for each person is an individualized matter, but a rough generalization is that people choose partners with similar levels of intelligence, backgrounds, age, and height. This is known as "positive sorting," and the search for a marriage partner has been compared to the search for a job on the labor market.[5]

The approach of non-intervention by law in marital choices makes sense for a number of reasons. First, legal institutions are ill-equipped to determine for others what types of marriages will maximize utility. Second, social goals when it comes to marriage are generally equivalent to private goals. The law does not need to channel people into attempting to find mates with whom they will be happy. Third, to the extent couples choose to have children, they are likely to want to provide for and assist in the development of those children.

Law does, however, nibble around the edges of the marriage market. As with all contracts, there are laws that limit the ability of minors to make marital commitments, which hopefully encourages judicious choice-making. Mandatory blood tests, premarital counseling, and waiting periods can also have an impact on ultimate compatibility and utility. As a technical matter, and as distasteful as it may seem, regulation based on race, social class and sexual preferences of partners could be explained on an economic basis (negative externality) if third parties find certain unions objectionable. Ultimately, individual choices of mates are far more deter-

5. Note that there are cultures in which the parents decide about the partners in marriage. (Could have superior knowledge when compared that of their children?). In a literal sense, at least, some level of similarity between the candidates is consistent with the organization and specialization that account for the efficiency of marriage.

mined by social norms and custom than by legal rules. These norms and customs are likely to have evolved to encourage the type of compatibility that is consistent with utility-increasing unions.

Although law does not have a great deal of economic significance to say about which individuals are selected as mates, it has something to say about the actual nature of the contracts that the parties make. For example, until relatively recently a man was not legally capable of raping a woman to whom he was married. Part of the marriage contract was that men could require wives to submit to sex. In fact, it was not until the late 1980's that the state of Maryland abolished what is called the "marital exception" to rape laws. The impact of this change has been to create a property right in women not to engage in sex with husbands. The economic question here is whether the reassignment of the "right to sex" is likely to be efficient by decreasing the husband's utility by less than it increases the wife's utility. Obviously, this measure of efficiency involves an interpersonal comparison of utility. From a wealth-maximizing perspective, the question is whether the husband or wife is likely to place a higher value on the wife's right to choose whether to submit to the husband's sexual desires.

An economic purist may question whether there is any need for judicial involvement in a situation like this. The reasoning would be that even if the default position is that the husband has absolute sexual rights, the allocation could be bargained around. The context would appear to be one involving low transaction costs and, from a Coasian perspective, prior to marriage the parties could agree to alter the default position. Practical considerations suggest that such an alternation may actually involve high transaction costs. First, until relatively recently, courts tended to disfavor contracts made by parties prior to marriage that would govern duties during marriage or the terms under which the marriage would end. Second, at the time of marriage it is doubtful that the couple will know or consider it relevant which party has the right to determine when the wife will have sex. In effect, values may change as the marriage progresses. By the time the wife discovers the state of the law, she may have accepted a non-income earning role in the relationship that makes it impossible to express her values. Plus, any leverage possessed prior to the marriage in the form of a threat not to marry has been lost. Thus, while it is impossible to know whether the reallocation was efficient, it is obviously a preferable allocation from a moral standpoint.

The more generalized question of judicial involvement is presented by the treatment of antenuptial agreements. An overall question is whether enforcement of these contracts is consistent with promoting marital efficiency. More narrowly, enforcing these agreements decreases judicial involvement in marriage. The problem is how do you both encourage marriage, with specialization and third-party efficiencies, and lend judicial support to agreements that 1) by their existence suggest an expectation that the marriage may not last and 2) lower the costs of dissolving the marriage? The inconsistency of antenuptial agreements with marital stability initially led courts uniformly to refuse to enforce them. Although the preservation of marriage was the initial basis for not enforcing antenuptial agreements, it is also clear that courts were concerned about the distributive implications of these agreements. The implication was that women would generally be losers as a distributive matter.

It is not clear that antenuptial agreements are always inconsistent with promoting marital efficiency. For example, although an antenuptial agreement may lower the cost of divorce, it paradoxically lowers the risks of marriage itself and may encourage unions, including ones in which both parties may feel more comfortable investing in children and each other. Second, a private agreement about the distributive outcome of a divorce may mean reducing post-divorce bitterness or impoverishment. Both of these factors could inure to the benefit of children.

Today, although it can vary substantially by state, the central focus of questions about antenuptial agreements is whether the parties maintained at least some level of an independent self-interested perspective.[6] Voluntariness is a key requirement, and this is obviously consistent with an interest in Pareto efficiency. As with contracts more generally, the analysis of consent or voluntariness is a fluid

6. See generally, "Marriage as Contract and Marriage as Partnership—The Future of Antenuptial Agreement Law," 116 *Harvard Law Review* 2075 (May, 2003).

matter and can be a function of a variety of factors including whether both parties understood the agreement, had access to full information about mutual assets, consulted legal counsel, etc. Limiting the analysis to consent is consistent with the generalized approach courts have with respect to avoiding interpersonal comparisons of utility. Sometimes the analysis is more substantive and looks to the actual division found in the agreement. Here, the level of intrusiveness can vary depending on whether substantive fairness is assessed at the time of drafting the contract, the time of executing it, or the time of divorce. As noted above, judicial interest in consent is obviously consistent with efficiency concerns. In the case of antenuptial agreements, the distributive consequences also may have efficiency concerns. For example, an antenuptial agreement that contains within it the terms for education of one of the spouses or the children may represent a distribution that permits efficient investment in human capital.

In effect, although it is generally accepted that there are inefficiencies associated with marriage, it is not clear that public involvement in determining the mates chosen or the nature of the agreements made would be beneficial. The case for outside regulation becomes even more difficult when the cost of public involvement is included in the analysis.

D.   THE ECONOMICS OF THE END OF A MARRIAGE

As you saw in the discussion of contracts remedies, the default remedy is expectancy. The goal of expectancy is to put the non-breaching party in the position he or she would have been in had there not been a breach. Subject to a number of qualifications, damages equal to expectancy encourage the efficient breach and discouraged inefficient breach. In effect, a contract breach is efficient only when one party finds it so advantageous to breach that he will be better off and the non-breaching party is no worse off.

The efficient divorce, it follows, would be one in which at least one party is better off and no one is worse off. In effect, as a couple the parties are better off. For example, suppose William and Kate marry and stay married for several years. Then William begins to think he would prefer not to be married or would at least prefer to violate a key provision of his marital contract by having an affair with Lo, a new work mate. In the world of the efficient divorce, William would contemplate what it would cost to give Kate her expectancy. Somehow this would be a monetary amount that would leave Kate indifferent between being married to a faithful William and receiving the compensation. He would then consider whether he could still do this and feel he had increased his own utility by leaving the marriage or by having the fling with Lo. If Kate and William have children, their disutility would have to be considered as well. For example, if Kate were likely to have custody, as a rational party contemplating a breach, William would have to contemplate payments to Kate as well as payments for child support. Obviously, the calculation of divorce damages would be more complicated than the vast majority of conventional contracts cases.

A solution to damages calculations is to grant literal expectancy in the form of specific performance. The discussion in Chapter Five suggested that specific performance could lead to efficient outcomes because the parties would bargain over the right to perform or the right not or perform. In the context of our example, if William wants out of the marriage, he could pay Kate to release him. (Theoretically, he could even pay her to allow him to have an affair with Lo.) That transaction would determine whether the benefits to William of the divorce were high enough to allow him to pay Kate and still be better off. There are some problems with this. The first is bilateral monopoly. For example, suppose William does approach Kate in order to buy her right to continue the marriage, but Kate, knowing that she presents a sympathetic picture to the courts, holds out for a particularly good settlement. The haggling that takes place can be costly to the couple and ultimately to the public and delay or prevent an efficient divorce.

The second problem stems from the fact that the relevant breach is not so much asking for the divorce, but the fact that William no longer loves Kate enough to not consider having an affair. In the typical specific performance case, actual performance is still possible and desired by the non-breaching party. The negotiation is a way of discovering the values the parties place on that performance. In the divorce context, simply avoiding divorce is not expectancy. Expectancy was being married to a loving and faithful William. This change in what is available to Kate even if William is forced to perform decreases her bargaining power in the transaction.

An additional problem with equating efficient divorce with efficient contract breach stems from the difficulty of determining who breached. For example, suppose William wants out of the marriage because of subtle changes in Kate's behavior. William's desire to leave the marriage does not necessarily mean that he was the one who first breached one of the many subtle understandings within the relationship. An efficient system of divorce would be one that makes the critical distinction between the party who is at fault in ending the relationship and the one who is the first to ask to end the relationship.

All this suggests that the notions of efficient divorce and an appropriate remedy are more theoretical than real. Still, the law of divorce has some facets that are consistent with the concept of efficient divorce and still others that are inconsistent with it. Moreover, the treatment of the parties at the end of a marriage will likely have an impact on their decision-making, and there is a public interest in some outcomes as opposed to others.

Interestingly, the law of divorce was probably more consistent with the theory of the efficient divorce in the early part of the 20th century. In that time, divorce was granted when one party could show that the other had violated the marriage agreement in one of several ways. What hinged on the finding of fault was not simply whether the marriage would end but the financial consequences in the form of alimony. Alimony derives from the traditional notion of marriage where the man works outside the home and the woman works in the home in a non-income-earning capacity. In effect, men were required after divorce to continue supporting the former spouse roughly consistent with the support expected during marriage and, thus, alimony had an expectancy-like quality. The possible payment of alimony worked in a manner similar to damages in that it theoretically discouraged divorce by increasing its cost.[7] Damages for women who breached the marital contract were in the form of low or no alimony.

It has been argued that alimony serves another beneficial economic function. The logic of the argument goes back to the idea of marriage permitting specialization. Presumably, if one spouse stays home to care for the children and run the household, it will be the spouse whose opportunity cost[8] of not participating in the market is lower and who is more skilled at domestic tasks. On the other

---

7. Despite common perceptions, even when popular, alimony was awarded infrequently and paid even less frequently. One estimate is that alimony was granted in about 15% of divorce cases. See generally, Krause & Meyer, Family Law 264 (2003).

8. Opportunity cost here is not only the wage one could have earned in a job, but also includes the utility (pleasure) from staying at home and taking care of the children versus the utility of finding a job and earning an income.

hand, a spouse who does not work outside the home and fails to develop human capital or use the human capital he or she possesses takes a risk by accepting the non-income earning role. In effect, alimony becomes like insurance that provides security against those risks should the marriage end.[9] In these instances, the measure of alimony is the difference between the spouse's post-divorce income potential and what that potential would have been if the time spent in the home had been spent acquiring human capital and working outside the home. This measure of alimony is not a measure of expectancy and cannot be seen as closely related to efficient divorce. It does, however, resemble reliance, a commonly awarded measure of contract damages when expectancy is unavailable for one reason or another.

Whatever the theory of alimony, it has not been used functionally like damages in traditional contract cases. In many states and for a substantial period of time, alimony was adjusted depending on the level of fault of the party breaching the marital contract. From an economic perspective, this looks a bit more like a tort remedy in that the stress is on the activity of the breaching spouse rather than on the damage to the non-breaching spouse. More recently, alimony has been awarded on the basis of the spouse's need and the means of the paying spouse with the objective of encouraging the spouse

9. See generally, Jana B. Singer, "Alimony and Efficiency: The Gendered Costs and Benefits of the Economic Justifications for Alimony," 82 *Geo. L. J.* 2423 (1994).

to return to the labor market and end dependency on his or her counterpart. Sometimes this means short-term payments lasting only long enough for the spouse to retool. Obviously, for someone who "expected" to be married for life and work within the home, this is not fully compensatory.

The unlinking of alimony to fault was made necessary by a variety of factors, the most important of which is unilateral no-fault divorce. This is now the prevailing regime and either spouse may ask for and be granted a divorce without demonstrating that the other spouse has breached the marital contract. In effect, no-fault reduces the cost of divorce and seems inconsistent with the policy of encouraging the continuation of the marriage. As a statistical matter, the no-fault regime is correlated with the increase in divorce. It may not be entirely accurate, however, to say that no-fault divorce has caused increased divorce rates. Nevertheless, given the huge incidence of divorce and the costs of administering a strictly fault system involving trials, attorneys, and judicial resources, a switch to no-fault makes economic sense. Still there is a chicken and egg quality about alimony and fault and no-fault systems.[10] Certainly alimony and divorce based on fault alone would provide an incentive to make a marriage work. On the other hand, once that battle is lost and divorce a certainty, a no-fault system is the less costly system of administration.

10. It is generally accepted that the fault system had failed before being formally replaced or augmented by no-fault. In the fault era, the common process was for the spouses desiring a divorce to collude and determine a fault to present to the court.

What all this suggests is that modern divorce rules have little to do with the efficient divorce and even less to do with encouraging efforts to make marriages work. Instead, while marriage has contract-like features, the end of a marriage for any reason, looks much more like what is called the dissolution of a partnership. In effect, the parties have accumulated wealth, and the issue is simply how to divide it so they can make a clean break.

This is not to say that the clean break itself is not characterized by many economic and non-economic challenges. A typical and difficult one involves the accumulation of human capital. Suppose one spouse works and takes care of the home while the other one attends medical school. After finishing school, he opens a practice and meets the ubiquitous Lo and wants a divorce. Dividing the human capital in which the former spouse invested is a far cry from dividing up the silverware or deciding who gets custody of Carmen, the cat.

In general, rather than attempting to divide the property equally or in a way that encourages efficiency, the tendency is to divide property "equitably" based on the parties' relative contributions, the economic position of the parties post-divorce, and the length of the marriage.

CHAPTER FIFTEEN

PUBLIC CHOICE

Most of this book and most of the applications of economic analysis to law involve implied or expressed *market* transactions. The implicit transactions concern issues like the "price" of driving negligently or the "price" of a contract breach. Expressed prices arise in the fields of antitrust, regulated industries, and some contract law. In these instances, preferences and choices are involved and resources allocated with the purpose, at least in theory, of maximizing individual utility.

Over the years, economists have studied another mode of choice-making and resource allocation—that which occurs through political action. In recent years, those who apply economics to law have also turned their attention to this area of inquiry. The study of "public choice" involves the application of economic analysis to political rather than market choices.

Three important factors distinguish decision-making in the political arena from typical market transactions. First, rather than spending dollars which are allocated unevenly, people "spend" or express their preferences with votes, which are often distributed evenly. Second, the voting takes place in the context of other voters whose preferences will affect the eventual outcome. Consequently, there is less certainty as to what one will get when his or her vote is "spent." Third, preferences are often expressed through intermediaries. These intermediaries may be elected officials, interest groups, or lobbyists. The presence of these intermediaries may dilute or amplify the preference expressed.

The study of public choice covers a number of topics.[1] Some are very broad like: why do individuals choose to have governments at all and is it rational to vote? Others are narrow and more technical, such as the advantages and disadvantages of various forms of voting. Still others involve efforts to predict how voters will vote on a given issue. In this Chapter, only a few of these topics can be discussed, and the discussion will only scratch the surface.

A.   WHY HAVE A GOVERNMENT?

The threshold question in the study of public choice is why individuals choose to have a government in the first place. "Government," in this context, means an environment in which one will not have free rein to exercise all of one's choices. In other words, it implies that there is some element of control by the government. To keep the discussion from veering too far from reality, it should be

1.   See generally Iain McLean, *Public Choice: An Introduction* (1987).

acknowledged that this is a choice few people get to make. They do have the choice, however, to escape from one form of government in favor of another and continually to press for more or less coercion within any given government.

In traditional economic terms, you will consent to an actual or potential loss of liberty when it appears to be utility-maximizing to do so. The basic reason for giving up some portion of your liberty is that it is a necessary part of an implicit or social contract with others who will be similarly limited. It is, in essence, what you must give up in order to induce the cooperation of others. Not only does the agreement to limit your freedom constitute the consideration in the "social contract" necessary for the formation of the government, it may actually increase your own power to influence others. For example, the knowledge that others have that you will keep a promise or observe certain rules of conduct may mean that others will depend and rely on you in their own behavior.

While giving up a portion of your own liberty may be necessary in order to "buy" some of the liberty of others, the question still remains: how could this make an individual better off? The basic reason can be traced to the notion of externalities—both positive and negative.

These concepts are discussed in Chapters Three and Ten, but by way of review, positive externalities occur when it is impossible for the producer of some benefit to keep others from enjoying those benefits.

The problem is that the producer's inability to "internalize" all the benefits may discourage production of something that all find valuable but are unwilling to pay for in hopes someone else will produce it. These goods are often called public goods.

An example of a public good might be a watchdog purchased by one neighbor, but whose barking actually frightens potential burglars away from the entire neighborhood. In instances in which the number of people involved is small, the production of public goods may come about through a series of private agreements. Each person could agree to contribute toward a fund to be used for the purchase or production of an item from which all would benefit. When the number of people involved becomes large, the transaction costs of a series of private contracts increases. In addition, there may be "hold-outs" who hope to benefit from the group effort without actually making a contribution. These factors are likely to make the private agreement route impractical.

As the terms suggest, negative externalities are the opposite of positive externalities. With positive externalities, the producer incurs all the costs of production but is unable to capture all the benefits. In the case of negative externalities, all the benefits of production are captured by the producer but the costs of production are incurred, in part, by others. The typical example is that of the factory that pollutes the air or water but does not incur any costs for the use of the air or water. The best illustration of how everyone is made worse off is the "tragedy of the commons." In this scenario, each firm produces as though it were the only user of fresh water. Of course, if they each operate accordingly, at some point the water supply will be used up and unavailable to anyone. Here again, there is some possibility that externalites could be controlled through private agreements, but this would be difficult without first taking the critical step of determining who has a right to use the water. In addition, when numerous parties are involved, more complex agreements are required, and the problem of transaction costs also arises.

The existence of public goods and the "tragedy of the commons" both suggest that the overall wellbeing of individuals may be improved through cooperation. The problem is that cooperation on a large scale is expensive to "produce" and is threatened by free-riders and hold-outs.[2] Consequently, even rational maximizers of self-interest may consent to the loss of liberty associated with being governed.

This discussion suggests that people may consent to being governed essentially because they are better off under a body of laws. Another way of putting this, which highlights the economic character of this choice, is that there are circumstances under which a system of government is more efficient than a "state of nature" or the absence of government. The amount of personal liberty individuals are willing to cede will be, in theory, determined by

2. Chapter Two includes a more detailed discussion of these concepts.

weighing the value of that liberty against the value to be gained by "pooling" each person's liberty in a "government."

The complexity does not end here. As noted in Chapter Two, "efficiency" has a variety of definitions or interpretations. If one is interested in Pareto efficiency, then the argument would be that there can be no government unless all of those subject to the government consent. On the other hand, the system would be efficient from a Kaldor–Hicks standpoint as long as those who benefit from the government could compensate those who are worse off, whether or not actual compensation takes place.

This means that a government that really coerces individuals would be unlikely to satisfy the Pareto test. On the other hand, the government might simply be established by a majority of people who felt they would be better off and agree to subordinate the wishes of the minority. This not only would not be Pareto efficient, but there is no guarantee that it would be Kaldor–Hicks efficient since it is impossible to know whether the benefits enjoyed by the majority would be sufficient to offset the losses incurred by the minority.

Using the notion of *ex ante* compensation, one might argue that those who stick around to be governed knowing they may later ultimately be part of a minority are actually consenting to the government and must, therefore, be better off. Whether this is consent in any meaningful way is questionable. The obvious point is that, even though the existence of government can be squared with the efficiency-oriented decisions of rational maximizers of self-interest, there is no guarantee that such efficiency will be achieved.

B. APPROACHES TO GOVERNMENT

The fact that rational self-interested people may choose to have some form of government does not mean they will agree on the proper role of government. This is true even if they are interested in the goal of maximizing individual utility. The central point of debate is just how much risk they are willing to expose themselves to in the quest for utility. Put differently and in an extreme fashion, do they prefer a society in which the advantaged may be extremely well off and the disadvantaged may be in terrible condition, or do they prefer a system in which even the worst off are taken care of? These two possibilities are, to some extent, illustrated by the two approaches discussed here: utilitarianism and John Rawls' *Theory of Justice*. They are not exhaustive of the possibilities by any means and the discussion is, by necessity, an overview.[3]

1. UTILITARIANISM

The model that fits a view that people are willing to "assume the risk" that maximizing society's util-

3. See David Barnes and Lynn Stout, *Cases and Materials on Law and Economics* 418–435 (1993).

ity will maximize their own utility is "utilitarianism." In its law and economics form, utilitarianism is closely related to Kaldor–Hicks efficiency, with "wealth maximization" substituting for "utility maximization."[4]

"Utilitarianism" as a model for social goals is beset with a number of problems.[5] Some of these are "boundary" problems. In other words, how large is the society for which utility is to be maximized? Are there specific geographical limits? If so, is there any rational or moral basis for imposing these limits? Also, do animals count, or is it only the utility of humans that is to be maximized?

Another problem is whether the goal is to maximize total or average utility. You can imagine a society with a huge population and a tremendous total utility even though everyone is miserable. On the other hand, maximizing average utility may require controlling the size of the population.

Perhaps the most difficult problems center around the possibility that one may find that her utility must be sacrificed in the interest of maximizing overall utility. The most extreme example of this is the so-called utility monster. This involves the individual who derives tremendous pleasure from activities that others find unpleasant. If the

4. There are differences between maximizing utility and maximizing wealth. For a discussion of the possible differences the reader may want to refer to Chapter Two.

5. J.J.C. Smart and Bernard Williams, *Utilitarianism: For and Against* 77–150 (1973); Richard Posner, *The Economics of Justice* 51–60 (1980).

pleasure derived is sufficiently high, it can "justify" whatever disutility the others may suffer. Of course, the utility monster may be a single person or even a small minority.

A case can be made that a wealth-maximization approach "solves" some of these problems. For example, the need to have money as a means of expressing oneself may lower the "utility monster" risk. And, since animals are unable to express themselves in the market, they will not count. Although wealth maximization provides answers to some of the problems, it can hardly be viewed as solving them in any way that has an independent moral basis.

The most common risk in a context in which there is majority control is that one will find that he or she is part of a minority whose freedoms must be limited in order to satisfy or increase the utility of the majority. For example, in *Bowers v. Hardwick*, 478 U.S. 186 (1986), a case eventually overturned, the U.S. Supreme Court, in upholding Georgia's anti-sodomy law, expressly relied on the "presumed belief of a majority of the electorate in Georgia that homosexual sodomy is immoral and unacceptable." Similar reasoning can be found in *Korematsu v. United States*, 323 U.S. 214 (1944) which dealt with the constitutionality of the internment of Japanese–Americans during World War II. The Supreme Court expressly weighed the hardship and disruption experienced by the internees against the perceived threat of espionage and sabotage.

What these cases illustrate is that in a utilitarian world there will be losers as well as winners. The same is true if the goal is wealth-maximization; depriving some of their property or wealth will be viewed as acceptable as long as the benefits to those to whom it is transferred value it more than the original owners. Of course, in a wealth-maximization world there is a further drawback in that maximizing wealth may or may not lead to maximizing overall wellbeing.

Obviously, a person's attitude towards the utilitarian model or wealth-maximization will depend on the position he or she is likely to occupy in that society. Will they tend to be net beneficiaries of rules or redistributions that are necessary in the name of utility or wealth-maximization, or will they tend, on balance, to be contributors? No one can be absolutely certain, and one's view will be shaped, in part, by an assessment of his or her own attributes and how averse she is to the risk that she will ultimately be a "net contributor" as opposed to a "net recipient." To those who are risk-averse, the possibility of being on the losing end of the "bargain" may make utilitarianism an unattractive option.

2. RAWLS' THEORY OF JUSTICE

An alternative to utilitarian reasoning, which expressly recognizes the aversion individuals may have to the risk of being members of a disadvantaged minority in a utilitarian system, is developed in what John Rawls calls "a theory of justice." Rawls addresses the question of what type of society individuals would choose if they did not know their personal attributes or the positions they would end up occupying in the society. They would be sheltered from any knowledge that would help them determine the likelihood that they would be "net contributors" or "net recipients" under the chosen system. The Rawlsian view is that the truly just state is the one selected when people do not know whether they are likely to be in the best or worse off group in that society.

Behind this "veil of ignorance," Rawls concludes that two principles would be chosen. The first would be that each individual would have a right to the most extensive basic liberty compatible with a similar liberty for others. The second would be that social and economic inequalities would be arranged so that they are reasonably expected to be to everyone's advantage.[6] This second principle—called the "difference principle"—would allow for inequalities in income and wealth, but those who become better off could only do so if those at the bottom of the distribution are also made better off. You can see the similarity between Rawls' difference principle and Paretian standards of efficiency. This is to be distinguished from utilitarianism and its Kaldor–Hicks counterpart, which permit individuals to be made worse off as long as overall welfare or wealth is increased.

6. John Rawls, *A Theory of Justice* 60–61 (1971).

Central to the Rawlsian model is the belief, which is somewhat supported in actual experience, that people are risk-averse. They are so risk-averse that they adopt a decision-making rule called "maximin." Under a maximin rule, the individuals assume they will ultimately be among the worst off in society and then choose the governing principles that would maximize the welfare of the worst off. Whether people would be so risk-averse behind the veil of ignorance that they would select the maximin decision rule is impossible to know.

In sum, there are sound economic reasons for individuals to express a preference for the existence of some form of a state. The exact form of a state that would be preferred is more difficult to predict. Moreover, imbedded in the decision about the guiding principles of a state is the moral and theoretical question of how much individuals should be permitted to know about their likely position in that state.

C. WHY VOTE AT ALL?

One of the issues that has perplexed social scientists for many years is why people bother to vote in the first place. Conventional economic analysis suggests that it is irrational to vote.[7] Under this analysis, the rational maximizer of self-interest compares the costs and benefits of voting. In the United States, voting requires that the individual undergo

7. Anthony Downs, *An Economic Theory of Democracy* 260–276 (1957); Gordon Tullock, *Toward a Mathematics of Politics* 110–112 (1967).

some inconvenience. The benefit from that vote is the probability that the vote will make a difference in the outcome times the change in one's wellbeing should the overall vote go the desired way. In any large election, the expected benefit is unlikely to out-weigh the cost of gasoline, parking, and the time consumed in the voting process.

In order to explain the decision to vote, you must expand the notion of the sorts of things from which people derive utility. One possibility is that people vote out of a sense of duty. In essence, they vote to avoid the feeling that they have shirked some responsibility. Another possibility is that they are not voting to enhance their self-interest narrowly speaking, but have a desire to look out for the welfare of others—children or the elderly. In this case, although the probability of a single vote affecting the outcome does not change, the benefit that accrues if the outcome is affected increases substantially.[8] In either case, the simplistic cost-benefit analysis does not apply.

More specifically, this suggests that the decision to express political preferences may be influenced by factors that are outside those that are traditionally viewed as consistent with self-interest. Not only may the decision *to* vote be affected by these factors, the decision about *how* to vote may also be affected. It has been suggested that the way people vote is likely to be influenced by generalized "values" while more traditional market transactions are

8. Harold Margolis, *Selfishness, Altruism and Morality* 88–95 (1982).

influenced by individual "tastes."[9] The decisions discussed in a study of law and economics probably fall somewhere between these two extremes.

D. PROBLEMS OF ASCERTAINING PREFERENCES THROUGH VOTING

1. UNANIMITY AND MAJORITY VOTING

As noted in Chapter Three, even in the traditional marketplace it is difficult to ascertain preferences. First, choices may not accurately reflect preferences. Second, since wealth and income limit one's ability to express preferences or their intensity, there is no guarantee that the eventual allocation of goods and services will maximize utility.

In the political context, rather than using money to express preferences, votes are the "currency." This too leads to problems in determining preferences, and different types of voting rules have different advantages and disadvantages in this regard.

The most basic rule and one that would seemingly appeal to the risk-averse would be the rule of unanimity. In other words, no actions can take place without the approval of all. Obviously, such a rule finds its economic counterpart in the form of Pareto efficiency, and its chief advantage is that it affords maximum respect to individual liberty. Even a strong majority is unable to subordinate a minori-

9. Kenneth Arrow, *Social Choice and Individual Values* 81–83 (1963).

ty or use the minority to achieve the majority's ends.

A number of things are, however, sacrificed under such a voting scheme. The obvious one is that complete respect for personal liberty may be inconsistent with utility maximization. It is not hard to imagine a situation in which 19 members of a group of 20 eligible voters feel very strongly that a certain policy should be adopted. The remaining voter disagrees but is almost indifferent. Still, he has, in essence, veto power. Of course, it is possible that the 19 voters in favor of the measure are just barely in favor of it and that the one voter in opposition is very opposed. In this case, the requirement of unanimity may not decrease an opportunity to raise total utility.

The veto possibility also raises a slightly different problem. Suppose voter number 20 really is indifferent about the issue or is actually slightly in favor of the majority view. Here there is a chance for that individual, by holding out, to force the others into certain concessions, and perhaps monetary compensation, in order to induce him to join the fold. Of course, every voter is a potential "voter number 20," and the probability of achieving unanimity—even in a situation in which all will be better off—may be reduced.

The obvious response to the problems inherent in a unanimity requirement is some form of majority vote. It could be a requirement for a simple majority or for a two-thirds or three-fourths majority. One of the advantages of these voting rules is that they lower the "costs" of reaching an outcome by greatly reducing the power of hold-outs. This follows from the critical feature of such voting schemes, which is that policies can be adopted without the consent of all those voting. In economic terms, it is more like utilitarianism or Kaldor–Hicks efficiency than Pareto efficiency.

This is not meant to imply that the elimination of the hold-out problem is altogether good. It is tempting to think of the problem as only arising when one voter acts opportunistically in a commercial context to extort payment from the other members of the electorate. This is, however, only one possibility. Another is that the hold-out honestly believes in her position and holds out in an attempt to convince the others that they are misguided. This might be the case when the voters are members of a jury. If the jury can render a verdict with less than a unanimous vote, the so-called hold-out with good ideas—ideas that might enlighten the majority—may be ignored.[10]

Similarly, one should be careful not to assume that some form of majority voting ensures utility or wealth maximization. There are no guarantees on this score at all. Just as one's ability to pay may be only tenuously connected to the utility he or she derives from that purchase, the capacity to cast one's vote for one alternative rather than another may be the result of only the slightest preference

10. *Apodaca v. Oregon*, 406 U.S. 404 (1972) (J. Douglas in dissent).

for that alternative. Similarly, the minority of voters, on the losing end of the vote, may have very strong desires for the alternative for which they voted. Voting rules that require more than a simple majority also fall short of assuring utility maximization, although they do lessen the risk.

Additional, such voting rules do not assure Kaldor–Hicks or wealth-maximizing results. Again, the fact that one position may be voted for by more people than the alternative tells us nothing about whether the net gainers from the vote could compensate those who lost. In fact, if the voting leads to a direct redistribution of income, there is no Kaldor–Hicks improvement, as the level of wealth in the community remains the same. And, to the extent the transfer involves incurring some costs, the redistribution may leave the community worse off. Of course, the redistribution could increase welfare or utility if the recipients value the additional dollars more than those from whom the dollars were taken.

This again raises the primary concern with majority voting, which is that the majority will exploit the minority. One can imagine a situation in which the majority votes to finance some project from which they will benefit by levying a tax on the consumption of a product that is consumed by a minority of the population. In fact, virtually every tax and spending decision has some redistributive effect. While it may be that the majority of voters are the net beneficiaries of many redistributions, it is also true that many publicly approved projects seem to be designed to assist relatively small groups.

In addition, when it comes to the issue of redistribution, it is more useful to think not in terms of majority and minority, but whether the redistribution tends to benefit the relatively rich or poor. For example, the use of general tax revenues to subsidize medical or legal education may mean redistribution in favor of the relatively well-to-do. On the other hand, the use of the same funds to finance a food stamp program redistributes income in favor of the poor.

The direction of any redistribution is important because, as a general matter, most people assume that the marginal utility of money declines. This means that a wealthy person will lose less utility when a dollar is taken than the poor person will gain if she receives that dollar. Thus, by answering the question of how funds have been redistributed, one may also answer the question of whether the majority has voted in a way that increases overall utility.

2. ARROW'S THEOREM AND POSSIBLE SOLUTIONS

One of the most discussed problems encountered in attempting to ascertain preferences through voting is called Arrow's Impossibility Theorem.[11] The Theorem can best be illustrated through the use of a simple example. Suppose a class of 36 law stu-

11.   Kenneth Arrow, supra note 9.

dents is asked to vote on what type of exam they will take. There are three possibilities: a three hour, open-book essay exam (OB), a three hour closed-book, multiple choice exam (CB), and a 48 hour open-book, take-home exam (TH). Suppose that 12 of the students prefer OB to CB and CB to TH. Twelve other students prefer CB to TH and TH to OB. Finally, the last group of twelve prefer TH to OB and OB to CB. Their preferences can be ranked as follows:

Group I:	OB > CB > TH
Group II:	CB > TH > OB
Group III:	TH > OB > CB

If the professor then asks them to vote, it is clear that 24 of the students prefer OB to CB. On the other hand, 24 students also prefer CB to TH. Finally, 24 of the students prefer TH to OB. The problem is that there is instability in the voting results; it is impossible to determine which alternative the group actually prefers because the answer changes depending upon how the alternatives are voted on. This problem is known as "cycling."

If cycling occurs, it opens the possibility that the order in which alternatives are voted on may determine the outcome. Power to set the agenda can then determine the outcome of the voting. For example, suppose in the test hypothetical, the professor wants to give a closed-book, multiple choice exam but also wants to be popular and give the students the sense they have participated in the decision about the type of exam they will take. The teacher may first pose the question of whether the students prefer an open-book three hour exam or an open-book take-home exam. The answer is that a majority favor the take-home exam. Then the take home exam is paired against the last possibility—the closed-book exam. Here the closed-book exam alternative wins.

The problem with the test hypothetical is not just that there is instability. Another problem, even if there were no instability, is that an ordinal ranking means that the accuracy of the vote is in question. As long as the voters are unable to do more than rank their preferences (engage in "ordinal" voting), the intensity of their preferences will not be gauged and a majority vote for one of the alternatives may not be consistent with what actually is consistent with overall welfare. Again, it is important to note that the accuracy problem may exist even if the rankings resulted in a stable outcome.

Returning to the test hypothetical, suppose each of the students voting is equipped with 10 "points" or votes that he or she can allocate to the three choices. Each group of twelve would then have a total of 120 votes. In casting their points or votes, the ranking would remain the same, but the students could reflect the intensity of their feelings by allocating the points in a manner consistent with their feelings. The outcome might be as follows (the numbers in parentheses represent the total votes for each of the choices):

Group I: OB(84) > CB(24) > TH(12)

Group II: CB(74) > TH(40) > OB(6)
Group III: TH(60) > OB(36) > CB(24)

Under the point system, the open-book classroom exam gets 126 points, the closed-book choice gets 122 votes and the take-home exam receives 112 votes. This outcome is both stable and permits voters to supply information about the intensity of their preferences.

"Cycling" has been offered as an explanation for seemingly inconsistent judicial decisions or instability in judicial positions.[12] In effect, the holding in a case may not represent the application of a majority rule but the ranking of two choices by nine Justices with different philosophies. For example, suppose the Court is faced with the issue of nude dancing. Three of the Justices are First Amendment absolutists and look upon all dancing as a form of expression (A), three feel as strongly about the First Amendment but do not believe that dancing is a protected form of expression (N), and three feel that dancing could be a form of protected expression but think the artistic efforts must be weighed against that part of the dancing that could be regarded as obscene (B). If these views are ranked by each group of three Justices, the possibility of cycling exists with respect to the "rule" that is adopted. This would be the situation if the rankings were as follows:

Group I: A > B > N

12. Frank Easterbrook, "Ways of Criticizing the Court," 95 *Harv. L. Rev.* 802 (1982).

Group II: N > A > B
Group III: B > N > A

The holding in the case will swing on the balance struck by those Justices who favor a balancing approach. It is important to note the holding is not the result of a "rule" requiring balancing. Whatever the outcome of one case, the next one may appear to be decided in an inconsistent manner. Of course, it is only inconsistent if one assumes that the first decision was the product of a rule the Court had adopted with respect to nude dancing.

The preferences of the Justices could be arranged and probably do often fall in a pattern that gives rise to a "majority rule." In the above example, a pattern like this would create such an outcome:

Group I: A > B > N
Group II: A > N > B
Group III: N > B > A

Here the outcome is stable, and the "majority" rule is A. Suppose, however, that the Justices in Group II are just barely in favor of A over N, mainly because they are not positive that dancing is a protected form of expression, and that the Group III Justices feel passionately that dancing is not protected by the First Amendment. Now, although there is a stable position, the question arises as to whether the majority rule is an accurate reflection of the "rule" once the intensity of feelings is considered.

a. Logrolling

As already discussed, judicial opinions have been described as exhibiting instability, possibly accounted for by the voting method used. On the other hand, legislative decisions, which are not supposedly guided by precedent, seem to exhibit greater stability. One explanation for why legislative decisions may be more stable is the potential for logrolling. Logrolling involves the practice of what is, in effect, trading votes. For example, a legislator from Florida may feel very strongly about a bill dealing with off-shore drilling and not really care about the outcome on a bill concerning subsidies for soybean farmers. A legislator from Iowa may have opposite interests and be relatively indifferent to off-shore drilling but feel strongly about the soybean subsidies. The Florida legislator may agree to vote in the manner desired by the Iowa legislator on soybean subsidies if the Iowa legislator will vote her way on the off-shore drilling issue. In effect, the legislators have traded votes giving the Florida legislator two votes on off-shore drilling and the Iowa legislator two votes on soybean supports.

Logrolling allows the legislators to exercise what is, in effect, more than one vote. By trading votes away in order to garner votes to cast on the issues they care about most, they will not be required to vote "yes" or "no" on a particular issue but will be able, indirectly, to indicate the intensity of their preferences. In this respect, logrolling can produce the same result as the point voting system described above. Outcomes will tend to be stable. In addition, there may be greater accuracy in that the votes of those caring the most will, in effect, count more than votes of those who do not have strong feelings.

b. Single–Peaked Preferences

Although Arrow's Impossibility Theorem is important to consider, it is also true that it does not apply in a wide variety of instances. One of the assumptions necessary for the Theorem to hold is that voters have a free range of choices.[13] This means that individuals may rank the alternatives in any order. This is not the case, however, with respect to many issues about which people are concerned. Instead, their choices will be arranged along a predictable spectrum. When this is the case, the individuals have "single peaked preferences." For example, suppose there are three positions on gun control: Ban all guns (B), ban some guns (SB) and ban no guns (NB). Three voters might express their preferences like this:

Voter I:	B > SB > NB
Voter II:	NB > SB > B
Voter III:	SB > B > NB

These combinations seem realistic since Voter I, who is greatly in favor of gun control, is likely to prefer at least some gun control to none. Similarly, Voter II, who favors no gun control, would favor some control as opposed to banning guns altogeth-

13. See David Barnes and Lynn Stout, supra note 3, at 465–466.

er. In this case, the stable and winning outcome is SB. Once again, it is important to note that stability does not mean that the result is the same as it would be if the strength of preferences could be determined.

E. THE ECONOMIC THEORY OF LEGISLATION

To this point, this Chapter has approached public choice as though each voter has the right to vote on each issue and the majority position becomes the law. As already indicated, the preferences indicated by voting may not be stable or accurate. Things become more complex when one considers the fact that the voters are typically voting for individuals who will then vote on legislation. Thus, much of the literature in public choice is devoted to the "theory of legislation." This area of discussion addresses the question of what motivates legislators. Are they wholly and exclusively interested in reelection? Do they vote in a manner that is consistent with an ideology that may at times be inconsistent with increasing the welfare of their constituents? How powerful are interest groups in influencing legislative outcomes? Can outcomes be, in effect, bought by means of campaign contributions and other inducements?

1. WHAT DO LEGISLATORS WANT?

As one might expect, the economic theory of legislation begins with the notion that legislators are rational maximizers of self-interest. The question then becomes: what are the sorts of variables that one might find in a legislator's utility function? One possibility is that the legislator is driven by the desire to be reelected. After all, whatever benefits are derived from office-holding are lost if the individual is not reelected. This is somewhat supported by empirical evidence that, in Senate reelection campaigns, candidates tend to move toward the positions held by the most recently elected Senator in their state.[14] On the other hand, this "flexibility" is quite limited. But this too could be consistent with the desire to be reelected, as voters may shy away from a candidate who is perceived as being too wishy-washy.

This leads to the question: what is the best way to ensure reelection? One possibility is that the legislator must make sure that, on balance, the legislation he supports would be supported by his constituents. And, assuming they are all rational maximizers of self-interest, this means he must vote in a way that benefits the majority. It is not clear whether this means that the legislator will only consider the narrowly defined economic well-being of the constituents or whether there will be some effort to gauge their more general values. The recent emphasis on abortion rights and sexual harassment by candidates suggests that more general values do motivate voters and, under this theory, political candidates. The basic problem with the

14. See A. Glazer and M. Robbins, "How Elections Matter: A Study of U.S. Senators" 46 *Public Choice* 163 (1985).

theory that the legislator must be careful to vote in a way that his constituents prefer is that it assumes a great deal about voter interest and information. For example, as already discussed, even the decision to vote seems irrational if one applies conventional economic reasoning. In other than very small elections, the costs of voting are likely to outweigh the benefits. In addition, for this theory to work, one would have to assume a fairly well-informed electorate that tended to keep track of how possibly obscure pieces of legislation affect them. Here again, the cost of information-gathering may be out-weighed by any possible benefit.

On the other hand, it may be that reelection really hinges on winning the support (or avoiding the disapproval) of specific interest groups that are capable of making political contributions and making sure those inclined to support the candidate actually do vote. When approached in this way, the legislator who wishes to be reelected may be seen as selling his votes to the interest group with the greatest clout. In fact, the theory of legislation is sometimes discussed in terms of the supply and demand for legislation, with interest groups being the primary demanders and legislators being the suppliers. A more detailed discussion of interest group theory is found below.

The economic theory of legislation has been criticized for offering too simplistic an explanation for legislative voting. In particular, Daniel Farber and Philip Frickey question whether legislators are directly responsive to their constituents or interest groups or whether they are also responsive to their own ideology. According to Farber and Frickey, the voting of legislators, as an empirical matter, is not fully explained by just the first two possibilities. Furthermore, other economic theories explain why one would expect some slippage between the interests of voters or interest groups and the votes of legislators. Thus, the authors propose a broader model in which votes are explained by constituent interest, special interest groups, and ideology.[15]

2.   INTEREST GROUPS

A concept that comes up frequently in the literature of public choice is "rent seeking." In the context of public choice, "rent" is the term for income that is received that is in excess of what would be received under competitive conditions. Much of the activity of interest groups can be seen as rent seeking. That is, the members of the group want to be sheltered from competitive conditions in the market.

For example, in the casebook favorite *Williamson v. Lee Optical of Oklahoma*, 348 U.S. 483 (1955), the Supreme Court reviewed an Oklahoma statute which prohibited opticians from providing lenses or eye glass frames without a prescription. This meant that most glasses would be sold by optometrists, who unlike opticians, were licensed to examine eyes and write prescriptions. In addition, any lenses that

15.   Daniel Farber & Philip Frickey, "The Jurisprudence of Public Choice," 65 *Tex. L. Rev.* 873.

were to be copied or duplicated for a customer would have to be provided by an optometrist. The legislation, which the Supreme Court held was not a denial of due process, was heavily supported by the Oklahoma Optometric Association. The intended economic effects were to limit competition in the market for eye glasses and, thereby, raise the prices that optometrists could charge. Any increase in price would be regarded as a form of "rent." A similar result would follow from the successful efforts by physicians or lawyers opposing the opening of a new medical or law school.

The existence of interest groups can be explained by rent seeking, but certainly interest groups may also be formed to support consumer interests and moral or religious values. The study of interest groups from an economic perspective is similar to the study of many other issues in public choice. Issues arise concerning when it is rational to support an interest group and the impact of free-rider problems.

A critical issue is whether the benefits of interest group formation and activity are outweighed by the costs. These costs, which can be quite high, are only justified if the group is able to influence the passage of some legislation or some of the details within the legislation. Moreover, this effort may take place in a competitive environment in which one interest group is pitted against another interest group. As in the case of the individual voter's decision to vote or not, the probability of having the desired effect must be taken into account.

A major draw of interest group participation would appear to be economies of scale. For a certain level of influence, it probably costs a number of individuals working together less than if they were involved in an uncoordinated effort. A drawback is that even in cases in which the financial gains of a successful effort may be huge, these benefits are not 100% certain and they must be divided among all the beneficiaries. When all is considered, even a successful effort may end up as a net loss.

Another problem stems from possible free-riding. The efforts of an interest group are like a public good in that the benefits produced typically cannot be restricted to those who have contributed. Thus, there is a temptation to sit on the sidelines and hope that the other interested parties will contribute. Obviously, if a number of interested parties take the same view, the "group" may never be formed or, if it is, the level if its "interest" may be understated.

3.   THE MARKET FOR LEGISLATION

Interest group activity and the likelihood that, all other things being equal, the interest group with the greatest financial clout will have greater influence leads to the issue of whether this is necessarily bad. After all, through participation in and contributions to interest groups, people are able to express the intensity of their preferences. This not only avoids cycling but seems, at first impression, to be consistent with maximizing wealth and, possibly, utility.

For example, suppose the "Save the Whales" group is able to collect $1,000,000 from contributors who want to be able to influence relevant legislation that will limit whaling. Suppose also that several producers in an industry are members of "Up With Industry," a group that opposes increased protection for whales and is able to collect $2,000,000. If this were an auction for legislation, the industry group would outbid the environmentalists and, one might say, they value the right to the whales more than the opposing bidders.

Obviously, there are several criticisms of such a view. First, as has been emphasized before, there is clear slippage between the willingness and ability to pay and utility. Thus, there are no guarantees that blocking the protective legislation increases overall utility.

Second, it is not clear that wealth will be maximized. To the extent free-riding exists by "supporters" of either group, the actual values will be understated. After all, the fact that one chooses to free-ride does not necessarily mean that she values the outcome any less than the next person; she may simply be attempting to maximize utility or wealth by enjoying the fruits of the efforts of others.

In addition, "Save the Whales" could be made up of hundreds of thousands of small contributors and "Up With Industry" may be made up of 12 producers. If so, free-riding is more likely to take place among supporters of "Save the Whales" because the diffuseness of the membership means that free-riders are likely to escape detection. Consequently, the likelihood that there could be sanctions or that they could be excluded from any benefits would be very low.

Members of "Up With Industry," on the other hand, would quickly know who the free-riders were, and there is a higher probability that they could react in a way that the free-rider would like to avoid. Thus, the relative contributions of the two groups do little to indicate the values attached to the legislation being "sold." This suggests that small groups composed of relatively affluent parties will be the most effective at achieving their aims.

The proposition that relatively small groups of intensely interested parties may be disproportionately "loud" in the market for legislation has some empirical support. Support for political action committees (PAC) tends to be less in industries with numerous firms, possibly due to free-riding fears. Increased industrial concentration leads to increased PAC activity up to a point.[16] After a point of concentration, the group may find that rent seeking efforts are more productive when directed to avenues other than political activity.

The possibility that expensive lobbying by a high powered interest group will somehow maximize

16. See Kevin Grier, Michael Munger & Brian Roberts, "PAC IT OR LEAVE IT: Concentration and Corporate Political Participation," paper delivered at the 1990 meetings of the Public Choice Society.

wealth is further reduced if the interest group is a rent seeker. Not only is a successful outcome inefficient, but the competition to achieve that outcome is also a loss since the efforts of competing groups may simply cancel each other out. In fact, even if the outcome could be viewed as otherwise efficient, the costs of achieving that outcome may be exceeded by the costs of getting there.

INDEX

References are to Pages

---

†